FOOD
FROM THE
COUNTRY

Also by Gail Duff:

Fresh All The Year
Gail Duff's Vegetarian Cookbook
Cooking on a Shoestring
Country Wisdom

To Jean.

lots of love from Ian & Jacqui

xx

28/6/85.

FOOD
FROM THE
COUNTRY

Gail & Mick Duff

**A celebration in words and pictures of the glories
of British food and the British landscape**

M

ISBN 0 333 27821 6

First published 1981 by
Macmillan London Limited
London and Basingstoke

Associated companies in Auckland, Dallas,
Delhi, Dublin, Hong Kong, Johannesburg,
Lagos, Manzini, Melbourne, Nairobi,
New York, Singapore, Tokyo, Washington
and Zaria

Graphic Design: Ray Hyden

Printed in Great Britain by
Butler & Tanner Ltd, Frome and London

For Patrick Duff
in loving memory

CONTENTS

INTRODUCTION

While the ploughman near at hand
Whistles o'er the furrowed land,
And the milkmaid singeth blithe,
And the mower whets his scythe,
And every shepherd tells his tale
Under the hawthorn in the dale.

(John Milton)

W E LIVE in the heart of a mixed agricultural area and all around us, at all times of the year, we watch the work that constantly takes place to provide the nation with its food and drink. Solid beef cattle graze contentedly, lambs grow fat under orchards of apples, fields of grain turn from green to gold and, morning and evening, dairy cows come home to be milked. We observe it with fascination and admiration and because of this we have written this book to show where our food comes from, how it is produced, and how we can do it justice by cooking it well. Although we have briefly traced some relevant pieces of history of our food and farming methods, we have not looked back with nostalgia as we believe that British food is as good today as it was in the past.

We have always loved traditional food best of all and, when we started, we already had a good stock of recipes that we had devised at home and enjoyed. We had to sift through them and, regrettably, leave out over half because of lack of space, but the ones that are left are a good representation. Most are based on traditional methods and traditional combinations of ingredients but others use the basic ingredients in new ways. They have given us and visitors to our house much pleasure, and we hope they will do the same for other people.

Most of the photographs have been taken specially for this book, certainly all of them have been taken within the past four years, and they record what is going on in the country at the present time. The pictures of the finished dishes we have set up to make as attractive as possible, using pottery and plates from our home kitchen, but we have been completely honest with the rest and if they show the countryside to be beautiful, that is how it actually is.

We had great fun (and probably spent too much time!) looking for quotations with which to illustrate the chapters. Much has been written in the past about British food, but we attempted to choose only those passages which seemed particularly relevant and recipes which are in the main workable, and combined them with amusing rhymes from children's books and with folk songs.

In the beginning, we listed the chapters and decided on what we

Every farmer's wife has recipes of her own, sometimes ones that have been handed down from generation to generation. Recipes are like folk songs; they are traditional to the countryside, part of the life of the village, the manor house, or the farm, and even if some of the ingredients and conditions necessary to their completion are not available today the recipes themselves should be kept alive.

(Kathleen Thomas, *Purse Barley*)

INTRODUCTION

Farmland on the Wales–Shropshire borders

thought would be interesting to include. We had some facts from previous research trips, but we needed a lot more, and to get background we also needed to see things going on at first hand. We had to talk to experts and to take many photographs. We made countless phone calls, wrote as many letters to find the right locations, and finally abandoned spaniel, cats and garden to the care of parents and friends and embarked on a series of research trips that took us north to Penrith in Cumbria, south to Devon, west into Wales and east to Essex.

We visited markets, cheese stores and cattle shows and even went on a course to learn how to keep pigs. We travelled miles and were fascinated by the way the landscape changes as you cross county boundaries, very subtly at first, but becoming more noticeable as you go in deeper. This does not apply only to scenery, but to livestock and crops as well. Hardy sheep and grass-fattened cattle are kept in the

FOOD FROM THE COUNTRY

Snow in the Yorkshire Dales in March

INTRODUCTION

The farm supplies the town – Church Stretton from the Long Mynd

Pedigree Jersey cows in the Eden Valley

Feeding time at a trout farm

upland hills; and in the fertile lowlands you find dairy cattle, fat lambs, vegetables and corn. Wherever we went, the scenery, the people and the atmosphere influenced us and we fell under their spell for the length of our visit. There was always something to enchant us, even if it were only a well-kept vegetable garden. We had some amazing luck, such as when we rounded a corner and came upon the most magnificent White Park cattle, or when we found our salmon fishermen on one of the best stretches of the River Wye. With the exception of one trip, the weather was always right. Even the snow came to order when we went looking for hardy sheep on the Yorkshire moors.

By the end of the last trip, when we had a bag full of exposed films and a notebook containing enough information to fill three books, we knew that there could be no more glorious a country than Britain and that from its fields, valleys and hillsides comes some of the best food in the world.

Gail and Mick Duff
Lenham Heath
1980

Note that all the recipes are for four people, unless otherwise stated.

PORK, HAM and BACON

Now pig is a meat,
and a meat that is nourishing and may be longed for,
and so consequently eaten; it may be eaten;
very exceedingly well eaten.

(Ben Jonson)

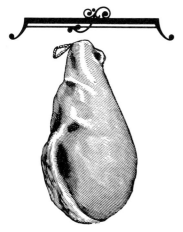

Pork, with two inches of fat, would be kept in brine for a year or more. Hams and sausages were hung on strings and cut down as needed, the hams having been hung in chimneys to be smoked by the smoke of wood fires.

(Marcus Woodward,
The Mistress of Stanton's Farm)

(left) Pedigree Gloucester Old Spot sow and offspring

THE GRUNTING, chops-smacking, comical, lovable pig must surely be the farm animal that has provided food for the most people with the least waste. Pigs were once kept on nearly every farm, where they were fed on the dairy by-products of whey and buttermilk. They were also the cottager's animal that could be fattened in a small sty in the back yard and fed on scraps and swill, to become the only type of fresh meat that was readily and cheaply available for everyday use.

When farming became more specialised, pig production centred on the dairying areas such as Wiltshire, Cheshire and Somerset, but in more recent years their feed has become more cereal based and so you are getting a greater number of pigs coming from the eastern arable areas such as East Anglia and the East Riding of Yorkshire. But there are no real restrictions and you will find pig farms all over Britain, from Cornwall to the North-East of Scotland.

Cottage pig keeping carried right on until the 1950s and many people between the wars belonged to pig clubs in which every member killed his pig at a different time. The meat was shared by special arrangement and so everyone had a regular fresh supply of pork. My uncle used to belong to one such club and I remember him in his boots boiling up swill in a big copper. Another memory is of walking through allotments in which were not only the usual vegetable plots but also a large number of pig sties. Great pleasure was to be had peering over the doors and watching the pigs go oinking round on their straw litter, rooting for food. They always smelt warm and not at all unpleasant. Pig clubs and single pig keeping died out rapidly as rationing disappeared for good and the butchers' shops and supermarkets became well stocked with vast quantities of reasonably priced pork. Recently, however, there has been another turn around. With the increased interest in self-sufficiency, the pig is once again becoming a popular animal to breed on a small scale and to keep in ones and twos for fattening.

At the beginning of this century, nearly every county had its own particular breed of pig that was most suited to the climate, living conditions and food available, and very often to the taste of the local population as well. Nowadays, with more controlled breeding conditions and a national rather than a local taste in food, there is just one type of

FOOD FROM THE COUNTRY

pig that tends to dominate where commercial breeding is concerned. He is white, with a long, lean, almost oblong body, and he produces the small, lean cuts of bacon and pork that are in greatest demand. He will be either a Large White (once called the Yorkshire Large White), or a British Landrace, developed from the Scandinavian Landrace which was first imported in 1949, or some sort of cross between the two.

There are all sorts of ways of keeping this type of pig, from the intensive-rearing systems to keeping the animals in open fields with arcs for shelter. One pig farm we visited is in between the two; it is an efficient system and the pigs are happy. The sows live in concrete yards covered with straw and are taken into small pens to farrow. At five weeks the baby pigs are put together in covered pens where they are warm but have room to run around. They seem, at this stage, to spend their lives eating! After this they are put into larger, airy pens, with straw-littered floors where they stay until they are big enough for market.

A small number of farmers use the free-range system for Landrace and Large Whites and have found it profitable, but it is mainly used for the older breeds. At Easthele Farm in Devon we found Gloucester Old Spots, white with black spots and lop ears and friendly, docile natures; rounded black Berkshires; sweet-tempered Middle Whites, with their squashed noses and button-bright eyes; and the prick-eared, red-bristled, intelligent, roguish Tamworths. Baby pigs were running around in gangs like unruly schoolchildren and pregnant sows rooted contentedly. Here we learned about feeding, ringing and every other aspect of pig keeping – and fell in love with pigs.

No animal could possibly have so many uses as the pig. Half a head, two trotters and the tail can be made into a tasty brawn; and the liver, lights and other bits and pieces into faggots or haslet. Unless you kill your own pig, it is unlikely that you will ever get the blood, but you can still buy genuine black puddings made with oatmeal. Any surplus fat can be rendered down to make dripping. The brown pieces that are left are called browsels, scraps or scran, and can be salted and eaten as a snack or mixed into cakes, as in the recipe below. The flead (fat from under the belly) often used to be made into flead cakes. It was finely chopped and then banged into the flour with the side of a rolling-pin. The result was light, flaky cakes, similar in texture to puff pastry. Chopped pork fat was also rendered down to make enough fat to moisten and swell oatmeal, which was seasoned with plenty of pepper, to make the white puddings that were popular in Scotland and the North of England.

Pork belly can be roasted in one piece or cut into rashers, marinated and grilled, and as it has a good proportion of fat to lean it makes the best sausages and raised pork pies. The hand, or front leg, of pork needs long, slow cooking and can be diced and casseroled, or boiled, which gives it a soft, melting texture. Boned and stuffed with herbs before boiling, as in the recipe below, it makes an attractive cold dish.

Here lies John Higgs,
A famous man for killing pigs,
For killing pigs was his delight,
Both morning, afternoon and
night.
(Gloucestershire epitaph)

PORK

Faggots

Pork scraps and trimmings, seasoned with sage, black pepper, chopped onion and salt, used to be sold hot on Saturday night in Week Street, at Mr Stuffins' shop, and also in Pudding Lane, Maidstone. (We well remember Mr Stuffins - such a marvellous name for a pork butcher! His pork was still the best in the area when he retired only about four years ago.)

Some people like the loin of pork in one piece for roasting, and others like it cut into chops. Roast it with the bone, or boned and rolled; cook the chops quickly and easily in the frying-pan, in the oven, or under the grill. You can flavour them with traditional herbs such as sage, or make a dish such as the one below, with cucumber.

Pork seems to be butchered in different ways depending on where you buy it. Sometimes you will find spare ribs (the ends of the rib bones with small amounts of meat on them) which are ideal for marinating and then grilling on a barbecue or roasting. Spare rib chops are oblong pieces of meat with one small piece of bone that can be fried, or grilled, or diced and made into a casserole. They come from the shoulder area, which can also be tied into rounded joints for casseroling or roasting. The best thing to do with a leg of pork is to roast it, and if you are clever you can bone it, stuff it with a moist sage and onion stuffing, sew it up and reshape it, to make the traditional dish sometimes called way-goose or mock-goose.

One year, more by luck than judgement, we learned how to roast a pig on a spit. Our neighbours decided to have a barbecue and were tired of the usual sausages and beefburgers, so they bought a 60-lb pig, rigged up a stout iron spit and gave the responsibility of getting the pig ready at the right time to us. All we knew was that it was going to take a long time, so, after rubbing it with salt, we set it over the fire at half past eleven in the morning and after that turned it every fifteen minutes. At nine o'clock, just as the smell was making everyone

This is a Suffolk method of curing hams, recorded by George Ewart Evans in *Ask the Fellows Who Cut the Hay:*

The ham was given first a dry salt-bath; salt was rubbed into it and it was left in the pot, covered with salt, for seven days. At the end of this period the ham was taken out; the ham-pot was emptied of the salt and a sweet pickle was made in it. This consisted of two pounds of real black treacle; two pounds of real dark brown sugar; one quart of thick beer or stout - this, at least, was Prissy Savage's formula. The beer or stout was heated and then poured over the sugar and treacle. After the ham had

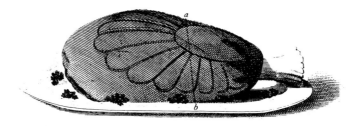

been thoroughly drained of the salt it would be placed in the pot and the mixture poured over it and then rubbed well into it. A big stone was then placed on top of the ham so that every part of it would be covered by the pickle. It was left in the pickle or sweet brine for

about six weeks; but every day it would be turned - flesh side up one day, skin side the next. When the six weeks were up, it was taken out, branded with the owner's initials - a blacksmith-made iron was usually the implement - and sent off to be dried.

FOOD FROM THE COUNTRY

hungry, it was done to perfection. The outside was smoky and crisp and as we cut slices away, the underneath gradually became cooked so we could keep up a constant supply of pig all evening. By the end of it, we smelled like a couple of kippers, but we can now say with confidence that a 60-lb pig takes $9\frac{1}{2}$ to 10 hours to cook!

Nowadays, when anyone buys half a pig, storage is no problem since the freezer is becoming a commonplace item in every home. But when the family killed their pig in the days before we had such luxuries, something had to be done to preserve the meat that could not be eaten immediately or processed into something like brawn. The answer was to salt it, and so developed the numerous local recipes for bacon and ham. Whole sides of pork were immersed in brine with other mixtures of sugar, treacle, honey, spices and herbs, and left until the salt had penetrated them completely. In the larger farmhouses they were then hung in the chimney to smoke over the wood fire, but those with no room took their joints to the local wheelwright. He had vast quantities of wood chippings and sawdust which enabled him to make smoking a sideline of his main business. Home curing died out for a time but, along with pig keeping, it is becoming popular again. The home-smokers rigged up by country do-it-yourselfers are original and varied, but the bacon that comes from them can be superb.

Many people are still confused as to what is bacon and what ham. The ham is really a term for the whole back quarter of the pig. If it is smoked as part of the side of pork, it is known as gammon or bacon, but if it is cut off and brined and smoked separately, it becomes ham. Every housewife once had her own special curing recipe, and certain famous ones can still be bought. The special flavour of Yorkshire ham is due to its having been smoked over oak sawdust. Cumberland ham is dry salted and rubbed with brown sugar and is usually green (un-smoked); and Bradenham ham is cured with molasses and spices to make it very dark and tasty. The type of cure used for most of our bacon today is the Wiltshire cure, which was first devised by the Harris Bacon Company in 1808. The sides of pork are first injected with brine to ensure even salting and then they are steeped in liquid brine for four days. They are taken out, drained and left to mature for a week in cool cellars. Just over half is sold as green bacon and the rest is smoked to give it a deeper colour and stronger flavour. You can buy British bacon in rashers, both lean and streaky, and in large joints for boiling. Look out, too, for the economical bacon pieces which are excellent for chopping and for mixing into pies and pâtés.

From the tip of its nose to the end of its tail there could be nothing more versatile than the British pig. As we heard one farmer say, 'The only thing wasted from a pig is his squeak.'

No pig for home consumption should be killed while the animal is in season. Market buyers, whose trade is chiefly in fresh unsalted pork, take but little notice of this restriction, but the farm housewife, who glories in the excellence of her home-cured meat, has a very great objection, well founded on experience, to having pigs killed at improper times. Further, if the meat is to be of the best quality, slaughtering must not be deferred too late in the spring of the year.
(R. E. Davies,
Pigs and Bacon Curing)

Recipes for Pork

Pork with apple and oatmeal crust

Pork shoulder is a very rich cut of meat and often needs the sharpness of apples. The oatmeal and apple mixture used here gives the meat a brown and crispy crust.

1 piece pork shoulder with the bone, weighing around 2½ lbs (1 kg)
1 large cooking apple
1 medium onion, finely chopped
pinch ground cloves
2 chopped sage leaves
3 tablespoons (45 ml) water
2 tablespoons (30 ml) fine or medium oatmeal
½ pint (275 ml) stock

Heat the oven to Reg 4/350°F/ 180°C. Cut the rind from the pork. Set the pork on a rack in a roasting tin, fat side up, and put the rind underneath it in the tin. Put the pork into the oven. After about 45 minutes, peel, core and finely chop the apple and put it into a saucepan with the onion, cloves, sage and water. Add 2 tablespoons (30 ml) fat taken from the pork tin. Cover and set on a low heat until you can beat the apple to a purée (about 10–15 minutes). Mix in the oatmeal and cook gently, stirring for about 3 minutes or until it has had time to swell and form a thick paste with the apple. Take the pan from the heat. Take the pork from the oven and spread the oatmeal mixture over the surface. Put it back into the oven for 1 hour 30 minutes.

Put the pork onto a carving plate. If any of the apple crust has slid off into the pan, press it back on. Discard the rind and pour off all the fat from the bottom of the tin. Pour in the stock and give it a good stir to incorporate any brown pieces in the pan. Bring the stock to the boil and simmer it for 5 minutes. Carve the pork, making sure each slice has a fair share of crust. Spoon the sauce over the top.

Preparation: 40 minutes
Cooking: 2 hours 30 minutes

Raised pork and apple pie

The apple in this pie makes it very moist as well as complementing the flavour of the pork. As a main meal it will serve 6–8 people.

2 lbs (900 g) belly of pork
1 large onion, thinly sliced
1 large Bramley apple (weighing about 12 oz (350 g))
1 oz (25 g) pork dripping
6 chopped sage leaves
sea salt and freshly ground black pepper
a little dripping for greasing a 2-lb (900-g) loaf tin or raised pie mould

PASTRY:
1 lb (450 g) 81% or 85% wheatmeal flour or wholemeal flour
½ teaspoon (2·5 ml) sea salt
freshly ground black pepper
4 tablespoons (60 ml) milk
2 tablespoons (30 ml) water
4 oz (125 g) lard
beaten egg for glaze

Heat the oven to Reg 3/325°F/ 170°C. Cut the rind from the pork. Finely dice the pork and the rind separately. Render a little of the rind down in a frying-pan to make 2 tablespoons (30 ml) fat to fry the onion. Discard the pieces of rind. Peel, core and dice the apple. Fry the onion gently in the rendered fat until it is soft. Mix the pork, apple, onion and sage in a bowl and season them well. To make the pastry, put the flour into a bowl with the salt and pepper. Put the lard, milk and water into a saucepan and set them on a low heat until the lard has melted. Make a well in the flour and quickly mix in the warm, milky mixture. Use your hands and knead it well, working quickly so it stays soft and warm. Set aside one third of the pastry for the top of the pie. Roll out the rest and line the tin or pie mould. Put in all the pork mixture and mound it up in the middle so it comes well over the top but does not fall off the edges. Roll out the remainder of the pastry and cover the pork with it. Pinch the edges of the pastry together, making sure they stay inside the edges of the tin. This will make for easier turning out. Decorate the top of the pie with trimmings and brush it with beaten egg. Bake the pie for 2 hours.

Take it out of the oven and let it stand for 10 minutes. Remove the pie mould or, if you are using a loaf tin, gently ease the edges with a round-bladed knife. Turn the pie out onto a wire rack and carefully lift it the right way up. If this looks, when you have started it, as though it might be disastrous, serve the pie straight from the tin. It isn't very elegant, but far better than damaging your carefully made pie. Let the pie stand for at least 6 hours in a cool place, before slicing it.

Preparation: 50 minutes
Cooking: 2 hours
Cooling: at least 6 hours

Boiled pork with herbs

Boiling pork in a cloth gives it a lovely soft texture and it also keeps in all the flavours of the herbs.

1 hand of pork weighing about 4 lbs (1·8 kg)
2 oz (50 g) chopped parsley
3 tablespoons (45 ml) chopped sage
3 tablespoons (45 ml) chopped chives

Cut the rind from the pork and cut away the bone, leaving the joint in one piece. Put the pork on a chopping board, fat side uppermost. Make long cuts across it $\frac{3}{8}$ inch (1 cm) apart and to within $\frac{3}{8}$ inch (1 cm) of the bottom. Season the insides of the slits well. Mix the herbs together and stuff them into the slits. Wrap up the pork either in muslin or in two linen tea towels and tie it securely with cotton string so it keeps its shape. Bring a large saucepan of water to the boil. Lower in the pork, cut side up. Cover it and simmer for 3 hours. Lift out the pork and leave it overnight in a cool place, still wrapped up in the cloth so that it sets in the right shape. Unwrap it and carve it across the top so you have slices that are striped with meat and herbs.

Preparation: 30 minutes
Cooking: 3 hours
Cooling: 12 hours

Golden 'apples'

If you buy your pork by the half pig, then you are most likely to have several enormous joints amongst the smaller ones. Roast them slowly and either have plain cold pork the next day or make the leftovers into these 'apples'. They are light and airy in the middle with a firm, crispy outside which seems to expand as they cook.

Serve them with any leftover apple sauce.

1 lb (450 g) cold roast pork
1 tablespoon (15 ml) chopped marjoram
3 teaspoons (10 ml) chopped sage
$\frac{1}{2}$ teaspoon (2·5 ml) ground mace
sea salt and freshly ground black pepper
2 eggs, beaten
COATING:
approximately 4 tablespoons (60 ml) seasoned wholemeal flour
1 egg, beaten
approximately 6 tablespoons (90 ml) browned granary or wholemeal breadcrumbs
deep fat for frying

Mince the pork finely. Mix it with the herbs, mace and seasonings and thoroughly mix in the beaten eggs. Form the mixture into eight small balls the size of new apples. Roll them in the flour, dip them in the beaten egg and roll them in the crumbs until they are thickly coated. Heat the fat in a deep fryer on a high heat. Put in the rissoles and cook them for 3–4 minutes so they are a crisp, rich brown. Drain them on kitchen paper before serving.

Preparation: 25 minutes
Cooking: 4 minutes

Sausages filled with chutney and cheese

Thin slices of farmhouse cheese and some homemade chutney can turn ordinary sausages into an attractive and special meal.

12 large, meaty sausages
12 thin, narrow slices Farmhouse Cheddar cheese
6 tablespoons (90 ml) sweet homemade chutney such as apple or damson

Heat the oven to Reg 4/350°F/ 180°C. Put the sausages on a rack in a roasting tin and put them into the oven for 45 minutes or until they are brown and well cooked through. Take them out of the oven and put them in a heatproof serving dish. Slit each sausage lengthways about three quarters of the way through. Insert a slice of cheese into each sausage and spoon in some chutney. Return the sausages to the oven for 5 minutes for the cheese to just melt. Jacket or creamed potatoes are the best accompaniment.

Preparation: 15 minutes
Cooking: 50 minutes

Bacon stuffed with leeks and mushrooms

These bacon rolls make an easily prepared family meal.

12 collar rashers bacon
6 oz (175 g) leeks
6 oz (175 g) flat mushrooms
1 oz (25 g) butter or pork dripping
2 teaspoons (10 ml) spiced granular mustard

Finely chop the leeks and mushrooms. Melt the butter or dripping in a frying-pan on a low heat. Put in the leeks and cook them until they are soft. Raise the heat, put in the mushrooms and cook them for 2 minutes, stirring. Take the pan from the heat and stir in the mustard. Heat the grill to high. Cut the rind from the bacon rashers. Lay the rashers out flat, stretching them slightly. Put a portion of the leek and mushroom mixture on each one and roll them up. Arrange the rolls on a large, heatproof serving dish. Put them under the grill for 7–10 minutes (depending on how well done you like your bacon), turning them once, halfway through.

Preparation: 20 minutes
Cooking: 10 minutes

Pork chops with fennel and cucumber

Fennel and lightly cooked cucumber make a summer dish of pork chops. The chops are glazed with the wine and adding the cucumber towards the end ensures they stay nice and moist.

4 loin pork chops
1 large cucumber
3 tablespoons (45 ml) chopped fennel
$\frac{1}{4}$ pint (150 ml) dry white wine

Trim away any excess fat from the chops, chop it and put it into a frying-pan. Render it down on a low heat until there are 3 table-spoons (45 ml) fat in the pan and then throw the pieces away. Raise the heat. Put the chops into the pan and brown them on both sides. Pour off all the fat. Set the pan back on the heat and pour in the wine. Bring it to the boil and scatter in the fennel. Cover the pan and set it on a low heat for 15 minutes. Peel the cucumber and cut it lengthways into quarters. Cut away the seeds and cut the pieces lengthways in half again. Chop them into 1 inch (2·5 cm) lengths. Add them to the pan and cook for a further 10 minutes. Serve the chops with the cucumber on top.

Preparation: 20 minutes
Cooking: 25 minutes

Pork and rabbit brawn

Half a pig's head and a pair of trotters have made many a meaty brawn; very often wild rabbit was put into the pot as well, to make a leaner mould with a more delicate flavour. Brawn is usually kept in a cool place and brought out for the lunchtime snack or sandwich, but if you want to make this one into a main meal, it will

serve eight people very well.

1 small unsmoked knuckle of bacon
$\frac{1}{2}$ pig's head, brains removed
2 trotters (each, if possible, with meaty ends)
1 small wild rabbit, weighing 12 oz–1 lb (350–450 g) after skinning
1 tablespoon (15 ml) black peppercorns
1 large onion, cut in half but not peeled
2 medium carrots, cut in half lengthways
1 stick celery, broken, plus a few leaves
1 large bouquet garni which includes sage
2 bayleaves
1 pint (575 ml) dry cider
water to cover
freshly ground black pepper
10 chopped sage leaves
2 tablespoons (30 ml) chopped parsley

Blanch, drain and refresh the knuckle of bacon. Put it into a really large saucepan with the head, trotters, rabbit, peppercorns, vegetables, bouquet garni and bayleaves. Cover them with cold water but leave room for the cider. Set the pan on a moderate heat and bring the water to the boil. Pour in half the cider and let the scum rise to the surface. Skim well. Add the remaining cider and skim again. Cover the pan and simmer everything for 2 hours. Strain the stock into another saucepan, having lifted out the meat first, if you find the pan too heavy to manage. Cut all the meat from the bones, discarding as much or as little of the fat from the head as you wish.

Meanwhile boil the stock to make it reduce to a jelly. Put the diced meat into a large dish or bowl, season it with plenty of pepper and mix in the chopped herbs. Press the meat down lightly and pour in as much stock

as will just about cover it. Leave the brawn for a while for the stock to sink down and then top it up as much as you like. I like the meat only just about covered so you get a very little jelly holding together a good, meaty brawn. Others like a more jellied finish. Leave the brawn for at least 6 hours in a cool place to set.

Preparation: 1 hour
Cooking: 2 hours 30 minutes
Cooling: 6 hours

Layered pork loaf

A simple sage and onion stuffing can make just a little pork go quite a long way. This loaf will serve about six people. It is moist and tasty and requires no sauce, although a little mustard goes very well.

1$\frac{1}{2}$ lbs (675 g) streaky pork, on the lean side if possible
10 chopped sage leaves
4 crushed juniper berries
4 crushed allspice berries
freshly ground black pepper
1 oz (25 g) pork dripping
1 large onion, quartered and thinly sliced
4 oz (125 g) fresh wholemeal breadcrumbs
sea salt
6 tablespoons (90 ml) dry cider or apple wine

Heat the oven to Reg 3/325°F/ 170°C. Dice the pork very finely (this gives a better texture than mincing). Put it into a bowl and mix in four of the sage leaves, the crushed spices and some pepper. Melt the dripping in a frying-pan on a low heat. Mix in the onion and cook it until it is soft. Take the pan from the heat and mix in the breadcrumbs and the rest of the sage. Season well and mix in the cider or wine. Put one third of the pork into a 2-lb (900-g) loaf tin or a 7-inch (18-cm) soufflé dish. Put in half the stuffing, another third of the pork, then stuffing and finally the remaining pork. Put the dish uncovered, into the oven for 1 hour 30 minutes. Take it out and cool the loaf completely in the dish or tin. (A cool larder is better for this than the fridge.) Turn it out before serving, and cut it into slices.

Preparation: 30 minutes
Cooking: 1 hour 30 minutes
Cooling: at least 6 hours

Bacon baked with damsons

A sharp fruit sauce counteracts the saltiness of bacon, and cooking it with fruit makes it moist and succulent. When damsons aren't available, sharp cooking plums can be used instead.

1 collar joint bacon weighing around 2½ lbs (1 kg)
FOR BOILING:
1 teaspoon (5 ml) black peppercorns
1 teaspoon (5 ml) cloves
1 small onion, cut in half but not peeled
1 small carrot, cut in half lengthways
1 stick celery, broken
1 bayleaf
1 bouquet garni
FOR COOKING:
8 oz (225 g) damsons
½ oz (15 g) butter
1 small onion, finely chopped
grated rind and juice of 1 orange
2 tablespoons (30 ml) red wine vinegar
¼ teaspoon (1·5 ml) ground cloves
2 tablespoons (30 ml) clear honey

Put the bacon into a saucepan with the boiling ingredients and cover it with water. Bring it gently to the boil, skim, cover it and simmer it gently for 1 hour. Lift out the joint and cut off the rind. Heat the oven to Reg 4/ 350°F/180°C. Stone and halve the damsons. Melt the butter in a flameproof casserole on a low heat. Stir in the onion and let it soften. Mix in the damsons, orange rind and juice, vinegar and cloves. Set the joint on top, rind side up. Spoon the honey over the bacon and put the casserole, uncovered, into the oven for 1 hour. To serve, carve the bacon and arrange it on a serving dish. Spoon all the damson mixture over the top.

Preparation: 35 minutes
Cooking: 2 hours

Scrap cakes

When I first made scrap cakes I was a bit dubious, as I had visions of everybody picking out the small pieces of fat. But in the cooking they just seem to melt into the flour, leaving only the flavour of pork. I found a very good description of the cakes in an old recipe book: 'A vulgar dish, but well tasted, and eats short.' Scrap cakes are best served hot instead of potatoes, but they will keep very fresh for two days. You can serve them cold like scones or even toast them for breakfast.

4 oz (125 g) flead (fat from the underside of the belly of pork)
8 oz (225 g) 81% or 85% wheatmeal self-raising flour
pinch sea salt
freshly ground black pepper
¼ pint (150 ml) water

Heat the oven to Reg 6/400°F/ 200°C. Chop the flead and put it into a small, heavy saucepan. Cover it and set it on a low heat for 15 minutes, turning the pieces and separating them once or twice. (Be careful as you do this as the fat may splash. Stand back when you take off the lid and wear oven gloves.) By the end you should have about ½ inch (1·5 cm) fat in the bottom of the saucepan and the flead pieces will be brown and crisp. Put the flour, salt and pepper into a mixing bowl. Add the scraps and stir in the water and 1 tablespoon of the rendered fat. Mix everything to a sticky dough and divide it into twelve small balls. Place them on a greased baking sheet and put them into the oven for 30 minutes.

Preparation: 45 minutes
Cooking: 30 minutes

Peas and ham in cream

Peas and ham always go well together as the slight starchiness of the peas soaks up the salt in the ham. This is a luxury dish for special occasions, but with the same basic combination of ingredients as pease pudding and bacon.

1½ lbs (675 g) peas, weighed before shelling
1 oz (25 g) butter
1 medium onion, thinly sliced
1½ lbs (675 g) lean ham, cut from the bone in thick slices
½ pint (275 ml) double cream
10 chopped sage leaves
2 teaspoons (10 ml) clear honey

Shell the peas. Melt the butter in a frying-pan on a low heat. Stir in the peas and onion, cover them and simmer them gently for 10 minutes. Add the ham and mix in the cream, sage and honey. Cover again and simmer for a further 10 minutes.

Preparation: 25 minutes
Cooking: 20 minutes

BEEF and VEAL

Boiled beef was eaten with suet pudding made with herbs.
Roast sirloin had Yorkshire pudding, rising to a height,
crisp and soft and golden.

(Alison Uttley)

Gail Duff with Charolais–Jersey crosses

Hereford bull at the Kent County Show

THE 'ROAST BEEF of Old England' is legendary, and over the years has earned itself a high reputation and much deserved praise. Nonetheless it has never been the mainstay of our diet, as romanticised history books would have us believe. Only the best cuts of beef can be successfully roasted and so, except in the houses of the rich, the traditional roast, dark on the outside and pink in the middle and with its accompaniment of batter or currant pudding, has always been looked forward to as a rare treat, to be eaten only on special occasions. It was these memorable meals that became famous while the everyday stews, puddings, pasties and pies were thought of as having no particular significance. Yet it was these that were the really traditional beef dishes. The beef that came into most country kitchens on ordinary working days was often in the form of the cheapest cuts or odds and ends such as feet or kidneys. The housewife had to use all her skill and imagination to eke them out with vegetables, pastry and suet crusts and to turn them into nourishing and acceptable meals for her working family. Renowned and unbeatable our roast beef may be, but we must not forget the steak and kidney puddings, aromatic stews with more vegetables than meat, tripe and onions, oxtail soups and cow heel brawn, which were made with all the other parts and probably fed a good many more people. In their way, they were just as good.

Until the middle of the eighteenth century, much of our beef came from cattle that were small and tough. Very few were bred purely for beef, but were looked on as dual-purpose animals, providing milk and meat. The most popular breed for this at the beginning of the eighteenth century was the docile Longhorn, attractively coloured with black sides and white markings on its back and belly and a speckled and white face. Robert Bakewell, who lived in Loughborough, realised its beef potential and bred it to accentuate its small bones and heavy flesh. Although the popularity of the Longhorn has since declined, it was Bakewell's achievements with this breed that encouraged owners of other types of cattle to follow suit, to give us the typical stocky animals that are the best beef producers today. The British beef industry has come a long way since then and roast beef is more common now than it has ever been. Our stews and casseroles are often more meat than vegetable and we never have to wrestle with odd bits and pieces.

Probably the finest textured and flavoured beef comes from cattle that grow in their own time on their own native pasture. This, in farming terms, is called single suckled beef. It is produced from a herd of cows of a beef breed that is put to a bull of the same breed or another

Sussex cattle grazing on what were once sea cliffs at Port Lympne, with Romney Marsh behind

Devon cows fattening on the rich pastures of the South West

BEEF AND VEAL

White Park cattle, Llwyncellin, Llandeilo

beef type. Each cow produces one calf per year and the calves stay with the mother for six to ten months, suckling all the time, besides eating grass and other types of cattle feed. They are then either reared on the same farm or sold as store cattle for somebody else to fatten.

Much of this single suckled beef is produced in the hill country of the North of England, Wales and Scotland, and the breeds are hardy and able to thrive on the poorer grass and in harsh weather conditions. The Aberdeen Angus has been largely responsible for spreading the fame of Scottish beef and it is still one of our most important beef breeds. Then there are the smaller, highly attractive, red, shaggy Highland cattle, and the black Galloways which, in the seventeenth and eighteenth centuries, were herded down the drove roads to be fattened on the rich pastures of East Anglia. The Belted Galloway, with a white strip running round its belly, has been popular in the North of England, and from Wales come the Welsh Blacks.

From further south comes the Hereford, still the most popular beef animal. Herefords are low and wide with a red-brown back and sides, white underparts and legs, and a broad white face which is handed down to all their progeny, whether pure or cross-bred. From the South-West come the russet-red Devon cattle or 'Red Rubies' and the South Devon, the largest British breed, which is light brown and still often used as a dual-purpose animal. Sussex cattle are smooth-coated and glossy and a dark, rich red with a white tip to the tail. They have big, wide, powerful shoulders and were used as draught animals in Sussex and Kent until the beginning of this century.

In the early sixties we started to bring in the enormous 'exotics' from the Continent, the Charolais being the most popular. They don't thrive on rough pasturelands and need a good deal of cosseting, but because of their rapid growth rate and lean meat, they have quickly become popular. We must confess to having been prejudiced against these imported breeds and resolute that we would only photograph those that we thought to be truly British. However, we visited a friend who was just about to sell his cattle, and he asked us if we wanted to see them before they went. They were three quarters Charolais and a quarter Jersey and we have to admit they were beautiful; mostly a soft biscuit colour, very large and solid and calm. It was the Jersey that gave them their soft eyes and appealing look but they helped to correct our idea of the Charolais.

Planked steak

BEEF AND VEAL

All beef cattle are quiet, patient, majestic creatures and it is always a delight to see them on their home ground: red South Devon cattle in green south-western fields, Herefords grazing by the River Wye, and Sussex on the high, wind-swept cliffs overlooking the Romney Marshes. But the most memorable cattle experience for us was one of those amazing pieces of luck that happen only very rarely. We were driving through Dyfed, near Dynevor Castle, not thinking about cattle at all, when we came across a small herd of magnificent White Park cattle, white, as their name suggests, large and long, and with big, spreading horns. They have been kept in the same area since the time of the Druids and when we spoke to the owner's father, Alcwyn James, he told us that they have been used as beef, draught and milking animals, and he remembers a herd of forty all being milked by hand. Now his daughter, Eleri, keeps them for their lean beef which is becoming popular. It was good to see a herd being preserved in its traditional surroundings.

The best places to see cattle together and to compare breeds is at the annual summer agricultural shows and winter fat-stock shows. These events are the farmer's shop window and if he can get a good placing, he is sure of a good price for his beef. For the shows he turns out his best stock; never have they been so well groomed. Their backs shine and the ends of their tails are combed until they are fluffy and they are led round the ring by their proud handlers.

These beef breeds alone, however, cannot supply us with the cheap and readily available beef that we have come to expect. This is achieved only through the close tie-up between our beef and dairy industries. Most of our dairy cows, unless the farmer is building up a pedigree herd, are crossed with one of the beef breeds to produce a sturdy calf that can be reared for beef instead of milk; about fifty-five percent of our beef is produced in this way. Our most common dairy cow is the Friesian and the main crossing animal, despite the increase in the Continental breeds, is still the Hereford, so you get a black and white calf with the characteristic wide, white Hereford face. The Aberdeen Angus is the next most popular for crossing and all his progeny are black; then comes the Charolais, who produces calves of various biscuit and grey colours. The calves are usually sold to another farm where they are fed a mixture of grass and concentrates until they are well grown and ready for market.

We have never been great veal producers in this country, partly because it has been more profitable to rear the animals until they are full-grown, and more recently because of public prejudice against the veal system. However, more farmers are now producing quality veal by a new method. Instead of being kept in pens, the calves are housed in open straw-littered barns and they drink from an automatic teat system rather than buckets. They need more attention than penned calves but the system is nevertheless economical. The meat is of excellent quality and certainly acceptable to many more people.

The quality of British beef has always been unsurpassable but tastes change over the years and now the trend is towards far leaner joints than our grandmothers would have approved of. Cuts, which once varied from district to district, are also becoming more standardised, as are their names. Even so, you still find the rump being called pope's eye in the west of Scotland and heuk bone in the east; and in Wales and the west of England it is called the pin bone. In some places, the front legs are called the shin and the back, the leg; in others, they are both called shin and in Scotland, hough or skink.

If you are looking for the best joint for roasting, then choose the fore rib. It always looks spectacular roasted on the bone and stays more moist and succulent this way than when it has been boned and rolled. It provides its own fat and needs no basting. Another popular cut for roasting is the very lean topside, but it needs to be basted well and is probably best for pot roasting with vegetables. Brisket on the bone, as long as it is put into a slow oven for a long time, makes another good roasting cut and it is exceptionally good cold with pickles and mustard. Boned brisket makes a succulent pot roast and you can also rub it with a dry salting mixture and leave it for a few days before rolling and boiling. For braising, choose chuck steak or top rump or the neglected, but very tender and juicy, skirt. For slow-cooking winter stews, buy shin or leg, which is very lean and makes a rich, dark gravy. And then there is the ever versatile mince with which you can make traditional cottage pies or modern-style beefburgers. Steaks are a relatively modern idea. All the old recipes that you find for sirloin are for roasting in one piece. Rump was usually roasted in the same way or cooked with wine and herbs in a pot roast.

Cooking on a plank

One old method of cooking thick slices of rump steak was on a plank. We had read about this method but had never come across anyone who had actually tried it, so we went to the local timber yard and purchased a sturdy piece of oak, 3 inches (7·5 cm) thick and just smaller than the size of our oven. A friend hollowed out the middle for us to a depth of about 1½ inches (3·75 cm) with his lathe, and then the rest was up to us. The essential ingredient was the steak, so we bought 1½ lbs (675 g) of the best rump steak in one slice about 1 inch (2·5 cm) thick, and cut it into four serving pieces. Then, we had to work on the plank. We rubbed the top and hollow very thickly with duck dripping (you could use pork, beef, goose, turkey or chicken dripping, or just butter). Next, we rubbed the hollow with a cut clove of garlic and scattered in slivers from another whole garlic clove. On top of this we put two bayleaves and the hollow was filled with herbs — thyme, lemon thyme, parsley, savory, marjoram and two rosemary sprigs.

We put the plank on a rack in the oven with the oven still cold and then turned the heat to Reg 6/400°F/200°C, closed the door and let the plank heat up with the oven. About half an hour after the oven had come up to the right temperature a delicious smell was wafting round the kitchen, there was a small pool of dripping in the hollow

At the other end of the scale to the large joints of roast meat are the simple country stews, with plenty of vegetables to make a small piece of meat go a long way:

Ten-Ty-Ones-Stew
Fur every ten slices of spuds you take a bit of meat. Put in some onion, salt and pepper and keep on until you get your old pot full. You won't be able to bring up a nice little family on a few shillings without this I lay a penny.

(Old Kent recipe)

BEEF AND VEAL

Baron of Beef

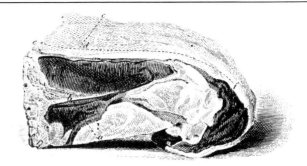

This weighs from forty to eighty pounds and is always roasted. The prime pieces of beef for roasting are the sirloin, or the fore rib, and before cooking it is always advisable to hang beef for a few days.

To roast beef before the fire, it is necessary first of all to make up a very good fire, and when the joint is ready, hang the joint on the roasting jack, wind it up and set it going with the beef quite close to the fire for the first ten minutes, in order to seal up the outside, forming a case to keep the red juices of the meat from escaping; then draw it back a little and cook steadily, basting the joint frequently. Allow fifteen minutes to the pound in the usual way; but if the joint is a very large one, twenty minutes would be better.

For the gravy, pour nearly all the dripping away from the pan, then sprinkle in a little salt and a dust of flour and stir with an iron spoon, then pour into it about $\frac{3}{4}$ pint of boiling water or, better still, boiling stock. Stir well and pour some round the joint when dished, and pour the remainder into a gravy boat.

(Helen Edden, *County Recipes of Old England*)

and the oak was gently singing to itself. We left it for a further half hour and then turned the oven off, leaving the plank inside. About two hours later, it was time to cook the steak, so we removed all the garlic slivers and herbs and replaced them with new ones, the same amount of garlic but fewer herbs. We also added another teaspoonful (5 ml) of dripping. This time we heated the oven to Reg 8/450°F/ 220°C, and when the plank was really hot we fitted the pieces of steak into the hollow, closed the oven door and left them for 5 minutes. The steak was then turned over and left for a further 15 minutes.

We have never had steak like it! It was deliciously tender, you could taste the herbs and the smokiness of the oak, and the fat was browned and melting. It also made its own rich, brown gravy that collected in the hollow of the plank. It is a completely different way of cooking steak from frying or grilling, since the steak is what could be described as 'well done', being cooked all the way through, but without having that hard quality of well-fried or well-grilled steak, the meat being unbrowned on the outside. It is done all the way through but should appeal to everyone's taste, even those who normally like steak rare.

After cooking, the herbs and garlic were removed from the plank and the wood, when it had cooled, was rubbed clean with kitchen paper. Never wash a plank, for that would make the wood split in the oven and cause the meat to simmer instead of sizzle. The second time you use it, rub it again with dripping and put in the garlic and herbs. Heat it up in the oven to Reg 8/450°F/220°C and leave it until it gets very hot (about 30 minutes). Then put in the steak and carry on as for the first time. Well cared for, the plank will last a long time, and if you cannot always afford steak, it works superbly with lamb or pork chops.

Recipes for Beef

A crust for roast rib of beef

Instead of roasting a piece of rib plainly, give it a savoury mustard and horseradish crust.

2 tablespoons (30 ml)
  mustard powder
1 tablespoon (15 ml) grated
  horseradish
4 tablespoons (60 ml) malt
  vinegar

Mix all the ingredients to form a stiff paste. Set the rib of beef upright in a roasting tin and spread the outer fat with the paste before putting it into the oven.

Preparation: 10 minutes

Beef and nutmeg casserole

This is a simple casserole but the magic is worked by the large amount of nutmeg.

1½–2 lbs (675–900 g) chuck
  steak
1 lb (900 g) small white
  turnips
8 oz (225 g) parsnips
8 oz (225 g) carrots
1 large onion
1 oz (25 g) beef dripping
1 pint (575 ml) stock
1 large bouquet garni
½ nutmeg, grated
sea salt and freshly ground
  black pepper

Heat the oven to Reg 4/350°F/ 180°C. Cut the beef into 1-inch (2·5-cm) cubes. Finely dice the vegetables. Melt the dripping in a large flameproof casserole on a high heat. Put in the pieces of beef and brown them well. Remove them, lower the heat and mix in the vegetables. Cover them and let them sweat for 10 minutes. Pour in the stock, bring it to the boil and add the grated nutmeg. Replace the meat, tuck in the bouquet garni and season lightly. Cover the casserole and put it into the oven for 1 hour 30 minutes.

Preparation: 30 minutes
Cooking: 1 hour 30 minutes

Light summer stew

Not every summer day is hot and a selection of garden vegetables can make a warming but light stew, ideal for a cool evening.

1 lb (450 g) shin of beef
1 tablespoon (15 ml)
  seasoned wholemeal flour
12 small, round onions, with
  tails (or large spring
  onions)
4 medium-sized new
  potatoes, weighing
  together 8–10 oz (225–275 g)
4 small white turnips
8 oz (225 g) French beans
8 oz (225 g) small new carrots
1 lb (450 g) marrow (about
  half a small one)
1 oz (25 g) beef dripping
½ pint (275 ml) stock
2 tablespoons (30 ml)
  chopped dill
2 tablespoons (30 ml)
  chopped marjoram
petals of four marigold
  heads (optional but they
  make it very pretty)

Heat the oven to Reg 3/325°F/ 170°C. Trim the beef and cut it into ¾-inch (2-cm) dice. Leave the heads of the onions whole and finely chop the tails. Wash and quarter the potatoes. Quarter the turnips and chop the beans into 1-inch (2·5-cm) lengths. If the carrots are very small leave them whole, if not, cut them into short lengths. Peel and de-seed the marrow and cut it into small, thin slices. Melt the dripping in a casserole on a high heat. Put in the beef, brown it well and remove it. Lower the heat and mix in the onion heads, potatoes and turnips. Cook them, stirring occasionally, until they are just beginning to brown. Pour in the stock and bring it to the boil. Add the carrots and beans and bring the stock to the boil again. Put in the meat, herbs and onion tails. Cover the casserole and put it into the oven for 30 minutes. Mix in the marrow and return the casserole to the oven for a further 1 hour 30 minutes. Serve the casserole scattered with marigold petals and with more new potatoes boiled in their skins.

Preparation: 30 minutes
Cooking: 2 hours

Christmas beef

I went to my butcher a few days before Christmas looking for something for one of the many celebratory meals of the season and he came out with the largest and leanest piece of leg of beef I had ever seen. It was really far bigger than I needed, but as it was so perfect and I was so full of the joys of the season, I bought it. I cut it into succulent slices and made a tasty marinade from the Christmas beer in which it stayed for 24 hours. The meal was perfect for the purpose, and if you ever tire of the inevitable turkey, it would make a festive Christmas dinner as well.

4 lbs (1·8 kg) shin of beef, in
  one piece if possible

MARINADE:
2 pints (1·150 l) best bitter
1 stick of celery and a few
  leaves
1 large carrot, roughly
  chopped
1 white turnip, roughly
  chopped
1 medium parsnip, roughly
  chopped
1 medium onion, halved but
  not peeled
2 bayleaves
1 large bouquet garni
2 teaspoons (10 ml) black
  peppercorns
1 clove garlic, finely chopped
COOKING:
2 oz (50 g) beef dripping
2 large onions, thinly sliced
12 oz (350 g) mushrooms,
  thinly sliced
4 tablespoons (60 ml)
  chopped parsley
2 bayleaves
1 large bouquet garni

Cut the beef into slices about $\frac{1}{2}$
inch (1·5 cm) thick. Put all the ingredients for the marinade into a
saucepan. Cover them, bring
them to the boil and simmer them
for 10 minutes. Let them cool.
Put the beef into a large bowl and
pour the marinade over it (the
vegetables as well as the beer).
Leave the beef for 24 hours in a
cool place.
  Heat the oven to Reg 4/
350°F/180°C. Lift out the beef
and strain the marinade. Put the
beef into a large colander and let
any liquid from it drain into the
marinade. Heat half the dripping
in a large flameproof casserole on
a high heat. Put in the beef and
brown the slices well on both
sides. Do this in several batches,
adding more dripping as and
when necessary. Remove the
beef, lower the heat and put in the
onion. Cook it until it is soft. Mix
in the mushrooms. Pour in the
marinade and bring it to the boil.
Add the parsley, bayleaves and

bouquet garni. Replace the meat.
Cover the casserole and put it into
the oven for 2 hours.

Preparation: *for marinade:* 30
  minutes plus 24 hours
  for beef: 30 minutes
Cooking: 2 hours

Potted beef and onion

Potted beef can be served for
lunch or tea with brown bread
and butter, or with a salad it
can make a main meal.

$1\frac{1}{2}$ lbs (675 g) leg of beef
10 black peppercorns
6 allspice berries
1 medium onion, finely
  chopped
1 small carrot, cut in half
  lengthways
2 bayleaves
1 large bouquet of parsley,
  savory, marjoram and
  thyme
1 clove garlic, finely chopped
2 tablespoons (30 ml) sherry
1 tablespoon (15 ml) chopped
  parsley
1 tablespoon (15 ml) chopped
  thyme

Heat the oven to Reg 2/300°F/
160°C. Trim any fat from the
meat in one piece and put this fat
into an earthenware casserole.
Stand the casserole in a roasting
tin of water and put it into the
oven while you prepare the rest of
the ingredients. Cut the beef into
small dice. Crush the spices
together. Take the casserole from
the oven and mix in the beef,
spices, onion, carrot, herbs, garlic
and sherry. Leave in the fat. Put
the casserole back into the tin of
water and put it into the oven for
3 hours. Strain all the contents,
reserving the juices that have run
from the meat. Discard the bayleaves, bouquet garni, pieces of
carrot and fat and let the rest cool.
Skim the juices. Shred the meat
and pound it to a paste with the

onion (a large pestle and mortar
is the best implement for this).
Beat the reserved juices and the
chopped parsley and thyme into
the beef. Press the mixture into a
dish and leave it in a cool place
for 12 hours. Turn it out and slice
it for serving.

Preparation: 40 minutes
Cooking: 3 hours
Cooling: 12 hours

Braised beef and anchovy cabbage

Brisket of beef becomes
meltingly tender if it is braised.
The anchovies and spices in
this recipe give it an
eighteenth-century flavour.

1 piece lean rolled brisket of
  beef, weighing about $2\frac{1}{2}$ lbs
  (1·225 kg)
1 oz (25 g) butter
1 large onion, quartered and
  thinly sliced
3 flat anchovy fillets
1 January King cabbage
  weighing about $1\frac{1}{2}$ lbs
  (675 g)
6 tablespoons (90 ml) dry
  white wine
$\frac{1}{2}$ teaspoon (2·5 ml) ground
  mace
little freshly grated nutmeg

Heat the oven to Reg 4/350°F/
180°C. Melt the butter in a flameproof casserole on a high heat.
Put in the beef and brown it all
over. Remove it and lower the
heat. Put in the onion, cover it
and cook it gently for 7 minutes.
Pound the anchovies to a paste
and stir this into the onions. Mix
in the cabbage. Pour in the wine
and bring it to the boil. Add the
mace and nutmeg. Put the beef
into the casserole and surround it
with the cabbage. Cover the casserole and put it into the oven for
1 hour 30 minutes.

Preparation: 20 minutes
Cooking: 1 hour 30 minutes

Boiled beef and pickles

Cold beef is always improved by pickles and here they are cooked together to give the meat a spicy flavour. The cooking liquids can be made into a warming soup which you can have before the beef.

2 lbs (900 g) beef skirt, in one thin piece
3 pickled dill cucumbers
6 pickled onions
freshly ground black pepper
1 small carrot
1 small onion
1 stick celery and a few leaves
6 black peppercorns
6 allspice berries
6 cloves
½ pint (275 ml) stock
water to cover

Remove any skin and fat from the beef. Lay it out flat and grind over it plenty of black pepper. Lay the gherkins on one end of the beef so they are in a line, parallel to the short side. Roll the beef over once. Lay the onions beside the first roll and continue to roll up the beef. Tie the roll up with fine cotton string at regular intervals and tie round two pieces lengthways so the pickles do not fall out of the ends. Put the vegetables, spices, stock and enough water to cover the beef into a large saucepan and bring them to the boil. Put in the beef and bring it back to the boil. Cover and simmer the beef for 1 hour 30 minutes. Cool it in the liquid, take it out and leave it until it is completely cold. Serve it cut into slices ¾ inch (2 cm) thick.

Preparation: 30 minutes
Cooking: 1 hour 30 minutes

Soup:

2 pints (1·150 l) stock from boiling beef
2 oz (50 g) granary or wholemeal breadcrumbs
2 tablespoons (30 ml) Worcester sauce
6 oz (175 g) flat mushrooms, finely chopped
2 pickled onions, finely chopped
2 pickled dill cucumbers, finely chopped

Pound the breadcrumbs with the Worcester sauce and 4 tablespoons (60 ml) of the stock. Put the rest of the stock into a saucepan and bring it to the boil. Put in the mushrooms and simmer them for 15 minutes. Add the soaked crumbs and simmer for 5 minutes more, adding the chopped pickles for the final minute.

Preparation: 15 minutes
Cooking: 20 minutes

Beef and veal pasty

This delicious, crumbly packet of dripping pastry encloses a tasty filling of beef, veal and mushrooms. It is excellent hot or cold.

PASTRY:
8 oz (225 g) wholemeal flour
sea salt and freshly ground black pepper
4 oz (100 g) beef dripping (from a roast joint of beef)
cold water to mix
beaten egg for glaze
FILLING:
1 lb (450 g) shin of beef
12 oz (350 g) minced pie veal
8 oz (225 g) mushrooms
1 large onion, finely chopped
1 clove garlic, finely chopped
5 allspice berries, crushed
¼ teaspoon (1·5 ml) ground mace
sea salt and freshly ground black pepper
grated rind and juice ½ lemon
2 tablespoons (30 ml) chopped thyme
1 tablespoon (15 ml) chopped marjoram

Heat the oven to Reg 4/350°F/ 180°C. Make the pastry and set it aside in a cool place. Cut the beef into small, thin slivers. Finely chop the mushrooms. Heat a large, heavy frying-pan on a high heat with no fat. Put in the beef and veal and stir them about until they are brown. Mix in the mushrooms, onion and garlic. Lower the heat and cook for 2 minutes more. Take the pan from the heat and stir in the spices, seasonings, lemon rind and juice, and herbs.

Roll out just under half of the pastry and lay it on a floured baking sheet. Put the meat mixture on top, leaving about 2 inches (5 cm) all round. Roll out the remaining pastry a little larger than the first piece. Lay it over the meat and seal the edges. Decorate the top with any trimmings and brush it with beaten egg. Bake the pastry for 55 minutes.

Preparation: 45 minutes
Cooking: 55 minutes

Veal balls with orange

These meat balls are light and savoury and the sweet herbs give them an Old English flavour.

1½ lbs (675 g) minced veal
6 tablespoons (90 ml) chopped parsley
2 tablespoons (30 ml) chopped lemon thyme
grated rind ½ large orange and juice of 1
1½ oz (40 g) butter
1 medium onion, finely chopped
sea salt and freshly ground black pepper
approximately 8 tablespoons (120 ml) seasoned flour
¼ pint (150 ml) stock
¼ pint (150 ml) dry sherry

Put the veal into a bowl and mix in the herbs, orange rind and half the orange juice. Melt $\frac{1}{2}$ oz (15 g) of the butter in a small frying-pan on a low heat. Put in the onion and cook it until it is soft. Beat it into the veal. Season the mixture lightly and form it into twenty-four small balls. Roll them in the seasoned flour. Melt the remaining butter in a large frying-pan on a moderate heat. Put in the veal balls and brown them all over. By this time they should be just cooked through. Pour in the stock, sherry and remaining orange juice. Bring them to the boil and simmer gently, uncovered, for 10 minutes.

Preparation: 20 minutes
Cooking: 20 minutes

Stuffed leg of veal

This is based on an eighteenth-century recipe called 'To Coller a Breast of Veal'. It works beautifully with leg of veal and covering it with bacon as it cooks keeps it soft and moist.

1 piece leg of veal weighing, with the bone, about 2½ lbs (1·125 kg)

2 flat anchovy fillets
4 oz (125 g) thinly cut lean bacon rashers
STUFFING:
2 oz (50 g) granary or wholemeal breadcrumbs
grated rind and juice ½ lemon
4 tablespoons (60 ml) stock
¼ teaspoon (1·5 ml) ground mace
little freshly grated nutmeg
2 tablespoons (30 ml) mixed chopped thyme, marjoram, parsley
FOR ROASTING:
4 oz (125 g) streaky bacon rashers
SAUCE:
1 egg yolk
freshly ground black pepper
1 teaspoon (5 ml) mustard powder
juice ½ lemon
½ pint (275 ml) stock
1 tablespoon (15 ml) wholemeal flour

Heat the oven to Reg 5/375°F/ 190°C. Remove the bone from the veal, keeping the joint in a round shape. Pound the anchovies to a paste and spread them round the cut surface of the veal where the bone was removed. Line the hole with thin pieces of bacon. Thoroughly mix together all the ingredients for the stuffing and fill up the hole with them. Tie the joint round with fine cotton string, reshaping it as much as possible. Place it in a roasting tin and cover it with the streaky bacon rashers. Put it into the oven for 1 hour 30 minutes. Remove the bacon and continue roasting for a further 20 minutes.

Remove the veal from the roasting tin and keep it warm. There should be just enough fat in the pan to make the sauce. Set the pan on top of the stove on a moderate heat. Stir in the flour and cook it for 1 minute. Stir in the stock and bring it to the boil, stirring in any pieces of pan residue. Beat the egg yolk in a small saucepan with the pepper and mustard powder. Gradually add 2 tablespoons of the liquid from the pan. When it is well mixed, stir in the rest and add the lemon juice. Stir the sauce on a low heat, without letting it boil, until it thickens. Carve the veal and arrange it on a serving dish. Serve the sauce separately.

Preparation: 40 minutes
Cooking: 1 hour 50 minutes

Veal.

Beef.

LAMB and MUTTON

The mountain sheep are sweeter,
But the valley sheep are fatter;
We therefore deemed it meeter
To carry off the latter.
(Thomas Love Peacock)

SHEEP ARE the most self-sufficient of our farm animals. They thrive in all types of terrain from the rough hill pastures of Scotland to the damp, coastal marshlands of the South-East. They can survive in all weathers, often give birth to their lambs outside and alone, and are excellent mothers. They provide wool, skins, meat and sometimes milk for the consumer and breeding stock for the farmer. Very often a large flock can be put in the charge of just one caring shepherd.

There is no one, perfect, universal sheep, since the countryside in which they are kept varies so widely, but each breed is excellently well adapted to the land from which it comes. In the very early days of sheep keeping, the shape of the animal, its prolificacy and readiness to fatten took second place to the quality of the wool which, in medieval times especially, played an important part in our economy. It was not until the eighteenth century when Robert Bakewell, who did so much for British livestock, started crossing experiments with various breeds, in particular the Leicester, that animals were produced which became renowned for their meat. From the numerous local breeds that have been crossed, merged and improved over the years, we now, in this country, have over forty registered pure breeds of sheep and between them they produce over three hundred crossbreeds. The farmer can almost tailor his breed to suit his land.

From the mountains of Scotland and Wales and the hills of the North of England come the hill sheep. They are small, surefooted and alert, stand up well to the cold wind and snow and are especially adapted to eating the heather and poor grassland, though, not surprisingly, they take a long time to fatten. Of these, the hardiest is the Herdwick, but more common are the Swaledale, with its long wool, curly horns and speckled legs and feet, and the Scottish Blackface. The Cheviot comes from the hills of Northumberland and the Welsh Mountain from Wales.

Life is hard up in the hills, even for a long-coated sheep, and after three or four seasons producing lambs in these conditions, the ewes are sold to farmers with lowland pastures. Here they meet up with rams from the breeds of sheep that are kept specifically for crossing, such as the Blue Faced and Border Leicesters, the curly-coated Tees-

At four years the flesh of the Herdwick wether is calculated to serve the taste of the most fastidious epicure, being ripe, juicy, and unsurpassingly sweet.

(Thomas Farrall)

LAMB AND MUTTON

Hardy upland sheep in the snow-powdered Yorkshire Dales

water, the Colbred and the white-nosed Freisland, also called the British Milksheep. They then produce larger lambs which reach an earlier maturity but which still retain the leaner characteristics of the ewe. These crosses have been so frequent that the progeny now have their own breed names. A Masham is a cross between a Teeswater ram and a Swaledale, Dales Bred or Rough Fell ewe; and a Mule is a Blue Faced Leicester and Swaledale cross.

The crossing does not stop there, for from the rolling downs in the South of England come the Downland breeds, in particular the black-faced Suffolk whose rams are responsible for about three quarters of the lambs that are produced every year. Downland sheep are round and compact (like every child's idea of the sheep that he could take to bed with him) and they produce quick-fattening, sturdy lambs. There are also breeds that are adapted to grazing lush lowland pastures, such as the Kerry Hill from Wales, the Devon Closewool and the Clun Forest, and the large, heavy-woolled Romney, so at home on the wet, foggy marshes. Rare breeds such as the Soay and Portland are kept in small flocks by enthusiastic breeders, and the success story of the

(*above*) *Exmoor Horns at local fatstock show*

Shepherd with Friesland, or British Milk, sheep

LAMB AND MUTTON

Autumn lamb sales – 'Who buys must have a thousand eyes'

LAMB AND MUTTON

century must be that of the Jacob which was virtually saved from extinction by Lady Aldington and is no longer listed as rare. It is certainly the most handsome of all sheep, with its double horns, one pair long and upward curving and the other curled, and its striking markings of large brown spots.

Wherever you go in Britain you can't help coming across sheep. We have seen them waiting to lamb against the snow-grey skies of the Yorkshire moors; stopped the car for them to cross the sunny road to Porlock on an August holiday; walked among them on the blustery top of the Long Mynd; and shivered with them in the rain on the top of the Black Mountains. All around us in the spring they graze under apple blossoms; and a friend of ours nearly always has two orphans sleeping by the Aga! But we have never seen so many sheep as in the bright green, daffodil-dressed fields of the Welsh lowlands. We sat and watched them for a while. The lambs were at that unruly adolescent stage and were going round in cocky gangs playing 'King of the Castle'. But suddenly they would give a bleat which would draw a deeper baah in response from across the field. Mother and offspring would run towards each other and, after sniffing and establishing identity, the lamb bent to suckle, its woolly tail waggling in delight. Sheep might be called 'silly', but their mothering qualities are unmatched.

The sheep year begins in the autumn. One eager ram is put to a flock of ewes, after he has been painted underneath so that he will mark each one he covers. Twenty-one weeks later the lambs are born; the first appear in January in the warmer South-West. The hill farmer waits as long as he can to escape the worst of the winter weather, and his lambs arrive in April. The first January-born fat lambs provide sweet, tender spring lamb that can reach the shops by Easter. In June, supplies will increase, and will become cheaper and more plentiful from then until October.

The early autumn is the time for the sheep sales, where lambs from the farmer whose ewes produced them are sold as 'stores' to another who will fatten them, and ewes from the hills are sold to lowland farmers. In the crisp, bright air of an autumn morning, at country markets all over Britain, soft noses will poke gingerly out of trailers and lorries and the sheep will be herded in thirties into pens. There are no onlookers at sheep sales, just those who mean business. Farmers are inspecting, prodding and discussing. 'They want a bit o' feedin', some of 'em.' 'They seem much the same as they were last year.' The sheep wait patiently and the stockmen stand by them, eating bacon sandwiches from the steamy café. At half past ten there is just time to check the catalogue. At eleven o'clock a handbell rings and it is time to begin. The first lambs are sent in. 'Look at those beautiful lambs!' says the auctioneer. And off he goes, forcing the price higher and recognising by a wink, a casual nod or a wave of a catalogue, that a bidder is willing to better it. Never scratch your nose at a sheep sale, or you might walk away with a trailer load of lambs!

(opposite) Lamb chops with Red Leicester rarebit (page 41)

FOOD FROM THE COUNTRY

A lamb in its first year is only technically a lamb until the end of December. After that it becomes a hog or a hogget and is really mutton, but you may not notice until the new supplies of spring lamb arrive the following spring and for a while the two are on sale together. Neither meat is better than the other but it is worth remembering that winter 'lamb' needs longer, slower cooking and is probably more suited to seasonal stews and pot-roasts than to summer-type grills.

Most of our lamb these days comes from cross-bred sheep and it is very rarely that you will be able to compare the flavours and textures of the meat from one breed with another. The type of food, rearing conditions, and age also have an effect, but connoisseurs will tell you that there are definite meat differences between the breeds. We buy Friesland–Romney crosses from a shepherd friend and find that although the joints are large, they are very tender and lean. In the shepherd's words, 'they have walked on muscle for a year', but they can be grilled or lightly cooked like any spring lamb. Jacobs are also killed at a year old. They are very small and virtually fat-free, but they can be on the tough side and need to be cooked for a long time and, if possible, marinated first. Their flavour is superb, very sweet and gamey.

One meat that we would love to try is that of the Herdwick. This was the sheep that produced the legendary mutton of the Lakeland Hills. It came not from year-old hoggets but from wethers (castrated males) that were grazed in the hills for up to four years. This produced a deliciously flavoured meat, so good that it was served at the coronation dinner of Queen Elizabeth II. In Cumberland wether mutton used to be made into hot-pot, mutton pudding which included the kidney, Cumberland sweet pies filled with fat mutton and dried fruits, and the famous Tatie Pot, a bubbling stew of mutton and potatoes topped with sizzling black pudding.

Lambs' tails are now docked by means of a rubber ring. On the Romney Marshes, when they were all taken off at once with a docking iron, they were taken home by the shepherd for his wife to make lamb's tail pie. This recipe is taken from Whitbread's *Receipts and Relishes.*

Lamb's Tail Pie
This pie can be made only at lambing time since the tails have to be absolutely fresh.

Lambs' tails
Parsley or mint sauce
Short crust

Pour boiling water over the tails and skin after a few minutes. Cut up in pieces and lay in a pie dish. Make a parsley or mint sauce and pour over. Cover with short crust and bake in a moderate oven for 45 minutes.

LAMB AND MUTTON

Lamb is a very convenient animal for providing meat for today's small households as its cuts are not as large as those of beef or even pork. The leg is most often chosen for roasting but nowadays it needs to be well basted as the meat is getting leaner. It is best cooked in a covered casserole with vegetables to flavour and moisten it. The foot end of the leg is sometimes called the shank and the top end, the fillet. In the front of the leg comes the chump which can either be sold as part of the leg, or in one piece separately, or cut into thick, meaty slices and sold as boneless chops.

The loin (called in Scotland the double loin and in the North of England the middle loin) is usually cut into chops, but don't forget that one side is excellent boned, stuffed, rolled and roasted, and the two sides together can be roasted with herbs, as saddle. The best end neck is the continuation of the loin. Scotland is again different and calls it the loin or single loin, and in the North of England you may find it called fine end loin. Whatever its name, best end neck can be treated in the same way as the loin. It can also be boned out, together with the neck, into a long, meaty round. It is then known as fillet of lamb, not to be confused with the fillet end of the leg. Underneath the loin is the breast which, if lean, can be rolled and roasted, or it can be boiled and pressed, or cut into small pieces, steeped in a marinade and quickly roasted or cooked on a barbecue.

The front end gives the shoulder which can be sold in one large piece or cut into two to produce the shank or knuckle end and the blade. The shoulder is the best part of the lamb for roasting. It is very juicy, with more flavour than the leg, and needs little or no basting. You can leave it on the bone and roast it just as it is or cover it with sprigs of herbs and wrap it in greaseproof paper or foil. You can also bone it and stuff it; or cut it into cubes and use it for a casserole. On the top comes the neck which makes tasty stews and soups. It can also be boiled and the meat cut away from the bone and mixed into a sauce or salad.

If you are ever offered a sheep's head, don't refuse it as it makes a thick, rich, Scotch broth. Mrs Loudon's recipe for Scotch barley broth that we have quoted on page 130 cannot be bettered. In Kent, when lambs' tails were docked with a docking iron, the shepherd knew there was lamb's tail pie for supper. This is one delicacy that, because of more efficient modern methods, we are unable to have now, but all the other cuts of British lamb are in the shops the whole year round.

Recipes for Lamb

Marinated leg of lamb

This marinade is suitable for any leg of lamb, but it works particularly well with slow-growing breeds, such as Jacob, which take up to a year to mature.

1 leg of lamb weighing 4 lb (1·82 kg)

MARINADE:
½ pint (275 ml) dry red wine
2 tablespoons (50 ml) olive oil
2 carrots, sliced
1 medium onion, sliced
4 sprigs thyme
4 sprigs rosemary
4 sprigs parsley
1 clove garlic, finely chopped
10 black peppercorns
4 strips thinly pared lemon rind

COOKING:
if you have a breed of sheep with very little fat you will need 1 oz (25 g) lamb dripping

SAUCE:
juice 1 lemon
up to ¾ pint (450 ml) stock
1 tablespoon (15 ml) wholemeal flour
2 tablespoons (30 ml) redcurrant jelly
1 tablespoon (15 ml) chopped thyme
1 tablespoon (15 ml) chopped parsley
1 tablespoon (15 ml) chopped mint

Put all the ingredients for the marinade into a saucepan. Bring them gently to the boil and simmer them for 5 minutes. Let them cool. Put the lamb into a large casserole or deep dish. Pour the marinade over it and cover it. Let it stand for 36 hours in a cool place, turning it several times.

Heat the oven to Reg 5/375°F/190°C. Lift out the lamb, brush off any pieces of marinade and dry the lamb with kitchen paper. Put it into a roasting tin and, if necessary, spread it with dripping. Put it into the oven for 1 hour 50 minutes. Strain and reserve the marinade and add the lemon juice. Make it up to ¾ pint (450 ml) with stock. Pour off all but 1 tablespoon (15 ml) fat from the roasting tin. Put the tin on top of the stove on a moderate heat and dust in the flour. Cook it for 1 minute and stir in the marinade and stock. Simmer the sauce for 2 minutes and stir in the redcurrant jelly and herbs. Stir until the jelly melts. Carve the lamb and serve the sauce separately.

Preparation (1): 30 minutes
Marinade: 36 hours

Preparation (2): 20 minutes
Cooking: 1 hour 50 minutes

Grilled lamb chops with mint sauce

A sweet and sharp mint sauce is the best accompaniment for lamb, and adding it before the end of the cooking time flavours the meat more completely.

4 good-sized lamb chops
6 tablespoons (90 ml) chopped mint
1 tablespoon (15 ml) clear honey
4 tablespoons (60 ml) white wine vinegar

Heat the grill to high. Lay the chops on the hot rack and grill them for 7 minutes on each side, or until they are done to your liking. While they are cooking, mix the rest of the ingredients together. Spoon them over the chops and continue cooking for 1 minute more.

Preparation: 5 minutes
Cooking: 15 minutes

Stuffed shoulder of lamb with sorrel

This recipe combines the older flavours of anchovies, mace and sorrel with a modern ingredient like yoghurt. It is a beautiful looking, light and delicious dish, full of summer herbs.

½ shoulder of lamb
2 oz (50 g) wholemeal breadcrumbs
¼ pint (150 ml) natural yoghurt
6 sorrel leaves
1 tablespoon (15 ml) chopped thyme
1 tablespoon (15 ml) chopped marjoram
1 tablespoon (15 ml) chopped chervil
1 tablespoon (15 ml) chopped chives
¼ teaspoon (1·5 ml) ground mace
sea salt and freshly ground black pepper

GLAZE:
2 tablespoons (30 ml) natural yoghurt
1 egg yolk
1 tablespoon (15 ml) wholemeal flour

SAUCE:
6 sorrel leaves
2 flat anchovy fillets
¼ pint (150 ml) stock
¼ pint (150 ml) dry red wine

Heat the oven to Reg 6/400°F/200°C. Bone the lamb. Soak the breadcrumbs in the yoghurt for

15 minutes. Remove the stems from, and finely chop, the sorrel leaves and mix them into the breadcrumbs with the other herbs and seasonings. Stuff the lamb with this mixture. Then roll and tie it and put it on a rack in a roasting tin. Put it into the oven for 1 hour 30 minutes. Take it out and turn it onto a heatproof serving dish. Remove the string. Beat the ingredients for the glaze together and brush them over the lamb, using them all up. Return the lamb to the oven for a further 20 minutes so that it becomes a good, deep brown.

To make the sauce, remove the stems from, and chop, the sorrel leaves. Pound the anchovies to a paste. Pour off all the fat from the roasting tin and put the tin on top of the stove on a moderate heat. Pour in the wine and stock and bring them to the boil, stirring in any residue from the bottom of the pan. Add the sorrel and anchovies and let the sauce simmer for 5 minutes. Serve it separately in a warm sauceboat. As the lamb looks so good with its shiny brown glaze, carve it at the table.

Preparation: 45 minutes
Cooking: 1 hour 50 minutes

Lamb chops with Red Leicester rarebit

Lamb chops with a delicious melting topping of cheese make a simple but very attractive dish, suitable for any occasion.

4 good-sized best end neck or loin lamb chops
juice 1 lemon
1 tablespoon (15 ml) Worcester sauce
2 tablespoons (30 ml) chopped marjoram
2 tablespoons (30 ml) chopped thyme
4 oz (125 g) Farmhouse Red Leicester cheese

1 small onion, finely chopped
4 thick slices of tomato

Heat the oven to Reg 6/400°F/200°C. Mix the lemon juice with the Worcester sauce and brush the chops with the mixture, using up about a quarter. Put the chops on a rack in a roasting tin and scatter them with half the herbs. Put them into the oven for 30 minutes. Turn them over and scatter them with the remaining herbs and onion. Put them back into the oven for 15 minutes. Finely grate the cheese and mix it with the remaining Worcester sauce and lemon juice. Spread the chops with the cheese and put a slice of tomato on top. Return them to the oven for 10 minutes so the cheese melts over them.

Preparation: 20 minutes
Cooking: 55 minutes

Lamb and tarragon fricassee

Tarragon and tarragon vinegar turn a cheap cut of lamb into a light and special dish.

2 lbs (900 g) neck of lamb
FOR BOILING:
1 onion, cut in half but not peeled
1 carrot, cut in half lengthways
1 stick celery and a few leaves
1 bouquet garni including tarragon
1 teaspoon (5 ml) cloves
1 teaspoon (5 ml) black peppercorns
water to cover
SAUCE:
1 oz (25 g) butter
2 tablespoons (30 ml) wholemeal flour
½ pint (275 ml) stock from boiling
1 tablespoon (15 ml) chopped tarragon

2 tablespoons (30 ml) tarragon vinegar
sea salt and freshly ground black pepper

Put the lamb into a saucepan with the boiling ingredients. Bring it to the boil, cover it and simmer for 1 hour 30 minutes. Strain the stock. Reserve the lamb and throw the rest away. Cut all the meat from the bones and dice it quite finely. Melt the butter in a saucepan on a low heat. Stir in the flour and cook it for 1 minute. Pour in the stock and bring it to the boil. Add the tarragon, tarragon vinegar and lamb, and season. Simmer for 2 minutes and serve with plainly boiled potatoes.

Preparation: 30 minutes
Cooking: 1 hour 45 minutes

Lamb curry with crab-apples

You can't actually taste the crab-apples in this English-style curry but they lift what might otherwise be a slightly fatty flavour to make it deliciously light as well as hot. It is a lovely warming and warm-looking dish suitable for those chill autumn evenings that we have at crab-apple time. At other times of the year a large Bramley apple may be used instead.

2½ lbs (1·125 kg) neck of lamb
8 oz (225 g) crab-apples
1 lb (450 g) potatoes
12 oz (350 g) carrots
1 oz (25 g) butter
2 medium onions, thinly sliced
1 tablespoon (15 ml) Hot Madras curry powder
2 teaspoons (10 ml) ground turmeric
2 oz (50 g) sultanas
1 pint (575 ml) stock (made from the bones if there is time)

Heat the oven to Reg 4/350°F/ 180°C. Cut all the meat from the bones and cut it into 1–1½-inch (3–4 cm) pieces. Quarter the crab-apples and cut away the cores. Scrub but don't peel the potatoes and chop them and the carrots into ¾-inch (2-cm) dice. Melt the butter in a large flame-proof casserole on a high heat. Put in the pieces of lamb and brown them. Remove them, lower the heat and stir in the onions, potatoes, carrots, curry powder and turmeric. Cover them and let them sweat for 10 minutes. Stir in the crab-apples and sultanas. Pour in the stock and bring it to the boil. Mix in the lamb. Cover the casserole and put it into the oven for 1 hour 30 minutes. Serve the curry with plainly boiled rice or potatoes boiled in their skins.

Preparation: 30 minutes
Cooking: 1 hour 30 minutes

Lamb's liver, bacon, swede and onions

Liver, bacon and onions have made many a satisfying supper. The grated swede in this recipe makes a thick and tasty sauce.

1½ lbs (675 g) lamb's liver
6 oz (175 g) lean bacon pieces
8 oz (225 g) swede, grated
1 oz (25 g) dripping or bacon fat
2 medium onions, thinly sliced
1 tablespoon (15 ml) chopped thyme
½ pint (275 ml) stock
freshly ground black pepper

Cut the liver and bacon into small dice. Finely grate the swede. Melt the dripping in a large frying-pan or shallow casserole on a high heat and brown the liver very quickly. Remove it and lower the heat. Mix in the onions and bacon and cook them until the onions are brown. Stir in the swede, thyme and stock, and season with the pepper. Bring them gently to the boil, cover, and simmer them for 15 minutes. Stir in the liver together with any juices that have run out of it and simmer for 10 minutes more.

Preparation: 30 minutes
Cooking: 25 minutes

Raised lamb and gooseberry pie

Raised mutton pies and raised gooseberry pies were both country favourites, and they work very well when they are combined. This savoury pie will serve six to eight people and it's just right for picnics.

1½ lbs (675 g) lean, boneless lamb, cut from the shoulder
8 oz (225 g) gooseberries
1 large onion, finely chopped
¼ nutmeg, grated
1 tablespoon (15 ml) chopped marjoram
PASTRY:
1 lb (450 g) 81% or 85% wheatmeal flour
¼ teaspoon (1·5 ml) sea salt

4 oz (125 g) lard
6 tablespoons (90 ml) water
beaten egg to glaze
a little lard for lightly greasing a 2-lb (900-g) loaf tin or raised pie mould

Heat the oven to Reg 3/325°F/ 170°C. Chop the lamb into tiny pieces. Top and tail and slice the gooseberries. Put both ingredients into a bowl with the onion, nutmeg and marjoram. Put the flour and salt into another bowl. Warm the lard and water together until the lard has melted. Mix them quickly into the flour so the dough stays warm and workable. Reserve about one third of the pastry for the top. Roll out the rest and line the loaf tin or pie mould. Press in the lamb mixture. Cover it with the rest of the pastry and seal the edges, taking care not to let them hang over the sides of the tin or mould. Decorate the top of the pie with trimmings and brush the top with beaten egg. Bake the pie for 1 hour 30 minutes. Take it from the oven and let it stand for 10 minutes. Remove the pie mould or, if you are using a loaf tin, run a long, round-bladed knife very carefully round the edges of the pie. Turn the pie onto a wire rack and quickly and carefully turn it the right way up. Leave the pie in a cool place for at least 6 hours and preferably overnight.

Preparation: 45 minutes
Cooking: 1 hour 30 minutes
Cooling: 6 hours or overnight

POULTRY

Young things of tender life again
Enjoys thy sunny hours
And gosslings waddle oer the plain
As yellow as its flowers
Or swim the pond in wild delight
To catch the water flye
Where hissing geese in ceaseless spite
Make childern scamper bye

(John Clare)

If you eat goose on Michaelmas Day you will never want money all the year round.

(Old saying)

HENS, DUCKS AND GEESE once added colour and interest to every farm. They were a profitable sideline for the farmer's wife, supplying her with eggs and meat, down for cushions and pillows, and quills for pens. They have also always been kept on a small scale on smallholdings and in country gardens and, far from dying out, poultry keeping is becoming ever more popular.

In early times, chickens scavenged at will round the farmyard. Different breeds crossed with one another and also with pedigree game cocks that were often allowed to run amongst them. Some good layers were produced from this motley selection and some proved excellent eating, but most often they were all used for both purposes. When a chicken became too old for laying she was taken as a boiling fowl; and if the family wanted a special treat, a young cock was killed. For Christmas, the farmer's wife would castrate young cocks at a very early age and rear them up as plump, fat capons. Chicken was by no means the cheap and readily available meat that it has become today. In the 1850s, new breeds were developed, some more suited to laying and others specifically for the table. They were put for safety and ease of management into hen-houses and runs, and this, in some cases, led to the development of commercial poultry farms.

One of the first table breeds was the plump, wide-breasted Dorking which was reared in Surrey. It was either pure bred or crossed with other suitable types and from its offspring were produced the famous Surrey capons. Kent produced the Buff and Black Orpingtons which were very wide and stout; and a whole fattening industry grew up in Sussex round their table birds, known because of their colours as the Light, Speckled and Red Sussex. Until the 1950s, these breeds and those such as the Rhode Island Red from America and others from France were kept both on a small scale by country people and as the basis of the commercial poultry industry. You can still find them on smallholdings and in back gardens and they provide succulent, well-flavoured meat, but they are not as common as they were. Over the past few years, new hybrids have taken over. They were originally developed by breeding companies for rearing in batteries and have a remarkably efficient food conversion rate. Provided they are well looked after, they can also survive outside in chicken runs.

Whenever you are shopping in country markets always look out for the poultry stalls where you can buy superb, fresh, free-range birds; after trying them you will probably agree that it is best to live as we once did, having the best quality meat occasionally rather than frequent supplies of the cheaper, battery kind.

Turkeys, which have become an essential part of our Christmas festivities, have also suffered from a degree of intensive farming. Hybridisation has produced a number of quick-fattening breeds, the flesh of which is sometimes so dry that the producers deem it fit to inject it with butter or chicken stock! However, at Christmas time especially, a number of naturally reared, slow maturing fresh ones are available and if you try these you will find a moister, tastier flesh, particularly if they have been hung for about a week before you eat them. It is best to avoid the monsters. Generally, the smaller the turkey, the more succulent it will be.

The vast majority of turkeys that are produced today, whether naturally reared or not, are white, but originally it was the Norfolk Black that was most common. This came into the country in the sixteenth century and was originally a game bird, but it was gradually domesticated and became fairly widespread. From a gourmet's point of view it is hard to see why it died out, but it was just not suitable for modern production systems. The birds take a long time to reach maturity and then only weigh around twelve pounds. We were determined to track down these elusive birds and finally found a breeder through the Rare Breeds Survival Trust. We went to see them in early

County Down Goose ... *the birds to be killed spent the last 10–14 days of their lives in a barn and were fed only on milky foods, potatoes, etc., instead of rooting round the farmyard. Their flesh when cooked was pale in colour and mild and delicious to eat.*

(Florence Irwin, *The Cookin' Woman*)

You cannot have a grander recipe for poultry than this *Yorkshire Christmas Pie:*

First make a good Standing Crust, let the wall and bottom be very thick; bone a Turkey, a Goose, a Fowl, a Partridge and a Pigeon. Season them all very well, take half an ounce of Mace, half an ounce of Nutmeg, a quarter of an ounce of Cloves, and half an ounce of Black Pepper, all beat fine together. Open the Fowls all down the Back, and bone them, first the Pigeon, then the Partridge, then the Fowl, then the Goose, and then the Turkey, which must be large. Season them well, and lay them in the Crust, so as it will look like a whole

turkey. Then have a Hare ready cased, and wiped with a clean cloth. Cut it in pieces, on the other side Woodcock, more Game and what sort of Wild Fowl you have. Put at least four pounds of Butter

into the Pie, then lay on your lid which must be a Thick One, and let it be well baked. These pies are often sent to London in a box as Presents.

(Hannah Glasse, *The Art of Cookery made Plain and Easy*)

Black turkey cock

summer when the Christmas birds were still small chicks, cheeping away together in an outdoor pen. It was just at the end of the breeding season and the males were losing their tail feathers; nevertheless they were magnificent birds, with the sun shining on their backs and making them gleam in black and various colours of deep bronze. They gobbled contentedly away at one another. We had meant only to take photographs, but we came away with a better prize – a plucked black turkey for the oven. And it really was good. The meat, even that on the breast, was darker and moister than that of any white turkey we have ever cooked, and it was just as good cold as it was hot.

The other turkey-like bird that is beginning to be popular with the aspiring, self-sufficient countryman is the guinea fowl. They are rather silly, highly strung birds with tiny heads and thin necks and bodies covered with a thick layer of brown feathers with white tips, looking very much like animated feathered hats. Nevertheless they can be prolific layers and when they reach the pot they are small, tender and moist, and taste like a cross between chicken and pheasant. A plucked bird will weigh about $2\frac{1}{2}$ lbs (1·125 kg) so, with a good stuffing, it will feed four very well. Roasted guinea fowl is also good cold in a decorative salmagundy-type salad.

Ducks have suffered far less from intensive rearing than chickens and turkeys, and geese not at all, since they do not adapt to any kind of small pen, let alone a rearing shed or battery cage. Duck keeping is very popular at the moment and whenever you find a house in the country with even the smallest of ponds there is more than likely to be a few ducks quacking about. A friend of ours has a smallholding, where he has dammed the stream, made a lake and a series of islands and stocked it with various breeds of ducks and geese. The ducks swim quietly quacking on the water, occasionally upturning and paddling down to the bottom. When they reach the islands they fluff their feathers and waggle their curled-up tails, sit and watch the world go by and occasionally make a nest. On the edge of the lake they paddle about in the mud and waddle up in a noisy flock when anyone comes out with a food bucket. There are brown Khaki Campbells, and the Muscovies with their red knobbly faces and black and white markings, both of which are kept mostly for their eggs. The table ducks are the Rouens and the Aylesburys. The Rouens are handsome birds with markings much like those of the wild mallard from which they are descended. They take a very long time to mature and their flesh is dark coloured and rich. But I have to be biased towards the Aylesburys, for I am an 'Aylesbury Duck' myself.

Aylesbury ducks were first bred by Mr Weston of Aylesbury in Buckinghamshire early in the nineteenth century. They are pure white birds with a deep breast, long broad body and straight back, yellow feet and a bill which should be flesh coloured rather than yellow. The beauty of them is that they mature very fast and, if they are fed well, at nine weeks they will weigh from seven to eight pounds. Mr Weston's farm was in the middle of the town and yet he managed to create ideal .

conditions for his ducks with running water, ponds and islands. Aylesbury ducks were always in great demand by the London market, particularly in spring and early summer, and to meet this, ducks were farmed out to people in Aylesbury itself and in the surrounding villages. The people who kept them were called 'Duckers' and the particular area of Aylesbury in which most of them lived was known as 'Duck-End'. Some kept stock ducks just to lay eggs and others bought the eggs and hatched them under Dorking or Cochin hens.

The young birds were very cosseted. They were fed on brewers' grains and horsemeat and were often brought into the houses to sleep. Every evening, a horse-drawn van went round Duck-End and the duck-keeping villages collecting crates of ready-plucked ducks so they could be put on the train to London in time to reach the early morning markets. On some days in the height of the season, as much as a ton of ducks would be sent off. The population of ducks declined considerably during the last war, and the last 'Duckie' Weston, great-grandson of the founder, died in 1961. Aylesbury ducks no longer come from Aylesbury, but wherever a quick maturing, good tempered duck is required you are likely to find them.

Geese are noisy, cantankerous and dirty, but nevertheless endearing, and can graze and thrive on rough areas of grassland. The most popular and typically British breed is the large, white Embden, and the smaller grey is the Toulouse from France. In a mixed flock you generally find white, grey and speckled crosses like the beautiful female that we found on a smallholding protectively guarding her eggs inside an upturned oil drum. Geese were once our most popular Christmas bird. They were bred mainly in East Anglia and were driven down to London in December with the soles of their feet tarred to stop them from wearing out. But they became very uneconomical to breed on a scale large enough to satisfy the huge Christmas demand for poultry that exists today. They have to be free-ranged on pastureland and one goose can eat more than one sheep. Most commonly, one or two breeding pairs are kept by farmers mainly for themselves and friends, and a frequent sight in orchard country in the spring is to see mother and goslings in a line under the blossoms. They can, however, be reared in flocks of up to a hundred and fifty to appear on the market at Christmas, but if you want one, ask your butcher well in advance. A goose is a good size for Christmas. It will feed up to twelve people without giving you the problem of what to do with the leftovers for several days afterwards. It is really more traditional than turkey and once you have tried its rich, dark flesh, you will probably try to buy another one the next year. Goose is always thought to be fatty, but it need not be. One trick I learned from my aunt is to put a lemon right up inside the body cavity and then either serve or cook it with apples. Accompany it with braised red or white cabbage or make a stuffing with sage, onion and chopped apple. Another good idea is to surround it with baked apples filled with rowanberry or redcurrant jelly.

We have tried all kinds of ways when it comes to roasting any type

Four ducks on a pond,
A grass bank beyond,
A blue sky of spring,
White clouds on the wing.
(William Allingham)

Chicken with celery and cheddar cheese stuffing (page 48)

of poultry and have come to the conclusion that the best method is this. First heat the oven to Reg 6/400°F/200°C. It sounds high, but it works. Put the stuffed and trussed bird on a rack in a roasting tin and if it is a chicken, guinea fowl or turkey, spread a little butter on its breast. Ducks and geese benefit from being pricked all over with a fork and rubbed with fine sea salt. Then cover the bird completely with foil and put it into the oven. A small guinea fowl will need 1 hour, with an extra 15 minutes with the foil removed, to brown; a duck will need 2 hours and then 30 minutes browning; a chicken wants 1 hour and then 30 minutes; a small turkey, 2 hours and then 15 minutes, and a 16-lb turkey 2½ hours and 30 minutes. The meat will be very tender and still moist and the foil will have kept in all the flavour.

Chickens are the most versatile of all poultry and they can be successfully poached, grilled, casseroled or fried. Guinea fowl can be treated like chicken, but the joints are very small. They can also be split down the back, opened flat and grilled whole. Ducks are really best roasted, although boiling them makes them less rich and keeps them very juicy. For parties where a special cold buffet dish is required, turkeys and geese can be boned, stuffed and rolled and then either roasted or braised. This makes them look extremely attractive, they go further and they are very easy to carve. They are also exceptionally delicious.

Recipes for Poultry

Chicken with celery and Cheddar cheese stuffing

The cheese in this deliciously rich stuffing stays in small, distinguishable, melting pieces and the chicken is moist and very tender with a crispy brown skin.

1 roasting chicken weighing 3–3½ lb (1·350–1·575 kg)
4 sticks from the inner heart of a head of celery
2 oz (50 g) grated Farmhouse Cheddar cheese
2 tablespoons (30 ml) rendered chicken fat or ½ oz (15 g) butter
1 small onion, finely chopped
2 oz (50 g) wholemeal breadcrumbs
2 tablespoons (30 ml) chopped parsley
1 tablespoon (15 ml) chopped thyme
2 tablespoons (30 ml) dry white wine
½ pint (275 ml) stock

Heat the oven to Reg 6/400°F/ 200°C. Finely chop the celery and cut the cheese into tiny dice. Heat the fat or melt the butter in a frying-pan on a low heat. Mix in the celery and onion and cook them until the onion is soft. Take the pan from the heat and mix in the breadcrumbs and herbs and finally the cheese, taking care not to mash it or break it up. Bind everything together with the wine and use the mixture to stuff the chicken. Sew up and truss the chicken and put it on a rack in a roasting tin. Cover it completely with foil and put it into the oven for 1 hour. Take off the foil and continue the cooking for a further 30 minutes so the chicken becomes a beautiful golden brown. Lift the chicken onto a serving dish and pour away any fat from the roasting tin. Set the tin on top of the stove, pour in the stock and stir to incorporate any residue from the bottom of the pan. Let the sauce simmer while you cut the chicken into four serving portions. Arrange them on a dish with the stuffing and serve the sauce separately.

Preparation: 30 minutes
Cooking: 1 hour 30 minutes

Chicken and nasturtium salad

For a salad, a poached chicken is the best as it will keep moist and delicately flavoured. This salad is creamy coloured and decorated with bright red nasturtium flowers. The flavours are a gentle hint of lemon and ginger.

1 roasting chicken weighing 3–3½ lb (1·350–1·575 kg)

FOR BOILING:
4 nasturtium leaves
2 bouquets garnis
½ lemon, thinly sliced
1 teaspoon (5 ml) ground ginger
1 small onion, cut in half but not peeled
1 small carrot, cut in half lengthways
4 cloves

FOR SALAD:
¼ pint (150 ml) natural yoghurt
1 teaspoon (5 ml) ground ginger
16 nasturtium leaves, finely chopped
2 teaspoons (10 ml) chopped pickled nasturtium seeds or capers
1 clove garlic, crushed with a pinch of sea salt
1 medium-sized lettuce, shredded
½ medium-sized cucumber, quartered lengthways and sliced
8 nasturtium flowers

Put two nasturtium leaves, one bouquet garni and the half lemon inside the chicken. Truss the chicken and rub the ginger into the skin. Put the chicken into a saucepan with the remaining boiling ingredients. Cover it with water to the top of the legs. Bring it to the boil, cover and simmer for 1 hour. Lift out the chicken and let it cool completely. Strain the stock and save it for soup.

Take all the meat from the bone and dice it. Put the yoghurt into a bowl and mix in the ginger, chopped nasturtium leaves, pickled seeds or capers and garlic. Fold the dressing into the chicken. Arrange a bed of lettuce and cucumber on a serving plate and pile the salad on top. Decorate the salad with the nasturtium flowers.

Preparation: 45 minutes
Cooking: 1 hour
Cooling: 1 hour

Chicken in a dish with herbs

Take a walk in the herb garden and cut as many different herbs as you can find and use them with homemade wine to enhance a simple dish of chicken.

1 roasting chicken weighing 3–3½ lb (1·350–1·575 kg)

$\frac{1}{2}$ oz (15 g) butter
1 large onion, quartered and
  thinly sliced
6 tablespoons (90 ml) dry
  white wine
8 tablespoons (120 ml)
  freshly chopped mixed
  herbs

Heat the oven to Reg 6/400°F/
200°C. Cut the chicken into
twelve small serving pieces. Melt
the butter in a large frying-pan on
a moderate heat. Put in the pieces
of chicken and brown them.
Then pack them into a large pie
dish. Lower the heat under the
pan and put in the onion. Cook it
until it is soft. Pour in the wine
and bring it to the boil. Stir in the
herbs. Spoon the onion, wine and
herbs over the chicken, cover the
dish with foil and put it into the
oven for 1 hour. Serve the
chicken straight from the dish.

Preparation: 40 minutes
Cooking: 1 hour

Chicken, leek and bacon pie

This raised pie will feed up to
eight people. It smells
absolutely superb while it is
cooking and it is a temptation
not to eat it straight away, but
it is best if it is left to cool.
Serve it with a salad or with
hot vegetables, or take it on a
picnic.

1 small chicken weighing
  about 3 lbs (1·350 kg)
4 oz (125 g) streaky bacon
12 oz (350 g) leeks
3 tablespoons (45 ml)
  chopped parsley
6 chopped sage leaves
freshly ground black pepper
pinch sea salt
PASTRY:
1 lb (450 g) wholemeal flour
$\frac{1}{2}$ teaspoon (2·5 ml) sea salt
freshly ground black pepper
4 tablespoons (60 ml) milk

3 tablespoons (45 ml) water
5 oz (150 g) lard
beaten egg for glaze

Heat the oven to Reg 3/325°F/
170°C. Joint the chicken, take the
meat from the bones and dice it.
Dice the bacon. Cut each leek in
half lengthways and slice it
thinly. Mix all these in a bowl
with the parsley and sage, and
season. Put the flour into a bowl
with the salt and pepper and
make a well in the centre. Put the
lard, milk and water into a saucepan and set them on a low heat
for the lard to melt. Pour the
mixture into the flour and quickly
mix everything to a workable
dough. Set aside about one third
of it for the top. Use the rest to
line a 2-lb (900-g) loaf tin or
raised pie mould. Press in the
chicken mixture and cover it with
the reserved pastry. Seal the
edges, making sure they come inside the rim of the tin. Decorate
the top of the pie with trimmings
and brush it with beaten egg.
Bake the pie for 2 hours. Take it
out of the oven and let it stand for
10 minutes. Remove the mould or
loosen the pie from the sides of
the tin with a rounded knife.
Turn it onto a wire rack and
quickly turn it up the right way.
Let the pie cool for at least 6
hours before serving.

Preparation: 50 minutes
Cooking: 2 hours
Cooling: 6 hours

Sage and onion stuffing for duck

The traditional stuffing for a
duck is sage and onion.
Softening the onion in milk
first gives a very mild onion
flavour and the stuffing is soft
textured and not at all
puddingy as some sage and
onion stuffings can be. The
same stuffing can be doubled in
quantity to use for a goose.

1 large onion
$\frac{1}{4}$ pint (150 ml) milk
1 bayleaf
4 oz (100 g) wholemeal
  breadcrumbs
8 chopped sage leaves
sea salt and freshly ground
  black pepper

Quarter and thinly slice the
onion. Put it into a saucepan
with the milk and bayleaf.
Cover and simmer for 15
minutes. Remove the bayleaf.
Mix in the breadcrumbs and
sage leaves and season well.

Preparation: 25 minutes

Boiled duck with apples

Boiling is a way of cooking
duck which keeps the meat soft
and juicy but which eliminates
any fattiness. The apple sauce
makes a good sharp
accompaniment to the slightly
rich meat.

1 duck weighing $3\frac{1}{2}$–4 lb
  (1·575–1·800 kg)
12 oz (350 g) Bramley apples
8 sage leaves
1 onion, cut in half but not
  peeled
1 carrot, cut in half
  lengthways
1 stick celery, broken
4 cloves
1 teaspoon (5 ml) black
  peppercorns
$\frac{1}{2}$ teaspoon (2·5 ml) sea salt
6 fl oz (175 ml) dry cider
1 oz (25 g) butter
1 large onion, quartered and
  thinly sliced

Put two sage leaves inside the
duck and truss the duck. Put it
into a large saucepan or casserole with the peelings of the
apples, two more sage leaves,
the onion, carrot, celery, cloves,
peppercorns, salt and $\frac{1}{4}$ pint
(150 ml) of the cider. Add water
to cover and bring everything

to the boil. Cover and cook gently for 1 hour 30 minutes, or until the duck feels tender when pricked with a fork.

To make the sauce, finely chop the apples and remaining sage leaves. Melt the butter in a saucepan on a low heat. Mix in the onion and cook it until it is soft. Add the apples, sage leaves and remaining cider. Cover and cook gently for 15 minutes or until the apples are soft and pulpy. Carve the duck, discarding the skin. Spoon a little of the cooking liquid over it and serve the apple sauce separately.

Preparation: 30 minutes
Cooking: 1 hour 30 minutes

Duck, mint and cherry salad

Roasting a duck with mint flavours it gently all the way through. The dark meat and glossy cherries make a colourful summer salad.

1 duck weighing $4\frac{1}{2}$ lb (2 kg)
8 large mint sprigs
2 teaspoons (10 ml) fine sea salt
8 oz (225 g) red cherries
3 tablespoons (45 ml) chopped mint
2 tablespoons (30 ml) olive oil
juice $\frac{1}{2}$ lemon

Heat the oven to Reg 6/400°F/ 200°C. Put two sprigs of mint inside the duck. Truss the duck, prick it all over with a fork and rub the salt into the skin. Put it on a rack in a roasting tin and cover it with the remaining mint sprigs. Wrap the duck all round with foil and put it into the oven for 1 hour 30 minutes. Remove the foil and mint sprigs and continue cooking for a further 30 minutes so the skin turns dark brown. Take the duck from the oven and let it cool completely. Take all the meat from the bones and cut it into 1-inch (2·5-cm) dice. Stone the cherries. Put the duck, cherries and mint into a bowl. Beat the oil and lemon juice together and fold them into the salad.

Preparation: 45 minutes
Cooking: 2 hours
Cooling: 2 hours

Guinea fowl with spiced pork stuffing

Guinea fowl can be small, so they are best filled with a meaty stuffing.

1 guinea fowl weighing around 2 lb (900 g)
8 oz (225 g) lean pork (shoulder or spare rib chops)
4 prunes
$\frac{1}{4}$ pint (150 ml) dry red wine
1 small onion, thinly sliced
4 chopped sage leaves
6 black peppercorns, crushed
4 allspice berries, crushed
4 juniper berries, crushed
little sea salt
1 oz (25 g) butter
$\frac{1}{2}$ pint (275 ml) stock (made from the giblets)

Soak the prunes in the wine for 2 hours. Heat the oven to Reg 5/ 375°F/190°C. Chop the pork very finely. Blanch the onion in simmering water for 5 minutes. Strain the prunes and reserve the wine. Stone and finely chop the prunes. Mix the pork with the prunes, onion, sage and spices. Use the mixture to stuff the guinea fowl. Truss the guinea fowl and spread it with the butter. Put it on a rack in a roasting tin and cover it completely with foil. Put it into the oven for 1 hour. Remove the foil and continue cooking for a further 20 minutes. Place the guinea fowl on a carving plate and remove the trussing string. Put the roasting tin on top of the stove on a moderate heat and pour in the wine from the prunes and the stock. Bring them to the boil, stirring in any residue from the bottom of the pan. Carve the guinea fowl at the table and serve the gravy separately.

Marinade: 2 hours
Preparation: 45 minutes
Cooking: 1 hour 20 minutes

Brandied apricot stuffing for turkey

This is a luxury Christmas stuffing, just as good cold as it is hot. It is enough for a 16–20-lb (6–9-kg) bird. Make it on Christmas Eve and store it in a covered container in the refrigerator until Christmas morning.

2 oz (50 g) dried unsulphured apricots (or, if you cannot find these, ordinary dried apricots)
4 tablespoons (60 ml) brandy
8 oz (225 g) chestnuts
6 tablespoons (90 ml) rendered turkey fat or $1\frac{1}{2}$ oz (40 g) butter
3 large onions, quartered and thinly sliced
1 lb (450 g) streaky pork, minced, or good quality sausage-meat
4 oz (125 g) fresh wholemeal breadcrumbs
grated rind and juice 1 large orange
4 tablespoons (60 ml) chopped parsley
6 chopped sage leaves
1 tablespoon (15 ml) chopped thyme
1 tablespoon (15 ml) chopped marjoram
sea salt and freshly ground black pepper

Finely chop the apricots and soak them in the brandy for 12 hours. Blanch the chestnuts and simmer them for 2 minutes. Take them from the heat and peel them, leaving them in the water until you are ready for them. Finely chop them. Heat the fat or melt the butter in a large frying-pan on a low heat. Mix in the onions and cook them until they are soft. Put the pork into a large bowl and mix in the onions, bread-crumbs, orange rind and juice, herbs and apricots. Season and mix everything together well. (The best way of making sure that all the ingredients are evenly distributed is to roll up your sleeves and mix the stuff-ing with your hands!)

Marinade: 12 hours
Preparation: 30 minutes

Black turkey with walnut and apple stuffing

I have only ever been lucky enough to cook one black turkey and this is the way I did it. The savoury-sweet stuffing flavoured with herbs goes beautifully with the slightly richer meat, but it is also very suitable for an ordinary turkey.

1 black turkey weighing 12–14 lb (5–6 kg)
4 oz (125 g) chopped walnuts
1 oz (25 g) butter
4 large sticks celery, finely chopped
1 large onion, finely chopped
1 large cooking apple, peeled, cored and chopped
4 oz (125 g) wholemeal breadcrumbs
2 oz (50 g) sultanas
2 tablespoons (30 ml) chopped parsley
2 tablespoons (30 ml) chopped thyme
2 tablespoons (30 ml) chopped marjoram
4 tablespoons (60 ml) dry white wine

GRAVY:
½ pint (275 ml) stock, made from the giblets
¼ pint (150 ml) dry white wine

Heat the oven to Reg 6/400°F/ 200°C. To make the stuffing, melt the butter in a frying-pan on a low heat. Mix in the celery and onion and cook them until the onion is soft. Mix in the apple and cook for 1 minute more. Take the pan from the heat and mix in the breadcrumbs, sultanas and herbs. Bind them together with the wine. Stuff and truss the turkey. Place it in a roasting tin and cover it completely with foil. Put it into the oven for 2 hours, then remove the foil and cook it for a further 15 minutes until the skin is brown and crisp. Take out the turkey and put it on a carving plate. Skim any fat from the juices in the tin. Set the tin on top of the stove on a moderate heat and pour in the stock. Bring it to the boil, add the wine and simmer for 2 minutes. Serve the gravy separately.

Preparation: 45 minutes
Cooking: 2 hours 15 minutes

Boned and braised goose

This is a really festive dish of braised goose, and boning it out makes both cooking and carving easier. You can have it hot for a Christmas dinner or cold for a party.

1 small goose weighing 6–8 lbs (3–4 kg)
STUFFING:
1 lb (450 g) good quality sausage-meat
1 lb (450 g) minced pork
the goose liver, finely chopped
1 tablespoon (15 ml) chopped parsley
1 tablespoon (15 ml) chopped thyme

4 chopped sage leaves
pinch ground allspice
pinch ground mace
1 medium onion, finely chopped
1 oz (25 g) butter
4 tablespoons (60 ml) dry sherry
BRAISING:
2 medium onions, sliced
2 medium carrots, sliced
2 sticks celery, chopped
1 small turnip, chopped
1 bouquet garni
6 black peppercorns
½ pint (275 ml) dry red wine
½ pint (275 ml) stock
FOR SERVING:
¾ pint (450 ml) cooking liquid
pinch ground mace
4 tablespoons (60 ml) chopped parsley

Bone out the goose and make stock from the bones. Mix the sausage-meat, pork, chopped liver, herbs and spices together. Lay the boned goose out flat. Cover it with the pork mixture and then reshape it. Sew it up with strong thread. Heat the oven to Reg 5/375°F/190°C. Grease a large casserole with butter or dripping, add the braising vegetables, cover them and set them on a low heat for 5 minutes. Place the goose on top and put in the bouquet garni and peppercorns. Pour in the wine and stock and bring to the boil. Cover the casserole and put it into the oven for 2 hours.

Take out the goose and put it onto a heatproof dish. Return it to the oven for 20 minutes. Strain the juices from the cas-serole and skim them well. Measure off ¾ pint (450 ml) and put it into a saucepan with the mace and parsley. Simmer it for 2 minutes and pour it into a sauceboat to serve separately.

Preparation: 1 hour 15 minutes
Cooking: 2 hours 20 minutes

GAME

*The truth of the matter is that a sportsman should
not be content with a good gun and a good dog,
but also needs an intelligent and willing cook
who can bring game to the table in a manner worthy
of the best traditions of the art.*

(Major Hugh Pollard)

THE TWELFTH of August, the 'Glorious Twelfth', heralds the start of the game season. From then until the first of February, tweeds will be worn, eager dogs will be packed into the backs of Land-Rovers and estate cars, birds will be shot and some will escape, and game larders will be well stocked.

The countryman has always derived a great deal of pleasure from game. There is all the enjoyment of a day out in the air accompanied by friends and a faithful dog; there is the satisfaction of actually having to work for your food and pit your wits against nature to get it; there is the contentment of sitting round a fire in the evening, with a warming drink in hand, discussing the best kills of the day and those wily birds that lived to fight again; and then there is the final pleasure of enjoying the food that you went out to win.

Shoots, of course, vary tremendously, and few have illustrated it better than the cartoonist Thelwell in his drawings of the Rough Shoot and the Smooth Shoot. In the Smooth Shoot, tweeds are definitely the order of the day and a professional photographer has been hired to take the photograph of the well-ordered shooting party with their picnic hampers and their immaculately groomed, perfectly behaved labradors and airedales. The photograph of the Rough Shoot is being taken by one of their members on an amateur camera. They are wearing a various selection of hats and thornproof coats and leggings and are sitting in a happy, slightly untidy group with a motley collection of eager-faced springer spaniels. Neither shoot is really more enjoyable than the other and the safety and the quality of the shooting is generally the same. It really depends on your means and the situation you happen to find yourself in.

The large, well-organised shoots cover many acres of farmland and moorland. They are generally run by a keeper who has the responsibility of maintaining the land to provide the optimum conditions in which game can thrive and breed, and, in the case of pheasants and partridges, he replaces the stock by rearing and releasing young birds. He organises beaters and decides on the plan of action for the day. He makes sure all the shot birds are picked up and, at the end of the day, he sells surplus birds to a butcher or a game dealer. Members

The odd thing about rabbit is that, though it may be low, it's deuced good.

(Major Hugh Pollard)

GAME

Walking up pheasants on a rough shoot

The dog picks up the pheasant, carries it ...

The gamekeeper and his dog picking up pheasants on an organised shoot

... and retrieves to hand

of the shoot pay a certain amount a year and know they are going to have a full and successful day's shooting with a large bag at the end, be it on open grouse moors, in flat partridge country or in pheasant woodland.

Very often, the small shoots, covering far fewer acres, are do-it-your-self affairs. A group of guns may rent land from a farmer or the farmer may organise the shoot himself, and the members do their own rearing and keepering. On a day's shooting, they take it in turns to beat and shoot, and any game shot is immediately picked up and put into large, canvas game bags which are slung over the shoulder. They shoot the pheasants, partridge or duck that they have released on the land, together with any pigeons that their questing dogs happen to put up. At the end of the day, the bag is a mixed one, and is as evenly divided as possible. The cook waiting at home for the bag never knows what to expect. There may be one pheasant or a wild duck or just a couple of pigeons, or, if you are really lucky, there may even be a woodcock. You certainly cannot send your husband out with an order for, say, two brace of pheasants and a partridge, especially towards the end of the season when the birds are thin on the ground and any that are left are the wily ones that have avoided the guns on previous days. Yet it is these elements of uncertainty and surprise that make this type of shoot so enjoyable. No wonder the expressions on the faces of Thelwell's rough shooting characters are happy ones.

Pigeon shooting is a different matter. Pigeons are classed as vermin, but don't let the awful terminology put you off for they do make excellent eating. The beauty of their being vermin is that you can shoot them all the year round; they are plentiful enough for you to be able to do so without your doing any damage to the population whatsoever. One year when they were caught eating all our summer cabbages, we even shot three at the end of the garden! The serious pigeon shooter, however, takes his dog, his gun and a large bag to a spot under the flightpath. He erects a hide, puts out decoys and waits. By the end of the day he should be surrounded by spent cartridges, his dog will be tired from running up and down and retrieving, and the bag will be full. This is the man who has it all worked out. He does not take them all home by any means, but instead may sell them to a local butcher or to a middleman who sells them to a game dealer. From there they will reach town shops and also supermarkets all over the country, plucked and ready for the pot.

If the pigeon shooter's wife does get landed with a large number of birds to deal with, plucking them all straight away is out of the ques-

The Pheasant

OBSERVERS OF discrimination have often noted that in many cases the natural food of a bird or beast provided one of the best and most appropriate dressings with which to send it to table.... The pheasant is catholic in his taste, but he is a devotee of acorns, beechmast, and, above all, chestnuts; thus in the very nature of things it fitly comes about that though your exotic school of cookery may favour truffles and high sauces, there is nothing in plain cookery which goes so well with braised pheasant as chestnuts. Another peculiarity, too, may be noticed, which is that the little English edible chestnuts, which may be obtained in the same cover as the pheasant, are sweeter, better, and more delicate in flavour than the larger imported nuts from Spain and Italy.

(Major Hugh Pollard, *The Sportsman's Cookery Book*)

**A Buttered Rabbett:
Mrs Lord's Receipt**

Take your rabbett and fill the belly of it full of parsly, and when it is roasted mince the flesh with the parsly, then take butter and two spoonefulls of water, and some salt, and so boyle it allways stiring it, then take three spoonefulls of creame with the yolks of two eggs beaten with it, and put to it, then place the bones of your rabbett in the dish, and lay some sippetts in it and so poure your meat upon them.

(Rebecca Price,
The Compleat Cook)

tion. Instead, she makes a slit through feathers and skin and extracts only the plump, meaty breasts which can be sautéed or braised like chuck steak or made into terrines and pâtés. She can also freeze them, on the feather, exactly as they are. Just put them into polythene bags and the feathers will keep the meat moist. When you want to cook them, thaw them out at room temperature. The feathers practically fall off pigeons so, at your leisure, you can pluck them and cook them whole, or again just use the breasts. You can use the same method for all types of game if you have a glut; and if the birds need hanging, do so before freezing.

The first game to come into season is the red grouse which is shot on the high, bleak moors of Scotland and the North of England. They make an exciting day's sport as they wheel and turn swiftly in the air and demand a good deal of skill and an experienced eye. The best way of cooking young grouse is to roast them. You can also split them down the back, brush them with melted butter, sprinkle them with cayenne and grill them. Old grouse are best casseroled for about two hours. One grouse should feed two people.

Wild ducks and partridge both come into season on September 1st. Ducks are shot on estuaries, rivers and inland ponds. You need a good deal of patience for duck shooting, strong, waterproof clothing, and preferably thermal underwear! Wild ducks are much smaller than the domestic kind so you need a pair to feed four people, but they make up for this by having plump breasts and dark, flavoursome meat. Inland ducks never taste at all fishy, but if you ever receive one that has been shot on an estuary, take the precaution of putting a small, sliced potato and a slice of lemon into the cavity before cooking. Then you should have no trouble. Roasting, casseroling, and pot-roasting are all suitable cooking methods for wild ducks.

Partridge as a wild bird is declining in this country, but many shoots put down far more birds than they actually bag in a season and so, far from depleting the countryside, are doing their bit for conservation. Partridges thrive on flat land and you often find the best shoots on arable and horticultural farmland. A fair number of partridges do reach town shops and they ought to be labelled as being old or young. They have a delicate flavour which should not be masked by over-hanging (two days is about right) and which is best brought out in a young bird by roasting or grilling. Old partridges should be casseroled.

By far the commonest game bird is the pheasant and all through the season (October 1st to February 1st) it can be found hanging by the brace, one glossy coloured cock and one brown hen, in butchers, fishmongers and high class provision stores in town and country. They may look fairly expensive by the brace but if you work it out, one bird can often cost the same as a good quality chicken. If the shopkeeper won't split them up, buy the brace and cook them together, so you can have some cold the next day. Someone once said that cold pheasant should be served with Krug champagne for breakfast but, if you don't consider that a practical idea, make it into a winter salad with grapes, oranges and celery. We have tried all ways of cooking pheasant – marinating, braising and casseroling – but still consider that the best way of all is to roast it, covered with herbs, as in the recipe on page 58. One tip: if you only need, and are able to buy, one pheasant, choose the hen. She won't be as large as her mate and her feathers are by no means as spectacular, but she is generally plumper and moister.

There was a time when gamekeepers on country estates spent the whole of one afternoon hare shooting. Now, sadly, hares have declined considerably, and certainly when we see one on the farmland round us we are very glad he is there and would never shoot him. However, in other areas it is different and during the winter you can even find rich, dark hare meat in supermarkets. Jugged hare is still a country favourite. It got its name from being first made in a stoneware jug. Every game cook has her own recipe for jugged hare, but basically, it is marinated first and then browned with onions and carrots and small pieces of bacon. Then it is boiled up with stock and the marinade, herbs are added and the whole is poured into a jug or an earthenware crock. The jug is stood in a pan of water and put to simmer away gently in a slow oven. At the end of the cooking time, the blood of the hare can be added, together with port and lemon juice and perhaps some redcurrant jelly. There are many other ways of cooking hare, such as casseroling it in joints, roasting it whole, cutting the saddle into steaks or putting it into a pie; but somehow the jugged version is always the most memorable.

Don't forget rabbit. He is the poacher's game, available, like the pigeon, all the year round. Don't scorn him because of this, for he can be truly delicious. What could be more homely than a steaming rabbit pie or a rabbit stew with onions? You can also have a sauté of rabbit joints or a rich rabbit terrine that would grace the best of dinner parties. When we cook rabbit, we prefer to take the meat off the bone and use the bones for stock or soup, but it is very much a question of personal preference.

Venison is usually scarce and expensive. Some is sent directly to hotels and restaurants and most to butchers and game dealers; but occasionally the odd piece does arrive on the back doorstep! We place an order with a keeper at the beginning of the season for any spare, and usually forget all about it. Then out of the blue, the phone rings to say that it will be delivered in ten minutes. It is usually the pieces that hotels don't want such as the leg and shin, the neck or the loin. It arrives in huge joints that we hang as they are and then cut up for the freezer. So the recipes that we have in store are not for roasting a haunch or the saddle but for dealing with the less known parts. They are, however, exceedingly good everyday country fare.

Aged birds should be cooked by methods more closely akin to stewing than roasting, for an old cock (pheasant) can become nearly as tough as shoe-leather, and no amount of hanging will render him really tender.
(Major Hugh Pollard,
The Sportsman's Cookery Book)

Recipes for Game

Rabbit simmered with onions and finished with cheese

Wild rabbits vary tremendously in size and can be enough for from two to four people. The cheese topping in this dish can be made with more or less cheese, depending on the size of the rabbit. The sauce is deliciously creamy and a rich yellow colour and makes a humble rabbit into a special but still relatively cheap meal.

1 wild rabbit weighing 2–2½ lbs (900 g–1·125 kg) when skinned
1 thinly pared strip lemon rind
¾ pint (450 ml) stock
2 medium onions, thinly sliced
1 carrot, cut in half lengthways
1 stick celery, broken
a bouquet of sage, thyme, marjoram, rosemary and 2 strips lemon rind
sea salt and freshly ground black pepper
¼ nutmeg, grated
1 oz (25 g) butter
2 tablespoons (30 ml) wholemeal flour
2 egg yolks
4 oz (125 g) grated Farmhouse Cheddar cheese
3 tablespoons (45 ml) browned wholemeal breadcrumbs

Joint the rabbit. Cut the meat from the bones and cut it into ¾-inch (2-cm) pieces. Put these into a saucepan with the lemon rind, cover with water and bring to the boil on a moderate heat. Drain the meat, refresh it with cold water and drain it again. Put the rabbit meat back into the rinsed-out saucepan with the stock, onions, carrrot, celery and bouquet garni. Season well and grate in the nutmeg. Bring the rabbit gently to the boil, cover and simmer for 1 hour 30 minutes. Strain the stock and reserve the rabbit and the onions. Melt the butter in a saucepan on a moderate heat. Stir in the flour and cook it for 1 minute. Stir in the stock and bring it to the boil. Simmer the sauce for 2 minutes. Work the egg yolks together in a bowl and gradually stir in 8 tablespoons (120 ml) of the hot sauce. Stir the mixture back into the saucepan and continue to stir the sauce on a very low heat, without letting it boil, until it thickens. Mix the rabbit and onions into the sauce. Take the pan from the heat and leave it for 5 minutes. Pour the rabbit and sauce into a flat, heat-proof dish and scatter the cheese and breadcrumbs over the top. Put the dish under the grill for the cheese to melt and serve as soon as possible so it stays soft and bubbling.

Preparation: 45 minutes
Cooking: 1 hour 30 minutes

Rich rabbit and pork terrine

This is a good terrine – meaty and tasty and very cheap. As a main meal, with a salad, it will serve at least eight people.

the front and back joints of a wild rabbit plus the thick flesh from the lower back
the liver and heart of the rabbit
1 lb (450 g) streaky pork rashers
8 oz (225 g) good quality sausage-meat
1 tablespoon (15 ml) chopped thyme
8 chopped sage leaves
1 clove garlic, crushed with a pinch sea salt
freshly ground black pepper
8 oz (225 g) thinly cut unsmoked streaky bacon rashers
white flour and water for making luting paste

Heat the oven to Reg 3/325°F/170°C. Dice the rabbit meat. Finely mince the heart and liver with the pork. Mix the rabbit, pork and sausage-meat together and add the thyme, sage, garlic and pepper. Line a 2-lb (900-g) terrine or loaf tin with the bacon rashers and put in the rabbit mixture. Smooth the top, cover the terrine and seal it with luting paste. If you are using a loaf tin, cover it tightly with foil. Stand the terrine or tin in a roasting tin of water and put it into the oven for 2 hours. Let the terrine cool and remove the covering. Press the terrine overnight with a heavy weight, leaving it in a cool place. Remove any fat from the edges and turn it onto a large, flat plate, taking care not to lose any of the delicious jelly that will have set all round it.

Preparation: 50 minutes
Cooking: 2 hours
Cooling: 12 hours

Country pie

Game pies always call to mind pictures of old inns where the hunting or shooting party has just returned to warm up by a blazing fire, with a glass of strong drink and a hearty meal. When I first cooked this one for a family party, my uncle told me that it tasted of the country so that's how it came by its name. It is best served with braised red cabbage and jacket potatoes.

1 pheasant
1 hare
MARINADE:
$\frac{3}{4}$ pint (450 ml) dry red wine
1 large carrot, chopped
1 large onion, chopped
2 sticks celery, chopped, plus a few celery leaves
2 tablespoons (30 ml) red wine vinegar
1 clove garlic, finely chopped
FOR BRAISING:
1 carrot, chopped
1 medium onion, chopped
2 sticks celery, chopped
1 bouquet garni
1 bayleaf
liquid from the marinade
1 oz (25 g) butter
FOR PIE:
8 oz (225 g) flat mushrooms
3 tablespoons (45 ml) chopped parsley
rough puff pastry made with 8 oz (225 g) wholemeal or wheatmeal flour

Joint the hare and leave the pheasant whole. Put them together in a large deep dish or bowl. Put all the ingredients for the marinade into a saucepan, bring them to the boil and simmer them for 10 minutes. Let them cool completely and then pour them all over the pheasant and hare. Leave them for 24 hours in a cool place.

Heat the oven to Reg 4/350°F/180°C. Lift out the pheasant and hare and brush off any pieces of marinade. Strain the marinade and reserve the liquid, which by now should be lovely and rich with the blood of the hare. Heat the fat in a flameproof casserole on a high heat. Brown the pheasant and the hare joints all over. Lift them out and lower the heat. Put in the chopped vegetables, cover them and cook them for 7 minutes. Put the game on top and pour in the marinade. Bring it to the boil and add the bouquet garni and bayleaf. Cover the casserole and put it into the oven for 50 minutes. Take out the pheasant and put the hare back for a further 40 minutes. Cut the pheasant meat into 1-inch (2·5-cm) dice. When the hare is done, cut it up in the same way but leave the thin, muscular pieces from the rib cage. Raise the oven temperature to Reg 6/400°F/200°C. In a large pie dish, mix the pheasant, hare, mushrooms and parsley. Remove the bouquet garni and bayleaf from the casserole and spoon all the juices into the pie dish. Mix everything together well and put a pie funnel in the centre. Cover the pie with the pastry. Decorate the top with trimmings and brush it with beaten egg. Bake the pie for 45 minutes and serve it hot.

Preparation (1): 40 minutes
Marinade: 24 hours
Preparation (2): 1 hour
Cooking: 2 hours 15 minutes

Pheasant roasted with herbs

This is the best way I know of cooking young pheasants. It brings out all their natural flavour and makes the meat deliciously tender.

1 brace pheasants
6 sprigs each of thyme, marjoram, sage and parsley
thinly pared rind 1 medium orange
$\frac{1}{2}$ pint (275 ml) stock, made from the giblets
$\frac{1}{4}$ pint (150 ml) port

Heat the oven to Reg 6/400°F/200°C. Put a small sprig of herbs inside each pheasant and truss them. Place them on a rack in a roasting tin and cover them, together, completely with foil. Put them into the oven for 1 hour. Remove the foil and continue cooking for a further 30 minutes so that the skin becomes crisp and brown. While the pheasants are cooking, cut the orange rind into matchstick-sized slivers. Put them into a pan of cold water, bring them to the boil and simmer for $\frac{1}{2}$ minute. Drain them and refresh them with cold water.

Remove the pheasants from the oven and keep them warm. Pour off any fat from the roasting tin and set the tin on top of the stove on a high heat. Pour in the stock and bring it to the boil, scraping in any residue from the bottom of the pan. Add the port and pieces of orange rind and simmer for 2 minutes. Carve the pheasants at the table and serve the sauce separately.

Preparation: 25 minutes
Cooking: 1 hour 30 minutes

Pheasant braised with celery and chestnuts

This recipe follows Major Pollard's advice, and the pheasant certainly ends up well flavoured and moist.

1 large, well-hung cock pheasant
4 oz (125 g) chestnuts
1 head celery
1 oz (25 g) butter
1 medium onion, thinly sliced
$\frac{1}{2}$ pint (275 ml) good strong ale
large bouquet of parsley, thyme, marjoram, savory and sage

Heat the oven to Reg 4/350°F/ 180°C. Put the chestnuts into a pan of cold water, bring them to the boil and simmer them for 2 minutes. Peel them, leaving them immersed until you get to them, then chop them. Roughly chop the celery. Melt the butter in a large, flameproof casserole on a high heat. Put in the pheasant and brown it all over. Remove it and lower the heat. Put in the celery and onion and stir them about for 2 minutes. Pour in the ale and bring it to the boil. Mix in the chestnuts and set the pheasant on top. Tuck in the bouquet of herbs. Cover the casserole and put it into the oven for 1 hour 30 minutes. Joint the pheasant, arrange the joints on a serving dish and cover them with the chestnuts, celery and casserole juices.

Preparation: 30 minutes
Cooking: 1 hour 30 minutes

Pigeons and peas

So many game dishes contain only winter vegetables, but for a change, as pigeons are available all the year round, this is a light summer one with mint and peas.

4 pigeons
8 mint leaves
1½ lbs (675 g) peas, weighed
    in their shells
½ oz (15 g) butter or dripping
¼ pint (150 ml) dry red wine
¼ pint (150 ml) stock
2 sprigs mint
2 tablespoons (30 ml)
    chopped mint

Heat the oven to Reg 4/350°F/ 180°C. Truss the pigeons, putting two mint leaves inside each one. Shell the peas and reserve six pods. Melt the butter or dripping in a large, flameproof casserole on a high heat. Put in the pigeons and brown them all over. Pour in the wine and stock and bring

them to the boil. Add the mint sprigs and pea pods, cover and put the casserole into the oven for 1 hour 15 minutes. Remove the mint sprigs and pea pods and put in the chopped mint and peas. Cover again and put the casserole back into the oven for 20 minutes. Serve the pigeons with the peas and any juices from the casserole spooned over and round them.

Preparation: 30 minutes
Cooking: 1 hour 35 minutes

Venison marinated with beer and herbs

This is a homely country stew of very tender venison.

1½ lbs (675 g) leg of venison
MARINADE:
½ pint (275 ml) bitter beer
1 medium onion, thinly
    sliced
1 tablespoon (15 ml) chopped
    parsley
1 tablespoon (15 ml) chopped
    marjoram
6 chopped sage leaves
6 black peppercorns, crushed
pinch sea salt
COOKING:
1 oz (25 g) dripping
1 medium onion, thinly
    sliced
¼ pint (150 ml) bitter beer
1 tablespoon (15 ml) chopped
    parsley
1 tablespoon (15 ml) chopped
    thyme
1 tablespoon (15 ml) chopped
    marjoram
4 chopped sage leaves

Cut the venison into thin slices. Mix the ingredients for the marinade in a dish or bowl and put in the venison. Leave it for 36 to 48 hours in a cool place.

When you are ready to cook, heat the oven to Reg 4/350°F/ 180°C. Lift the venison from the marinade and drain it well, catching the liquid. Dry it on kitchen

paper. Melt the dripping in a flameproof casserole on a high heat. Put in the pieces of venison, brown them well and remove them. Lower the heat, mix in the onion and cook it until it is soft. Strain the marinade and pour it into the casserole. Add the beer and bring the liquids to the boil. Add the herbs and then the venison. Cover the casserole and put it into the oven for 1 hour 30 minutes.

Preparation (1): 15 minutes
Marinating: 36–48 hours

Preparation (2): 20 minutes
Cooking: 1 hour 30 minutes

Peppered venison chops

Loin of venison is very tender and the chops cook quickly and need only a simple marinade. The rich meat stands up well to a marinade flavoured with crushed peppercorns.

4 loin venison chops
¼ pint (150 ml) dry red wine
1 teaspoon (5 ml) crushed
    black peppercorns
1 oz (25 g) butter
2 tablespoons (30 ml)
    chopped parsley

In a flat dish, mix the wine with the peppercorns. Turn the chops in the dish and leave them for 24 hours at room temperature, turning them several times. When you are ready to cook, melt the butter in a large frying-pan on a low heat. Put in the chops (in two batches if necessary) and brown them well. Return all the chops to the pan, pour in the marinade and bring it to the boil. Cover the pan and keep it on a low heat for 45 minutes. The chops will be very tender and there will be just a little liquid left.

Preparation: 10 minutes
Marinade: 24 hours
Cooking: 55 minutes

Pupton

Pupton is a dish of pigeons layered with a savoury forcemeat and a selection of vegetables which vary according to the season, root vegetables in winter and artichoke bottoms and peas in summer. It is a delicious dish for any occasion. The pigeon breasts are meltingly tender underneath the gently spiced savoury breadcrumbs, and the high heat to finish off makes the topping brown and crisp.

4 pigeons
4 oz (125 g) streaky bacon
1 large onion, quartered and thinly sliced
4 oz (125 g) fresh wholemeal breadcrumbs
$\frac{1}{4}$ teaspoon (1·5 ml) ground mace
$\frac{1}{2}$ nutmeg, grated
grated rind 1 lemon
2 tablespoons (30 ml) chopped parsley
1 tablespoon (15 ml) mixed chopped sage and thyme
6 tablespoons (90 ml) stock, made from the giblets
8 oz (225 g) carrots
4 oz (125 g) open mushrooms

Heat the oven to Reg 4/350°F/ 180°C. Cut the breasts from the pigeons into halves. Cut off the legs, and remove and finely chop all the leg meat. Finely dice the bacon, put it into a frying-pan and set it on a low heat. When the fat begins to run, mix in the onion and cook it until it is soft. Take the pan from the heat and mix in the breadcrumbs, spices, lemon rind, herbs and stock. Finely chop the carrots. Halve or quarter the mushrooms, according to their size. Put one third of the breadcrumb mixture into the base of a large pie dish. Cover with half the carrots and mushrooms. Lay the pieces of pigeon breast on top in an overlapping line down the centre and lay the chopped leg meat on either side. Cover with the remaining mushrooms and carrots and then cover everything completely with the rest of the breadcrumb mixture. Cover the dish with foil and put the dish into the oven for 1 hour 30 minutes. Remove the foil, raise the heat to Reg 7/425°F/210°C and return the dish to the oven for 30 minutes. Serve straight from the dish.

Preparation: 40 minutes
Cooking: 2 hours

Wild ducks in cider

Wild ducks can be very small so you will need two for a meal for four people. You may have a little left over which can be served with sliced apples and celery as a first course. Apples and cider are good sharp accompaniments for rich meats and flaming the ducks in brandy makes the dish a lovely rich brown.

2 wild ducks, each weighing, when dressed, around 1$\frac{1}{2}$ lbs (675 g)
4 sage leaves
1 oz (25 g) butter
4 tablespoons (60 ml) brandy
$\frac{1}{4}$ pint (150 ml) stock, from the giblets
$\frac{1}{4}$ pint (150 ml) dry cider
1 small onion, peeled and left whole
1 small carrot, cut in half lengthways
1 stick celery, broken
1 bouquet garni
6 black peppercorns
2 tablespoons (30 ml) chopped parsley
apple sauce for serving

Heat the oven to Reg 4/350°F/ 180°C. Put two sage leaves inside each duck before trussing them. Melt the butter in a large casserole on a high heat. Put in the ducks and brown them all over. While they are browning, gently warm the brandy and set light to it. Pour it over the ducks and wait until the flames have died. Pour in the cider and half the stock and bring them to the boil. Add the onion, carrot, celery, bouquet garni and peppercorns. Cover the casserole and put it into the oven for 1 hour.

Take out the ducks and keep them warm. Strain the juices from the casserole into a sauce-pan. Add the parsley and the remaining stock. Bring it to the boil and let it simmer while you carve the ducks.

Preparation: 20 minutes
Cooking: 1 hour

RECIPES FOR GAME

Cartridges, cartridge bag, game bag and gun – and a dish of pupton

FISH

Where the pools are bright and deep,
Where the grey trout lies asleep,
Up the river and o'er the lea,
That's the way for Billy and me.

(James Hogg)

(*above*) *Fly fishing for salmon on the River Wye*

(*left*) *Fishing for char on Windermere*

THINK OF PEACE and tranquillity, the gentle swash of water at the edge of a lake or the running chuckle of a river, breathtaking scenery, the skill and excitement of the catch, and the full fish kettle. All these are combined in the sport of angling. In fact, nearly every fisherman to whom we have put the question 'Why do you fish?' has said that he would always put first the pleasures of being out in the open air, with time to think, and listen to the wildlife, and watch the world go by. Actually catching a fish is a bonus that makes his day even more pleasurable.

The largest proportion of anglers fish for coarse fish, like the huge, crafty, predatory pike, the fat carp, perch and grayling. These can be found in many English rivers, particularly those in the south and east of the country, such as the Thames, the Medway, the Great Ouse, the Trent and the rivers of Suffolk, Norfolk and Lincolnshire. Reservoirs and flooded gravel pits often hold large numbers of coarse fish; roach and bream in particular can be found in land drains on marshy land; and even the canals provide sport for the town dweller. Close seasons vary from county to county but the season for coarse fish is always a long one, starting some time in June and ending in March.

Much of the coarse fish is only valued for the sport it gives. Some, like the chubb, dace and barbel, are very bony and make poor eating, but others can be surprisingly good. A pike, so long as he is not too big, can be excellent; and several reservoirs are actually stocked with carp that are all caught to be eaten. We have never tasted any of the others but have been told that grayling, eaten fresh and cooked like trout, have a slight taste of thyme; and small gudgeon are delicious cleaned, coated in flour and fried in dripping, like sprats. Apart from these two, coarse fish has a slightly muddy flavour, so before you cook any of them, clean them and keep them in lightly salted water for up to two hours.

The game fishing season is shorter than that for coarse fish. Salmon, sea trout and trout are fished from April to October and char from March to September. The largest salmon ever caught came from the Thames. It was caught in 1821 by a Mr Richard Coxen of Twickenham, weighed 72 lb 8 oz and was sold to a fishmonger in Bond Street for

FOOD FROM THE COUNTRY

8s. 6d. a pound. For a long time the Thames has been far too polluted to carry any salmon, but due to recent endeavours to reverse the situation, the river is becoming cleaner again and experiments are now being made to reintroduce the 'King of the River'.

English salmon rivers include the Exe, Fowey, Tamar and Lyn in the South-West and the Whitby Esk and the Lune in the North, but the best salmon fishing is to be had in Scotland and Wales. The finest salmon river is reputedly the Tay and after this some would choose the Tweed and others the Aberdeenshire Dee. Then would come the Forth and the Spey. Wales also has a river Dee; and it has the Usk, the Conwy, and the Dovey among others and, of course, the Wye, which is often claimed by England but which is nevertheless under Welsh control. Wales's biggest salmon came from the Wye in 1923 and weighed 59 lb 8 oz.

The best time to catch a salmon is when it is just returning from the open sea to come up its home river to spawn. Then it will be in peak condition, its skin will be bright silver and its flesh, when cooked, a flaky pink. At this time it also makes the best, rich, deep-pink smoked salmon. The flavour of salmon is so superb that simplicity of cooking is always essential. Poach it in a court-bouillon, grill the steaks with knobs of butter, bake it whole or in steaks in a parcel of foil. Use lemon thyme, thyme, parsley and lemon for flavour, and plenty of butter, and never overcook.

Sea trout have a similar life cycle to the salmon, but stay near the estuaries of their home rivers instead of swimming out to the Atlantic. They are smaller than salmon and usually cheaper per pound but their flavour can be remarkably similar. Use the same methods for cooking. The native trout of the British Isles is the brown trout which can be caught in some western and northern English rivers, lakes and reservoirs, and in many Welsh and Scottish rivers. Until recently it has been left entirely to itself to reproduce its numbers, but now fishing grounds are increasingly being stocked with farmed brown trout. The rainbow trout, which came from America in the last century, is a completely introduced fish. Some breed in the wild, but it is restocked continually in rivers and reservoirs and is also being successfully farmed.

Knowing that possibly the best salmon fishing within a reasonable travelling distance was on the River Wye, we headed up river to see what we could find. It was a warm, April day and we went first of all to Builth Wells. Three different people had told us that eight salmon had been caught that week just outside the town where a tributary meets the Wye. So, in the cool of the late afternoon we sat and waited – and waited – and waited. We wandered up the tributary. A fisherman was just arriving. 'Are you out for salmon?' we asked him. 'No, trout.' He was a water bailiff from further upstream. The water was low, he said, there had been no rain for a week. The prospects for salmon were not as good as we had hoped.

So it was a mutual decision to move further down river. Just as we

My rod and my line,
my float and my lead,
My hook and my plummet,
my whetston and knife,
My basket, my baits,
both living and dead
My net, and my meat
for that is the chief;
Then I must have thread,
and hairs green and small,
With mine angling purse;
and so you have all.

(Izaak Walton,
The Compleat Angler)

There is one plain and simple rule about salmon which should be remembered by every cook. Salmon has a particular and specific virtue of its own. It is best plain, so do not attempt to better it. A clean-run spring salmon perfectly cooked is perfection in itself, and, incidentally, no bad test of a cook's skill.

(Major Hugh Pollard, *The Sportsman's Cookery Book*)

were giving up hope we came upon two fishermen complete with high waders and rods. They were definitely out for salmon, so we followed them down to the sparkling Wye. This stretch, they said, was perfection for salmon fishermen. There was a shingle bank so they could cast without obstruction and play the fish. The river was full and fast enough for the salmon to come up and yet not so deep that it came over your waders. The fishermen cast their rods, the sun was glinting on the gurgling river and behind us were the misty peaks of the Black Mountains. Everything was peaceful and calm. It was the perfect spot and the perfect evening for catching salmon. The same evening we found an old fishing inn with brown decor, and chairs that you sank into. So we sat back with a pint of beer and a hearty meal and listened to the fishing stories, the tales of the river and the talk of the one that got away.

When we left them, our fishermen presented us with a pike that they had caught that morning, and it survived a night in the fridge of the hotel and the journey home in our cold box. We had never seen one before, let alone eaten one, and had it not been for this there would have been no pike recipe in the book. He was a wicked looking creature, 27 inches long and with a large, wide head and strong jaws. His skin was coarse and dapple grey and he weighed $4\frac{1}{2}$ lbs. We must admit to having been a little dubious. You hear awful tales of pike tasting muddy and being dry and full of bones. Nevertheless, we cleaned him and soaked him in lightly salted water for a few hours. As the skin was coarse we didn't particularly want to bake or poach him whole so we decided on filleting, which was surprisingly easy to do, and then skinning, which was even easier, leaving around 2 lbs of clean, white fillets. Most fish cooks, from Izaak Walton to more recent ones,

Perch in Water Sokey

Scale, gut, and wash your perch, put salt in your water; when it boils, put in the fish, with an onion cut in slices, a handful of parsley picked and washed clean and as much milk as will make the water white; when your fish are done enough put them in a soup dish and pour a little of the water over them with the parsley and the onions, then serve them up with butter and parsley in a boat. Onions may be omitted if you please. You may boil trout the same way.

(An eighteenth-century recipe from May Byron's *Pot Luck*)

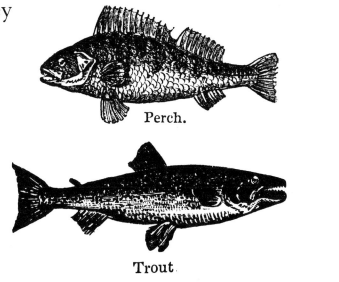

Perch.

Trout.

recommend using large amounts of butter with pike to keep it moist. Izaak Walton's recipe 'for anglers and very honest men' involves stuffing the belly with a mixture of butter, anchovies, oysters and herbs, sewing it up and roasting the fish on a spit. We liked the idea of the butter and herbs but, as it was the first time we had tried a pike, we did not want to mask the flavour too much, so we left out the anchovies. The result was the rich and delicious recipe below.

Chance also played a large part in our discovering about char fishing. Char are small fish, related to salmon that were left behind in certain lakes of the British Isles during the Ice Age. They are usually 6 to 10 inches long but can weigh up to 3 lbs, and they swim very deep down in the still, dark waters of lakes. That was all we knew about them until we went into a pub in Windermere that turned out to be

Salmon fisherman with his catch by the Wye – note the length of the rod

(**above right**) *Feeding time at a trout farm – the trout causing a stir in the water*

(**right**) *Pots of trout and almonds* (*page* **70**)

Pike.

the headquarters of the local char fishermen. They are a very secretive bunch and generally keep away from tourists, but the landlord was helpful.

All the baits, or lures, for char are handmade by the fishermen themselves from gold, silver, brass and stainless steel. One long line is hung into the water from a bamboo pole and from this come smaller lines to which the baits are attached. Although the season begins in March, the week when most of the fishing is done is the one before the spring bank holiday, before too many tourists appear in the area. In the evenings they take the fish back to the public bar, measure and weigh them, and talk of nothing but char. We were a week late for this but were told that the boats were still going out; they pushed off from the edge of the lake very early in the morning, at about half past five.

At five o'clock the next morning it was pouring with rain and photographs were out of the question. By eight o'clock it was drizzling, so we walked down to the far end of the lake. It was deserted, but then a small, wooden rowing boat came into view, moving very slowly, silently and steadily in a straight line through the deepest water. Fixed at right angles to the back of the boat, one on either side, were two bamboo poles. We had found our char fishermen. Apart from someone fishing for trout on the edge of the lake there was no one else around, and again there was an atmosphere of peace and calm. Most char find their way onto the plates of the fishermen. None ever reach the shops, but quite a large number are sold to hotels around the Lakes and are made into the local speciality of potted char. The fishermen themselves, however, prefer their char fried or grilled or baked in foil. The flesh of char is pinky brown and it tastes like a cross between trout and salmon. Don't mask the flavour with heavy spices; lemon and herbs are all you need.

Char and salmon are exclusive fish, enjoyed regularly only by those who catch them, but rainbow trout has in recent years become accessible to everybody because it is now produced on fish farms. This has made it relatively cheap and always available. We have two fish farms near us. One is centred on a natural lake surrounded by wild flowers and King Alfred reeds. It is fed from a spring that starts in the chalk of the North Downs and it produces both brown and rainbow trout that are sent out to angling societies to stock lakes and reservoirs. The other is small and on a farm near our own village. The trout is sold at the farm gate and only caught when you knock on the door and ask for it. Bright and sparkling, it is an absolute treat, but we have seen fish just as good stacked up by the boxful in Billingsgate market.

Trout is no longer an expensive, imported luxury, but a home-produced food that is no dearer by the pound than many types of white fish. It deserves to appear on everyone's table far more often than it does. You can grill trout, either whole or filleted; coat it in flour or oatmeal and fry it; poach it with a mint sprig inside it; bake it, either in wine or in a parcel of foil; or make it into a pâté. Izaak Walton was right: 'he may justly be said ... to be a generous fish'.

Recipes for Fish

Packets of salmon with lemon

This is a light way of cooking salmon that seals in all the flavour and keeps it very moist.

1½ lbs (675 g) salmon
2 tablespoons (30 ml) chopped lemon thyme
juice ½ lemon
sea salt and freshly ground black pepper
1 oz (25 g) butter

Heat the oven to Reg 5/375°F/ 190°C. Skin the salmon and remove the bones. Cut the flesh into pieces about 1 inch by ½ inch (3 cm by 1·5 cm). Put them into a bowl and mix in the lemon thyme and lemon juice. Season lightly. Use all the butter to grease four pieces of foil about 8 inches (20 cm) square. Divide the salmon between the pieces of foil. Seal the edges over the top of the salmon and lay the parcels on a baking sheet. Put them into the oven for 20 minutes. Take the un-opened packets to the table and unwrap them onto individual plates to preserve all the flav-oursome juices.

Preparation: 20 minutes
Cooking: 20 minutes

Salmon trout with fennel mayonnaise

Salmon trout topped with lacy sprigs of fennel makes a luxurious summer treat. This will serve four as a main course or eight as a first course.

1 salmon trout weighing around 1½ lbs (675 g)
COURT-BOUILLON:
water to cover

6 tablespoons (90 ml) dry white wine
2 bayleaves
1 bouquet garni which includes a fennel sprig
1 small carrot, cut in half lengthways
1 small onion, peeled and left whole
few celery leaves
1 teaspoon (5 ml) black peppercorns
MAYONNAISE:
2 egg yolks
freshly ground black pepper
1 teaspoon (5 ml) mustard powder
8 fl oz (250 ml) olive oil
juice 1 lemon
2 tablespoons (30 ml) chopped fennel
FOR SERVING:
1 lettuce
½ cucumber
4 fennel sprigs (or 8 if for a first course)

Clean the salmon trout. Put the ingredients for the court-bouil-lon into a saucepan, fish kettle or oval casserole. Cover them, bring them to the boil and sim-mer for 10 minutes. Put in the salmon trout and poach it, with the water just trembling, for 10 minutes. Lift it out onto a large piece of foil and immediately wrap it up. Let it cool com-pletely. Treating it this way, it won't be too dry to skin and all the juices will be kept inside. Make the mayonnaise, adding the chopped fennel at the end. Skin the salmon trout and divide it into four serving pieces (or eight if for a first course). Remove as many bones from each piece as possible. Arrange a bed of lettuce on a large serving plate. Put the

pieces of fish on top, coat them with the mayonnaise and deco-rate them with fennel sprigs. Surround the fish with thin, overlapping slices of cucumber.

Preparation: 40 minutes
Cooking: 10 minutes
Cooling: 1 hour 30 minutes

Grilled trout with sweet herbs

Chopped fresh herbs stuffed into the slits in the sides of whole, grilled trout make the final dish attractive as well as gently flavouring the fish as they cook.

4 small- to medium-sized trout
6 tablespoons (90 ml) mixed chopped thyme, marjoram, tarragon and parsley
¼ pint (150 ml) milk
approximately 6 tablespoons (90 ml) seasoned wholemeal flour
4 lemon wedges
2 oz (50 g) butter (optional)

Clean the trout but leave the heads on. Vandyke their tails. Make three diagonal slits in the sides of each one, running backwards from head to tail. Fill the slits with the herbs. Dip the trout in the milk and coat them in the flour. Heat the grill to high. Lay the trout on the hot rack and cook them un-til they are golden brown on each side and cooked through (about 12 minutes altogether). Serve plain with lemon wedges and, if you wish, dotted with butter.

Preparation: 30 minutes
Cooking: 12 minutes

Trout baked with lemon

These trout have a soft lemon flavour permeating through them.

4 trout
freshly ground black pepper
1½ lemons, the half cut lengthways down the lemon
4 sprigs lemon thyme
1 tablespoon (15 ml) chopped lemon thyme
1 oz (25 g) butter
1 tablespoon (15 ml) wholemeal flour

Heat the oven to Reg 5/375°F/190°C. Clean the trout and season the insides with pepper. Cut the half lemon into four long wedges. Cut the rind and pith from each one. Put a lemon wedge and a sprig of lemon thyme inside each trout. Lay the trout in a buttered, ovenproof dish. Squeeze the juice from the remaining lemon and put it into a small saucepan with the butter. Set it on a low heat for the butter to melt and then pour it over the trout. Sprinkle the trout with the chopped lemon thyme and then with the flour. Bake the trout for 30 minutes. Serve the trout straight from the dish and spoon the buttery lemon sauce over them.

Trout with orange and lemon sauce

Orange and lemon juices make a light, fresh sauce to go with rich, smoky-flavoured trout.

4 small- to medium-sized trout
¼ pint (150 ml) milk
6 tablespoons (90 ml) seasoned wholemeal flour
up to 3 oz (75 g) butter
juice 1 large orange
juice 1 lemon
¼ pint (150 ml) dry white wine
3 tablespoons (45 ml) chopped parsley
1 tablespoon (15 ml) chopped lemon thyme

Clean the trout, vandyke their tails and cut off the fins. Dip the trout in milk and then coat them in the flour. Melt 1 oz (25 g) of the butter in a large frying-pan on a moderate heat. Put in the trout, two at a time if necessary, adding up to 1 oz (25 g) more butter for the second batch if needed. Cook them so they are a good brown on both sides and cooked through. This will take about 10 minutes. Put them onto a warm serving plate and keep them warm. Put 1 oz (25 g) butter into the pan and let it melt. Pour in the orange and lemon juices and the wine and add the herbs. Cook the sauce for 1 minute, stirring in any pan residue, and then spoon it over the trout.

Preparation: 30 minutes
Cooking: 20 minutes

Grilled trout with sorrel sauce

If you catch your own trout or buy them from a fishing friend, you will not be able to choose the size that you may sometimes want. To prevent one person from ending up with a monster and another with a sprat, fillet the fish before cooking so you can even them out when you serve them. The sorrel and the mace in this sauce give an eighteenth-century flavour.

4 trout (all medium-sized if possible, but not essential)
juice ½ lemon
¼ teaspoon (1·5 ml) ground mace
freshly ground black pepper
SAUCE:
20 sorrel leaves
1 oz (25 g) butter
¼ pint (150 ml) dry white wine
¼ teaspoon (1·5 ml) ground mace

Fillet the trout and lay the fillets on a large, flat dish, overlapping as little as possible. Sprinkle them with the lemon juice, mace and pepper and leave them at room temperature for 30 minutes. Remove the back ribs from the sorrel leaves and finely chop the rest. Melt the butter in a saucepan on a low heat. Stir in the sorrel and cook it until it is a dull green and has 'melted' into the butter. Pour in the wine and bring it to the boil. Add the mace and simmer for 2 minutes. Keep the sauce warm while you cook the trout. Heat the grill to high and if you have an open, wire rack, cover it with foil. Lay the fillets, skin side down, on the hot rack and grill them until they are just beginning to brown and are cooked through (about 4 minutes). Serve the sauce separately.

Preparation: 30 minutes
Marinade: 30 minutes
Cooking: 4 minutes

Trout baked with thyme

Using red wine as the cooking liquid makes this dish much richer than the previous recipes.

4 small- to medium-sized trout
2 tablespoons chopped thyme
¼ pint (150 ml) dry red wine
one 4-inch (10 cm) piece cinnamon stick
1 medium onion, thickly sliced
1 tablespoon (15 ml) kneaded butter

Heat the oven to Reg 4/350°F/ 180°C. Clean the trout and van-dyke their tails. Lay them in a flat, ovenproof dish and use up to 1 tablespoon (15 ml) of the thyme by sprinkling it inside each one. Pour the wine over the trout, scatter the onion over the top and put in the cinnamon stick. Cover the dish with foil and put it into the oven for 25 minutes. Lift out the trout, making sure you leave all the pieces of onion behind, and lay them on a warm serving dish. Keep them warm. Strain the juices from the cooking dish into a saucepan and set it on a moderate heat. Bring to the boil, then whisk in the kneaded butter and the remaining thyme. Simmer the sauce for 2 minutes and pour it over the trout.

Preparation: 30 minutes
Cooking: 25 minutes

Pots of trout and almonds

Light and lemony pots of trout topped with crisp, browned almonds make a delightful first course.

2 large trout
2 large sprigs lemon thyme
little butter for greasing
1½ oz (40 g) butter
2 oz (50 g) almonds, blanched and split
juice 1 lemon
2 tablespoons (30 ml) chopped parsley

Heat the oven to Reg 4/350°F/ 180°C. Clean the trout and remove the heads. Put a sprig of lemon thyme inside each fish. Lay the trout in a lightly buttered, ovenproof dish and cover them with butter paper. Bake them for 20 minutes. Skin the trout and lift the flesh from the bones. Discard the lemon thyme. In a bowl, flake the flesh well. Divide it between four small cocottes or soufflé dishes. Melt

the butter in a small frying-pan on a moderate heat. Put in the almonds and stir them around until they brown. Add the lemon juice and chopped parsley and let the lemon juice bubble. Divide the mixture between the pots of trout. Put the pots into the oven for 5 minutes to heat through.

Preparation: 30 minutes
Cooking: 25 minutes

Grilled char with lemon butter

Until we went to Windermere, we had only heard of potted char, but this is made more in hotels than by the fishermen themselves. One of the most popular ways of cooking char is to grill them with butter. This is an excellent way if, as was our case, you are only able to obtain two fish, since it brings out all the natural flavour.

4 char
6 tablespoons (90 ml) seasoned wholemeal flour
4 oz (125 g) unsalted butter
sea salt and freshly ground black pepper
grated rind and juice 1 lemon
4 tablespoons (60 ml) chopped parsley

Clean the char and cut off the heads. Coat the fish in the flour. Beat the butter until it is soft and beat in the salt and pepper. Add the lemon rind and then the juice, drop by drop. Finally, beat in the parsley. Heat the grill to high and, if you have an open wire rack, cover it with foil. Lay the char on the hot rack and dot them with a quarter of the butter. Grill them for 3 minutes so that the top side is a good brown. Turn them over, dot them with a further quarter of the butter and grill the second side in the same way. Serve them hot and

put the remaining butter into a small dish to hand round separately.

Preparation: 20 minutes
Cooking: 10 minutes

Pike baked with butter and herbs

This recipe is very loosely based on a far more complicated one in Izaak Walton's *The Compleat Angler*. He ends, 'This dish of meat is too good for any but anglers, or very honest men.' Certainly, the orange and herb butter goes well with this very rich fish.

1 pike weighing around 4½ lbs (2 kg) to give, when filleted, 2 lbs (900 g) fillets
sea salt and freshly ground black pepper
50 g (2 oz) butter
2 tablespoons (30 ml) chopped parsley
2 tablespoons (30 ml) chopped thyme
2 tablespoons (30 ml) chopped marjoram
grated rind and juice 1 medium orange
1 teaspoon (5 ml) mustard powder

Fillet the pike and skin the fillets. Cut them into serving pieces and lay them in a large, flat, ovenproof dish, overlapping as little as possible. Put the butter into a saucepan with the rest of the ingredients. Set them on a low heat for the butter to melt, stir them together and pour them over the pike. Leave the pike for two hours at room temperature.

Heat the oven to Reg 4/ 350°F/180°C. Cover the pike with foil and bake it for 30 minutes. Serve it straight from the dish.

Preparation: 30 minutes
Marinade: 2 hours
Cooking: 30 minutes

EGGS

The clucking hen sat on her nest,
She made it in the hay;
And warm and snug beneath her breast
A dozen white eggs lay.

(A. Hawkshawe)

THE SOFT CLUCKING of hens as they scratch contentedly round the hen run or the farmyard, followed by the excited cackle and delighted cry of egg laying, are sounds so typical of the country. Eggs have always been an important part of cottage economy. They provide many a hearty meal for a hungry family and, in times of surplus, a sign can go up on the front gate – EGGS FOR SALE.

The Rhode Island Red has for a long time been the favourite garden hen as she is a prolific layer of brown eggs and a good mother, and any unwanted offspring make good eating. The black and white speckled Marans are becoming popular now amongst amateur chicken keepers since, although they are less heavy layers, their eggs are the most beautiful, deep, speckled brown. The white Leghorn can still be found but she is not quite so much in favour now as her eggs are white, although she is one of the most prolific layers. But in the commercial world these specific breeds are giving way to the hybrids developed by the egg companies. These will lay well kept in farmyard or garden conditions, but you will not get offspring with the same characteristics. To replace your stock you have to go back to the supplier and buy some more. So, in the backyard at least, the Rhode Islands, the Marans and the other egg-laying breeds will probably hold their own.

Chickens wandering round just where they please can lay their eggs in the most hard-to-find places, in boots and boxes and even inside the bonnet of an old car. The country housewife soon got round this problem by keeping them in a coop until a certain hour of the morning so they could lay where she wanted and not where they wanted. This also protected them from hungry marauding foxes during the night and gave them warmth and shelter. If you want to breed from your hens, then put a cock to run with them and put a clutch of eggs under a sensible and motherly hen. When they are hatched they will stay with their clucking mother for protection, following after her in a fluffy yellow cloud and learning how to peck, scratch and forage.

FOOD FROM THE COUNTRY

This sort of system is used universally by people who keep free-ranging chickens on a small scale, whether purely for their own use or to sell at the gate and to local shops. The best way to buy them is to stop when you see a sign or to enquire in village shops and wholefood shops if they ever have them available. Free-range eggs do reach towns but their production on a large scale means a lot of hard work and effort. The farm that is the biggest single producer of free-range eggs is Levetts Farm in Wiltshire. The owner buys most of his hens when they are one year old from a battery farm and successfully brings them round to being good layers on a more natural system. At any one time he has fifteen thousand laying hens. They are kept in large sheds with a long run at the front and back. Inside the sheds, the floor is covered with straw and there is a slatted upper storey so the hens can fly up or down and roost where they like. The feed comes in on a conveyor at certain times of the day and there are large comfortable nesting boxes. For most of the day, the door is open on one side of the shed so the chickens can come and go as they please.

A free-range system is more labour intensive than any other and it involves good stockmanship in watching out for any chickens that may be ill. All the eggs have to be collected by hand three times a day and then checked, graded and packed. The owner of the farm personally delivers his eggs to over a hundred London shops and also to hotels. You might think that town prices for free-range eggs are high, but they are well worth it. One restaurant in Windsor, for example, will not put soufflés on the menu unless these Wiltshire eggs are available, as they give perfect results every time. I poached some of the eggs that I took home from the farm. They stayed in a smooth, white round and the yolks were deep yellow.

The question of the battery egg is a difficult one. You cannot disregard it when writing about eggs since over ninety per cent of the eggs that are sold in Britain come from batteries and they are always cheaper than free-range. All we can say is that we prefer to eat free-range eggs, but everyone must make their own choice.

The lady at the farm where we buy our eggs also keeps bantams. In the early summer you might trip over a few chicks running about on the kitchen floor and if you are lucky you will be able to buy some of the eggs that are not put under the broody. If you have a hearty appetite, don't rely on a bantam's egg to fill you up; nevertheless, hard-boiled, they make delightful decorations for salads and for a first course you can bake them in a ramekin or a small soufflé dish without any danger of their overflowing. Silkies are another small bird producing small eggs. They have long, white, silky feathers, almost like fur. They are superbly decorative and suitable for the smallest of gardens.

The most prolific layers of all, however, are not chickens, but Khaki Campbell ducks. They are capable of laying three hundred eggs a year on a relatively small amount of feed. There is often a certain amount of prejudice against duck eggs, usually from people who have never tried them. They are just a little larger than most hens' eggs and the

The first thing to realise is that cooking bacon and eggs is a full-time job. You cannot, at the same time, make the coffee or toast; neither can you nip down to feed the hens.... Eggs should be cooked in hot, but not boiling, fat. Turn down the gas and replace the pan with the far edge over the flame. Tip it away from you so that there is a small pond of fat in the angle. Prop the pan in this position with a piece of coal or a fragment of that cup you've just dropped, and break two eggs into the fat, side by side. You can baste them either by flicking fat over them with the tip of the spatula, or by ladling it with a spoon - the idea being to cook the egg from both top and bottom at the same time, thereby avoiding a gelatinous top and leathery bottom. When an air bubble comes up over the yolk, take the egg out at once. It is cooked.

(W. M. W. Fowler, *Countryman's Cooking*)

EGGS

Breakfast eggs – omelette, boiled, coddled, scrambled; with lemon curd in a pot

Free-range eggs on a large scale. Hen-house, laying boxes and the door to the outside pen

shells are white with a slight blue tinge. If you hardboil them for 10 minutes, they will have a firm, almost translucent white and a beautiful orange yolk. If you poach or fry them they will keep a good, compact shape and you can use them in all types of cooking, from soufflés to simple cakes. But the best thing to do with a duck egg is to scramble it. All you need is a little butter melted on a low heat. Then stir in your beaten eggs and keep stirring until they set in a creamy purée which you can then pile onto wholemeal toast.

Of course, if you are feeling really greedy, you must go for a goose egg which is easily twice the size of a hen's. We have never actually had one fried, although we do know of someone who fills the pan for breakfast with one egg in the spring. Our favourite way of cooking goose eggs is to bake them. Use one ovenproof dish per person and butter it. Carefully break a goose egg into each one and cover it with grated cheese or double cream. Bake it in a hot oven for 25 minutes. With a baked potato and some vegetables on a separate plate, you have a substantial main meal.

FOOD FROM THE COUNTRY

Eggs will always make a substantial main meal, even if they are just plainly boiled at first:

TO FRICASSEE EGGS *Boil them hard, take out some of the yolks whole: then cut the rest in quarters, yolks and whites together. Set on some gravy with a little shred thyme and parsley in it, and when it boils up, put in your eggs, with a little grated nutmeg, and shake them up with a piece of butter till it is of a proper thickness. Serve it up hot.*

(From Susanna Stacey's Receipt Book, recorded in Marcus Woodward's *The Mistress of Stanton's Farm*)

From the owners of the black turkeys, we obtained some turkey eggs. They are smaller than you might expect, only about the size of a hen's egg. Their colour is buff, speckled with brown, and the pointed end is so defined that they are almost triangular. We boiled them, and the white was crumbly textured and the yolk golden yellow. Guinea fowl lay well in the spring and summer. Their eggs are small and speckled and, when boiled, have a soft, close texture. We once bought some quail eggs from the farm shop at Sissinghurst Castle. They are so tiny that you could eat them in two mouthfuls and they have a delicious, creamy texture. They are best boiled and used as decoration for salads and, if you can afford to buy enough, they would be delicious pickled. We ate them for lunch, with plenty of toast.

Recipes for Eggs

Hearty bacon and celery omelette

Eggs and bacon always make a good hearty meal and this is just a more interesting variation. To make more omelettes, simply increase all the ingredients in proportion. Cook the filling all together, but beat each batch of eggs separately and make the omelettes one at a time, keeping them warm in a low oven when they are finished.

FOR 1 OMELETTE:
2 eggs
1 tablespoon (15 ml) water
freshly ground black pepper
1 tablespoon (15 ml) chopped
    parsley
2 oz (50 g) bacon pieces
1 large stick celery
1 small onion, thinly sliced
up to 1 oz (25 g) butter or
    dripping
1 oz (25 g) grated Farmhouse
    Cheddar cheese

Beat the eggs with the water and parsley. Finely chop the bacon and celery. Put the bacon into a frying-pan and set it on a low heat. When the fat begins to run, mix in the onion and celery, adding up to $\frac{1}{2}$ oz (10 g) of the butter or dripping if necessary. Cook until the onion is soft. In an omelette pan, melt $\frac{1}{2}$ oz (15 g) of the butter or dripping on a medium heat. When the foam subsides, pour in the egg mixture. Give it a stir with a fork and then cook it, lifting the sides and tilting the pan slightly, so that as much of the mixture as possible gets to the sides and base. When the underside is brown and the top set, put the bacon mixture from the other pan onto one half of the omelette. Fold over the other side and slide the omelette onto a flat plate. Scatter the cheese over the top immediately so it melts deliciously into the hot egg.

Preparation and cooking: 20 minutes

Herbed eggs in a spinach nest

This is a perfect light summer meal in which the eggs are made into a creamy yellow and green scramble and put into a bright green spinach nest. A dozen eggs and a quarter of a pint of cream may sound a lot, but it still makes a very cheap meal for four people.

2 lbs (900 g) spinach
1 oz (25 g) butter
1 dozen eggs
4 tablespoons (60 ml)
    chopped parsley
4 tablespoons (60 ml) mixed
    chopped fresh herbs
2 oz (50 g) butter
$\frac{1}{4}$ pint (150 ml) double cream

Trim the lower stalks from the spinach, wash the leaves and put them into a saucepan with only the water that clings to them. Cover them and set them on a low heat for 15 minutes, turning them occasionally. Drain the spinach and press out any excess moisture. Beat the eggs with the parsley and other herbs. Melt 1 oz (25 g) of butter in a large frying-pan on a high heat. Put in the spinach and chop it into the butter. Keep chopping and turning until all the moisture has evaporated (about $1\frac{1}{2}$ minutes). Arrange the spinach round the edge of a large, flat serving plate and keep it warm. Melt 2 oz (50 g) butter in a large heavy saucepan on a low heat. Pour in the eggs and cook them, stirring all the time, until they are just about to set. Stir in the cream and keep stirring until the eggs are set and creamy. Pile them in the centre of the spinach to serve.

Preparation and cooking: 50 minutes

Scalloped eggs

This is based on an old Devon recipe in which single eggs were cooked in a scallop shell. The breadcrumbs make a crisp and tasty 'nest' while the eggs are just set in the middle.

4 rashers streaky bacon,
    preferably unsmoked
$\frac{1}{2}$ oz (15 g) bacon fat or
    dripping, if necessary
2 medium onions, finely
    chopped
6 oz (175 g) granary or
    wholemeal breadcrumbs
3 tablespoons (45 ml)
    chopped parsley
freshly ground black pepper
8 eggs
8 tablespoons (120 ml)
    double cream

Heat the oven to Reg 6/400°F/ 200°C. Lightly grill the bacon under a high heat and then chop it finely. Drain any fat from the grill pan into a frying-pan and add a little extra if necessary. Set it on a low heat. Put in the onions and cook them until they are soft and just beginning to turn golden. Take the pan from the heat and mix in the bacon, breadcrumbs and parsley. Season with the pepper. Use the mixture to line a large pie dish. Break in the eggs and fold any breadcrumb mixture above them over the edges, to form a border round the eggs. Spoon 1 tablespoon (15 ml) double cream over each egg yolk and put the dish into the oven for 30 minutes.

Preparation: 25 minutes
Cooking: 30 minutes

Swede, bacon and egg tart

The idea for this tart came from a Cornish pasty recipe using swede, chopped bacon and chopped hardboiled eggs. The combination of these ingredients is a savoury and flavoursome one.

shortcrust pastry made with 6 oz (175 g) wholemeal flour
FILLING:
3 oz (75 g) lean bacon
½ oz (15 g) butter
1 medium onion, finely chopped
12 oz (350 g) swede, grated
10 chopped sage leaves
4 eggs
4 tablespoons (60 ml) double cream

Heat the oven to Reg 6/400°F/200°C. Line an 8-inch (20-cm) flan ring with the pastry. Bake the pastry blind for 20 minutes. Chop the bacon and put it into a heavy frying-pan. Set it on a low heat and when the fat begins to run, put in the butter. When it has melted, stir in the onion and swede and cook them until the onion is soft, stirring frequently. Add the sage and season with the pepper. Pile the mixture into the flan ring, smooth it over and make four indentations in the surface. Break in the eggs and pour a tablespoon (15 ml) double cream over each yolk. Bake the flan for 25 minutes.

Preparation: 30 minutes
Cooking: 45 minutes

Egg and mushroom soufflé

Mixing chopped hardboiled eggs into well-beaten raw eggs makes a soufflé with a far more interesting texture than the original type, although the mixture does not rise so well. You have soft-textured hardboiled eggs surrounded by a light and spongy soufflé mixture.

8 eggs
8 oz (225 g) mushrooms
1 oz (125 g) butter
1 large onion, finely chopped
1 tablespoon (15 ml) chopped thyme
1 teaspoon (5 ml) chopped rosemary
1 teaspoon (5 ml) mustard powder
pinch sea salt
freshly ground black pepper
3 tablespoons (75 ml) chopped parsley
2 oz (50 g) grated Farmhouse Cheddar cheese
butter and crumbs for preparing a 2-pint (1·150-l) soufflé dish (no greaseproof paper is needed)

Heat the oven to Reg 6/400°F/200°C. Hardboil four of the eggs. Finely chop the mushrooms. Melt the butter in a frying-pan on a low heat. Mix in the onion, thyme and rosemary and cook them until the onion is soft. Raise the heat, mix in the mushrooms and cook them briskly for 1½ minutes so that their juices are sealed in. Take the pan from the heat and let the contents cool. Chop the hardboiled eggs. Whisk the remaining four eggs with the mustard and seasonings until they are very light and fluffy. Fold in the mushroom mixture, the hardboiled eggs, the parsley and the cheese. Pour the mixture into the prepared

soufflé dish and put it into the oven for 25 minutes so it is light and spongy and the top is golden brown.

Preparation: 30 minutes
Cooking: 25 minutes

A spring egg salad

Duck eggs always remind me of spring. They hardboil beautifully and are excellent for the first salads of the season. Chive flowers, which come during May, make an attractive decoration.

8 duck eggs
4 boxes mustard and cress
12 spring onions
1 tablespoon (15 ml) English Vineyard mustard
4 tablespoons (60 ml) olive oil
4 tablespoons (60 ml) dry white wine
8 chive flowers

Hardboil the eggs and let them cool. Cut the cress from the boxes and finely chop the onions. Mix them together and lay them on a serving plate. Cut the eggs in half and set them, cut side down, on the salad. Put the mustard into a bowl and work in first the oil and then the wine. Spoon the dressing over the eggs and decorate the dish with the chive flowers.

Preparation: 15 minutes
Cooking: 10 minutes

Bantam eggs baked with cheese and chervil

Bantam eggs are good for first courses. They are so small that you can add cheese to the dishes when you bake them without any fear of their overflowing. Chervil is a lovely herb with eggs and it is at its leafiest in May just as the bantams are laying well.

4 bantam eggs
butter for greasing
4 oz (125 g) grated
Farmhouse Cheddar
cheese
4 tablespoons (60 ml)
chopped chervil
4 tablespoons (60 ml) double
cream

Heat the oven to Reg 6/400°F/ 200°C. Lightly grease four in- dividual soufflé dishes or rame- kins and divide the cheese between them. Scatter the chervil over the top. Make a small indentation in the centre of the cheese and break a ban- tam egg into the centre of each dish. Spoon the cream over the top. Bake the eggs for 10 minutes.

Preparation: 5 minutes
Cooking: 10 minutes

Goose eggs baked with lettuce

One goose egg makes a meal for one person. This is a lovely spring dish with the eggs sitting on a light, lemony base of softened lettuce.

1 large Density or Cos
lettuce
6 large spring onions
butter for greasing
2 tablespoons (30 ml)
chopped parsley
juice 1 lemon
4 goose eggs
¼ pint (150 ml) double cream

Heat the oven to Reg 6/400°F/ 200°C. Shred the lettuce and chop the spring onions. Lightly grease a large, flat ovenproof dish and arrange the lettuce and onions in the base. Scatter the parsley over the top and pour in the lemon juice. Break the eggs on top and spoon in the cream to cover both the eggs

and the lettuce. Bake the eggs for 30 minutes. The yolks should be firm on the outside but soft in the middle.

Preparation: 15 minutes
Cooking: 30 minutes

Honey mould

This sweet custard is made in a similar way to crème caramel, but the honey gives it a much better flavour. Children love it, and you could just as easily serve it to guests at a dinner party.

4½ oz (125 g) honey
1 pint (575 ml) milk
2 eggs
2 egg yolks
¼ nutmeg, grated

Heat the oven to Reg 5/375°F/ 190°C. Melt 4 oz (100 g) of the honey and pour it into a 1½- pint (850-ml) soufflé dish. Tip the dish to and fro so the honey coats the sides and then put it into the refrigerator for about 15 minutes for the honey to set. Put the milk into a saucepan with the remaining honey and stir on a low heat until the honey has dissolved into the milk. Beat the eggs and yolks together lightly in a bowl. Pour the milk onto them and stir. Strain the mixture into the honey-coated dish. Add the nutmeg and stir it in, taking care not to touch the sides and base of the dish. Cover the dish with foil and stand it in a bak- ing tin with enough water to come half way up the sides. Put the custard into the oven for 1 hour or until it is completely set. Remove the dish from the tin, take off the foil and leave the custard until it is lukewarm. Turn it out carefully onto a high-sided dish.

Preparation: 30 minutes
Cooking: 1 hour
Cooling: 1 hour

Little apple custards

These rich, creamy, golden- yellow custards look lovely baked in white dishes.

1 lb (450 g) Bramley apples
6 tablespoons (90 ml) apple
wine, dry cider or water
4 cloves
one 2-inch (5-cm) piece
cinnamon stick
2 tablespoons (30 ml) honey
2 oz (50 g) sultanas
2 eggs, beaten
½ pint (275 ml) single cream

Heat the oven to Reg 3/325°F/ 170°C. Quarter, core and finely chop the apples, and put them into a saucepan with the cider, cloves and cinnamon. Cover them and set them on a low heat until they are soft and pulpy (about 15 minutes). Rub them through a sieve and stir in the honey, sultanas, eggs and cream. Pour the mixture into individual soufflé dishes, mak- ing sure each one gets an even share of sultanas. (They will sink to the bottom but this won't matter as they make a plump, sweet surprise at the end.) Stand the little pots in a dish of water and put them into the oven for 1 hour. Let the custards get quite cold before serving.

Preparation: 20 minutes
Cooking: 1 hour 15 minutes
Cooling: 3 hours

Rich rhubarb custards

Rhubarb purée, mixed with egg yolks and cream, makes browny-yellow custards with a brown top. They are creamy and refreshing at the same time.

1 lb (450 g) rhubarb
4 tablespoons (60 ml) water
one 3-inch (8-cm) piece
cinnamon stick
4 tablespoons (60 ml) honey

2 egg yolks
¼ pint (150 ml) double cream
freshly grated nutmeg

Heat the oven to Reg 3/325°F/160°C. Chop the rhubarb and put it into a saucepan with the water and cinnamon stick. Cover it and set it on a low heat for 15 minutes, or until it is soft and pulpy. Remove the cinnamon stick and rub the rhubarb through a sieve or the fine blade of a vegetable mill. Return the resulting purée to the rinsed-out pan and stir in the honey. Set the pan on a low heat and stir until the honey dissolves. Let the rhubarb cool. Beat the egg yolks and cream together and mix in the rhubarb. Pour the mixture into four small ramekins or soufflé dishes and stand them in a dish of water. Bake the custards for 1 hour. Lift them out of the dish and grate a little nutmeg over the top. Put them into a cool place (but not in the refrigerator) until they are completely cold.

Preparation: 40 minutes
Cooking: 1 hour
Cooling: 3 hours

Lemon curd

Any surplus butter and eggs often used to be made into a smooth and creamy lemon curd. It can be spread on bread for tea, on toast for breakfast, sandwiched between layers of a sponge cake or made into curd tarts.

4 eggs
8 oz (225 g) sugar
8 oz (225 g) butter
grated rind and juice 3 large lemons

Beat the eggs together. Put the sugar, butter and lemon rind into a saucepan and set them on a low heat. Stir until both the butter and sugar have completely melted. Stir in the eggs and immediately follow them with the lemon juice. Keep stirring on a moderate heat until the mixture is thick. Let it bubble – the eggs won't curdle. Pour the curd into warm jars and cover it while it is still warm. The curd should keep well for two months.

Preparation: 30 minutes

RECIPES FOR EGGS

Free-range eggs on a small scale – after the eggs have been collected in the morning the chickens are let out to scratch in the farmyard

DAIRY PRODUCTS

The friendly cow, all red and white,
I love with all my heart:
She gives me cream with all her might,
To eat with apple-tart.
(Robert Louis Stevenson)

(left) Beestings cheese and Beestings custard tart (see recipes on page 90)

EARLY IN THE MORNING and again in the afternoon, the cows come home from the fields to be milked. Driven by the farmer and often herded by a gentle collie dog, they amble across the grass and trot down the lanes to come eventually to the farmyard where they wait their turn to enter the milking parlour. Some are patient, others rattle the door, knowing that, once inside, they will be fed as well as milked.

The dairy cow that has become the most popular throughout England and Wales is the black and white British Friesian. In Scotland there are also large numbers of brown and white Ayrshires. These two breeds dominate in the dairy world but you can also find smaller numbers of other once favoured breeds. There are red and white Dairy Shorthorns and Northern Dairy Shorthorns, distinguished one from the other mainly by the angle of their horns. The now rare Gloucester cows are red with a white stripe running along the back, round the tail and underneath the belly, and the rich milk from these alone can be made into Double Gloucester cheese. There are two other breeds, set apart from the rest by their rich, golden milk which is much higher in butterfat. These are the Channel Island cattle, the Jerseys and the Guernseys, with their big ears and large eyes and faces that remind you of butter and cream.

In the past, the milkmaid balanced her pails on a yoke and carried them and her stool out to the fields where she milked the cows where they stood. At the beginning of this century the familiar 'Coup! coup! coup!' of the farmer called the cows home to the farmyard and we have met many older farmworkers who can remember milking a herd of up to forty by hand only thirty years ago. Now, almost all milking is done by machine. Once inside the parlour, each cow has her own separate pen and she chews away contentedly while her milk is drawn off through pipes and a filter to mix with the milk from the rest of the herd in a large, stainless steel tank in the dairy. The creamy white, frothing sea is kept very cool and agitated continuously by an automatic paddle until the

FOOD FROM THE COUNTRY

large, blue Milk Marketing Board tanker rumbles up the road to collect it. From the farm the milk may be taken to a bottling plant, or to a creamery to be made into yoghurt, cheese or butter, or to be separated into skimmed milk and cream.

That is the familiar pattern on most dairy farms. On farms where farmhouse cheese is made, all the milk is kept and used in the home dairy the same day, sometimes with milk from neighbouring farms. There are also some large farms, usually with herds of Channel Island cows, who prefer to keep the milk for making, on a small scale, their own brands of butter, yoghurt, soft cheeses and cream. At the other end of the scale, on smallholdings where there are only one or two cows, the milking will be done by hand in spotlessly clean sheds. The milk is kept for the family to drink and for making into cheese, butter or yoghurt, mostly for home use, but sometimes for selling locally.

By far the largest percentage of milk comes from cows, but in recent years there has been an increased interest in goat keeping, and goat's milk is sold at the farm gate and also through wholefood shops. It is a light, easily digested milk; and it makes delicious cheese, both soft and creamy and firm and crumbly. In Devon there is also a herd of British Milk Sheep, which are kept solely for milking, and a soft, tangy sheep's milk cheese has even found its way into London shops.

There was also Cornish cream and honey, and the butter was as golden as if King Midas had had a finger in putting up the pats.

(Richard Dehan,
Maids in a Market Garden)

Webster's Dairy at Saxelby, near Melton Mowbray – the smallest and the last privately owned Stilton dairy

DAIRY PRODUCTS

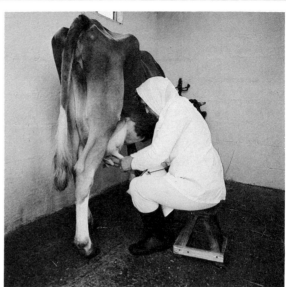

(*above right*) *Milking the house Guernsey cow by hand*

(*above left*) *Pedigree Jersey cows*

We spent a day at Calthwaite Hall in the Eden Valley of Cumbria where all the milk from a herd of pedigree Jerseys is made into a wide range of products in the farm dairy. The first impression in any dairy is one of cleanliness. Everyone who wasn't occupied in making something was scrubbing and cleaning and getting the utensils ready for the next batch of milk. From the milking parlour, the milk ran through a cream separator so the smooth, yellow cream ran out through one pipe and the frothy white skimmed milk through another. In one room this was heated until it was thick and bubbly, then cooled and mixed with a culture and left in the warm until it became a smooth, set yoghurt which was either put straight into pots as 'natural', or mixed first with one of eight different types of fruit. In another dairy the skimmed milk was made into white heaps of well-flavoured cottage cheese. The cream was left unpasteurised and cartoned as thick yellow double cream, or mixed back with varying proportions of the skimmed milk to become whipping, pouring or coffee cream. To some was added a culture to make it into a light tasting but creamy-textured soured cream.

But the process that we really wanted to watch was the butter making. Butter is one of the most natural fats we have and, whether factory or farm produced, is made only from churned cream. Thirty-five gallons of cream were poured into a huge wooden butter churn. Until electricity came to the farms, all butter churns had to be patiently worked by hand, but at the touch of a switch, this one started to revolve. The skilled butter maker can tell by the noise just what is happening inside the churn. When it starts, the liquid cream swashes around, when it is stiffly whipped it makes no sound at all, a gentle thud indicates that the butter is beginning to 'come', and a bang tells that the butter is made. It is rinsed through twice with cold water and, to keep the taste fresh, a little salt is added just before the churn is rolled to let

FOOD FROM THE COUNTRY

the water out. It was the end of May and the milk was rich, which made the butter the deepest golden you could possibly imagine. It was lifted out of the churn in large, yellow handfuls and was later worked into blocks and wrapped up ready for sale. Butter was once sold in round pats which were stamped with the emblem of the farm. Now it is oblong, and the emblem of the farm is on the greaseproof wrapping. Most of the butter is sold from the farm, but when there is some left over it is made into fresh lemon curd, Cumberland rum butter and melting fudge in a variety of flavours. The buttermilk (the liquid left over after the butter is made) is sold to a lady for mixing the scones that she sells at the local market.

Pedigree cheeses ... are born in the round – they live on round stands in country houses and hotels, and in wooden bowls in cottages and inns.
(Dorothy Hartley, *Here's England*)

We drink more liquid milk now than we ever have, mainly because of efficient transport systems, refrigeration and the speed with which it finally reaches our doorsteps. Before this system evolved, it was more economical for the farmer to make all his milk into butter and cheese on the farm. Every farmer's wife or dairy maid had her own recipe for cheese and almost every county had its own type. Besides the well-known regional cheeses of today, there were once others that were equally well admired. Banbury cheese was known all over England until the eighteenth century and was once so prized that it was sent abroad as a gift to a king. The cheese of Cambridgeshire was soft and unripened. There was a Wiltshire cheese, and the ill-reputed Suffolk, which was made from skimmed milk for the unmarried farm workers who 'lived in'. By all accounts it was a dreadfully hard cheese, but if it was melted in front of the fire until slivers could be scraped off with a knife and then slapped with fat bacon between two slices of bread, it became a breakfast fit to keep the cold away from any man.

But in the latter part of the nineteenth century, things began to change. In the 1860s a disease spread through much of the cattle population of the British Isles, causing many to die. The milk yield dropped, quickly and sharply, and very little cheese could be made. At the same time, a more gradual change was taking place. The industrial revolution caused the towns to grow. More people moved into them to find work, and urban populations cannot produce their own food. For a time, a bland, mousetrap, Cheddar-type cheese had to be imported from America, until English cheese-makers got together and decided that the solution was to set up cheese factories, which later became known as creameries, to take in milk from miles around and make cheese on a large scale. This saved the British cheese industry but it reduced the importance of the traditional farmhouse cheese.

The old cheesemaking methods did not disappear, but the farm cheeses only reached local shops and markets. In 1934, the Milk Marketing Board realised their potential and decided to set up the Farmhouse Cheese Scheme to revive and promote the distinctive qualities of the remaining regional cheeses. The number of farmhouse dairies, however, dropped considerably during the war and, at the end of rationing in 1954, only one hundred and twenty-six were registered. You were a very lucky person indeed if you were able to find any. The

DAIRY PRODUCTS

JUNKET is one of the most simple of desserts to make and yet everyone loves it. If you can't get milk warm from the cow as in this recipe, warm it up to blood heat.

We used junkets very often, and we never tired of them. Creamy milk fresh and warm from the Jersey cow was brought into the house for junkets. It was poured in a glass dish and a little sugar added and a drop of vanilla essence. Then a large teaspoonful of rennet to a pint of milk was stirred in and the milk left to set. A little nutmeg was grated over the surface as soon as the junket was ready.

Sometimes we had individual junkets, the original junket being mixed in a jug and then poured into glasses.

When set, thick cream topped each glass.

(Alison Uttley, *Recipes from an Old Farmhouse*)

Milk Marketing Board returned to its pre-war activities and now almost twenty thousand tons of farmhouse cheese are produced every year. It is sold through supermarkets, special cheese stores, delicatessens and wholefood shops, and sometimes even the shop on the corner.

We can all choose from the salty, crumbly Cheshire and the rare, creamy tasting Blue Cheshire; mild or mature Lancashire; mellow, loose-textured Red Leicester; the creamy millstone-shaped Double Gloucester; and the rich, red, strong Orkney. No makers of Farmhouse Wensleydale are registered with the scheme but we have come across one or two that have seemed far above the average creamery Wensleydale. Farmhouse Caerphilly is made no longer in Wales but in Somerset; and there are other cheeses, such as Swaledale, Eskdale and Cotherstone, which are made on such a small scale that they are only available locally.

We have missed one out – Cheddar – probably the most famous English cheese and certainly the one that is the most copied. Most of the farms that make cheese are small and the work is done by the family and a few employees. For Cheddar, the milk is poured into a large cheese vat, the culture is added, the curds and whey separated and the curds cut into large, wobbling lumps. At this stage it has a slightly rubbery texture when you eat it and a fresh, salty flavour. These blocks are constantly turned by hand for an hour (a process known as Cheddaring) until they become flatter and the moisture is lost. Then they are broken up by hand and put into cloth-lined moulds. In these the cheeses are pressed for a day, the cloth is removed and the cheese is spread with lard and coated with muslin. On wooden shelves in a cool store on the farm the cheeses mature for three months.

They are turned every day at first, but less frequently as they age. After this they are sent to large cheese warehouses where row upon row of maturing cheeses are left until they are nine months old. While the cheese is in the warehouse, the grader tests it by inserting a cheese iron and pulling out a plug of cheese. He can tell a fine grade just by looking at it and smelling it, but often he can't resist tasting it as well! Only the fine grade becomes branded as Farmhouse Cheese and it is given a label of three white cheeses on a black ground. Look out for it. You will taste a British tradition.

Stilton has been called the 'King of Cheeses' and when it is creamy tasting, well blued and mature, it lives up to it. Stilton, like the rest, was once only a farmhouse-made cheese, but now it is made mostly in large creameries. There is only one small dairy left and it has been a family business for over thirty-four years. It is in a pretty village near Melton Mowbray and when we went to look for it we drove past it twice because from the outside it looks like a private house. But inside we found the curds for the day's batch of cheese being milled and put into moulds. When the dairy first started, all the milk came from neighbouring farms but most of the dairy herds are now gone from the area and the Milk Marketing Board supplies milk from north-east Leicestershire. The staff in the dairy were friendly and happy and obviously worked on the cheese with loving care. In the two storeys above, cheeses were slowly maturing and acquiring the characteristic Stilton flavour and blue-ing. The future for the dairy is uncertain as there is no one, as yet, willing to carry on the business, but the owner still remains optimistic. He knows his cheese is some of the best that is produced and is not prepared to give up yet.

On our way back south down the A1, we decided to call in at the village of Stilton and see the Bell Inn whose landlord was first responsible for selling the cheese to travellers on the Great North Road and for spreading its fame. It was a beautiful building of yellow stone but to our dismay it was derelict and deserted. On the wall was a sign saying that it would be 'restored to its former glory' in 1980. That bodes well for the village of Stilton. Perhaps our dairy will have the same sort of luck.

Making Farmhouse Cheddar – on the right, Cheddaring, or turning the blocks of curd; on the left, filling round cheese moulds with milled curd

Recipes for Dairy Products

Pots of celery and cheese

This recipe only works well with the tender inner sticks of celery. It is quick and easy to prepare and makes a delightful first course suitable for any occasion. The cheese combines with the milk and melts deliciously round the delicate, flavoured celery.

the heart and inner sticks from a large head of celery
4 tablespoons (60 ml) chopped celery leaves
4 oz (125 g) grated Farmhouse Cheddar cheese
8 tablespoons (120 ml) milk

Heat the oven to Reg 6/400°F/ 200°C. Finely chop the celery and divide it between four individual soufflé dishes, together with the leaves. Cover the celery with cheese and spoon 2 tablespoons (30 ml) milk into each dish. Put the dishes into the oven for 15 minutes until the cheese is melted and just beginning to brown.

Preparation: 15 minutes
Cooking: 15 minutes

Bacon, Stilton and Cheddar pie

This is a lovely savoury pie made with the finest of English cheeses. It is best hot, either for lunch or as a main meal.

shortcrust pastry made with 8 oz (225 g) wholemeal flour, seasoned with freshly ground black pepper
4 oz (125 g) streaky bacon
½ oz (15 g) butter
2 medium onions, finely chopped
3 large sticks celery, finely chopped
4 oz (125 g) Stilton cheese
4 oz (125 g) Farmhouse Cheddar cheese
1 tablespoon (15 ml) chopped thyme
4 chopped sage leaves
beaten egg for glaze

Heat the oven to Reg 6/400°F/ 200°C. Dice the bacon. Melt the butter in a frying-pan on a low heat. Mix in the bacon, onions and celery, and cook them until the onion is soft. Take them from the heat, turn them into a bowl and cool them. Grate the two cheeses and mix them into the bacon, together with the herbs.

Roll out two thirds of the pastry and line an 8-inch (20-cm) diameter flan tin. Fill it with the bacon and cheese mixture. Make the top of the pie with the remaining pastry and seal the edges. Brush the top with the beaten egg and bake the pie for 35 minutes. Serve it hot so the cheese is soft and melting.

Preparation: 40 minutes
Cooking: 35 minutes

Spring cabbage and Red Leicester

Red Leicester cheese makes light spring cabbage into a tasty and colourful dish. With the amount of cheese below, it is served as a vegetable with lamb, poultry or white fish, but if you add more cheese it can make a meal in itself.

1 large spring cabbage
4 tablespoons (60 ml) olive oil
2 oz (50 g) Red Leicester cheese, finely grated

Shred the cabbage. Heat the oil in a saucepan on a moderate heat. Stir in the cabbage and, when it is well coated with oil, turn down the heat and cover the pan. Cook the cabbage for 10 minutes by which time it should be a light, fresh green and just tender. Take the pan from the heat and scatter the cheese over the cabbage. Cover the pan again and let the cabbage stand for 1 minute so the cheese softens and melts. Transfer the cabbage to a serving dish and fork the cheese lightly into it.

Preparation: 15 minutes
Cooking: 10 minutes

Cottage cheese mould

A light cheese, a rich cheese, and eggs make a very moist, light and fluffy-textured loaf, suitable hot for a main meal and delicious sliced cold as a snack or with a salad.

12 oz (350 g) cottage cheese
2 oz (50 g) Farmhouse Cheddar cheese
1 oz (25 g) butter, softened
2 tablespoons (30 ml) chopped parsley
2 tablespoons (30 ml) chopped chives
2 chopped sage leaves
4 eggs, beaten
butter for greasing a 2-lb (900-g) loaf tin

Heat the oven to Reg 4/350°F/ 180°C. Rub the cottage cheese through a sieve and grate the Cheddar. Mix them together and beat in the butter. Gradually stir in the eggs and herbs. Pour the mixture into the prepared tin and stand the tin in a pan of water. Bake the mould for 1 hour. For serving hot, turn it out of the tin when it comes out of the oven. If you want it cold, let it cool completely in the tin first.

Preparation: 20 minutes
Cooking: 1 hour
Cooling: 2 hours

Potatoes baked with soured cream

Potatoes cut into thin rounds and baked with soured cream make a creamy and gently spiced vegetable dish to go with plainly cooked meats, particularly roast or grilled lamb.

2 lbs (900 g) even-sized
   potatoes
butter for greasing a 2-pint
   (1·150-l) soufflé dish
sea salt and freshly ground
   black pepper
1 clove garlic, very finely
   chopped
½ nutmeg, grated
¼ pint (150 ml) soured cream
½ pint (275 ml) stock

Heat the oven to Reg 6/400°F/ 200°C. Scrub the potatoes but don't peel them. Cut them into very thin rounds, using a mandoline cutter if you have one. Thickly butter the soufflé dish. Put two overlapping layers of potato slices in the bottom of the dish. Season them well and scatter them with a little garlic and nutmeg. Continue layering until all the potatoes have been used up. Don't season the top layer. Beat the cream and stock together and pour them into the dish, making sure the potatoes have a creamy topping. Put the dish into the oven for 1 hour 30 minutes, so the top layer of potatoes is deliciously browned and the rest are soft.

Preparation: 30 minutes
Cooking: 1 hour 30 minutes

Beetroot and apple cheese

Beetroot, apples, curd cheese and yoghurt make a refreshing and beautifully coloured salad for a first course.

1 raw beetroot weighing
   about 6 oz (175 g)
1 large Bramley apple (or
   two small ones)
6 oz (175 g) curd cheese
¼ pint (150 ml) natural
   yoghurt
1 small lettuce
4 sprigs parsley

Peel and grate the beetroot. Peel, core and grate the apple. Mix them together and beat in the cheese and yoghurt so that you have a smooth, deep pinky-red mixture. Arrange a bed of lettuce on four small plates. Pile the cheese on top of each one and decorate with a sprig of parsley.

Preparation: 20 minutes

Double Gloucester and radish salad

This is a brightly coloured, robust and crunchy salad, ideal for either lunch or a main meal and excellent with brown bread and beer.

8 oz (225 g) Farmhouse
   Double Gloucester cheese
1 bunch radishes
6 medium-sized spring
   onions
freshly ground black pepper
4 tablespoons (60 ml) olive
   oil
2 tablespoons (30 ml) malt
   vinegar
1 small Density or Webbs
   lettuce

Cut the cheese into ⅜-inch (1-cm) pieces. Thinly slice the radishes and chop the spring onions. Put all these into a bowl and season them with the pepper. Beat the oil

and vinegar together to make the dressing and fold them into the salad. Line a salad bowl with whole lettuce leaves and pile the cheese mixture in the middle.

Preparation: 20 minutes

Cheshire cheese and watercress toasts

By the addition of watercress and beer, simple cheese on toast can be quite transformed. The amounts here make a substantial snack but you can double them for a main meal.

6 oz (175 g) Farmhouse Red
   Cheshire cheese
2 tablespoons (30 ml)
   Worcester sauce
1 bunch watercress
¼ pint (150 ml) beer (bitter or
   light ale)
8 small or 4 large slices
   wholemeal bread

Grate the cheese and chop the cress. Mix them with the sauce and beer. Toast one side of the slices of bread and lay them in a flat, heatproof dish, toasted side down. Put the cheese mixture on top and put the dish under a high grill so the cheese melts and browns.

Preparation and cooking: 25 minutes

Potted cheese with walnuts

This potted cheese is rich and delicious and best served either as a first course or with watercress sprigs and toast for lunch or supper. It is really too much for serving after dinner.

4 oz (125 g) Farmhouse
   Cheddar cheese
4 oz (125 g) good, creamy
   Stilton
2 oz (50 g) shelled walnuts
2 tablespoons (30 ml) port
watercress sprigs for serving

Finely grate the Cheddar and either grate or cream the Stilton, depending on its texture. Finely chop the walnuts. Put them all into a blender with the port. Work the mixture in several short bursts, stirring it about after each one. Half the mixture should end up smooth and the rest quite chunky. Press the mixture into four small ramekins or soufflé dishes.

Preparation: 30 minutes

Summer fruit dessert

Yoghurt is superb with summer fruits. This simple dessert is sweetened by the dried fruits instead of with sugar.

12 oz (350 g) raspberries
4 oz (125 g) black cherries
1 large ripe peach
2 oz (50 g) sultanas
½ pint (275 ml) natural
    yoghurt

Put the raspberries into a bowl. Stone the cherries and stone and finely chop the peach. Mix these and the sultanas with the raspberries. Fold in the yoghurt and let the dessert stand for 1 hour before serving.

Preparation: 20 minutes

Elderberry cream

Just a few elderberries, some cream and some honey make a deep purple, creamy dessert. It won't set completely but will be the consistency of thick custard. It is superb served quite plain but you could decorate the top with a piped rosette of whipped cream.

6 oz (175 g) elderberries
    (weighed before taking
    them from the stems)
4 tablespoons (60 ml)
    elderberry wine (or any
    other full-bodied red wine)

½ pint (275 ml) double cream
2 oz (50 g) honey

Take the elderberries from their stems and put them into a saucepan with the wine. Cover them and set them on a low heat for 15 minutes so that there is a large amount of juice in the pan. Press the elderberries in a fine sieve to extract as much juice as possible, but taking care not to let through any of the tiny pips. Let the elderberry liquid cool. Whip the cream stiffly and then whip in the honey and the elderberry liquid. Pour the cream into individual glasses and leave it in a cool place for 1 hour.

Preparation: 30 minutes
Cooking: 15 minutes
Chilling: 1 hour

Ginger soufflé

This is a light, fluffy, golden soufflé with a contrasting creamy sauce, and both have the delicious hint of ginger.

1 pint (575 ml) Gold Top
    milk
25 g (1 oz) butter
1 tablespoon (15 ml) flour
4 tablespoons (60 ml) ginger
    syrup (from a jar of
    preserved stem ginger)
grated rind 1 large orange
grated rind 1 lemon
4 eggs, separated
butter for greasing

Heat the oven to Reg 6/400°F/ 200°C. Pour off all the cream from the milk, then use the milk to make it up to 150 ml (¼ pint). Reserve it for the sauce. Measure out ¼ pint (150 ml) of the remaining milk. Melt the butter in a saucepan on a moderate heat. Stir in the flour and cook it for 1 minute. Pour in the ¼ pint (150 ml) of the skimmed milk all at once and stir until you have a good, thick, bubbly sauce. Take the pan from the heat and beat in the rinds of

half the orange and half the lemon, 2 tablespoons (30 ml) of the ginger syrup and 3 of the egg yolks. Butter a 7-inch (18-cm) diameter soufflé dish and tie buttered greaseproof paper round it to come at least 2 inches (5 cm) above the top. Stiffly whip all the egg whites and fold them into the sauce. Quickly pour the soufflé mixture into the prepared dish and bake it for 30 minutes.

While the soufflé is cooking, make the sauce. Beat the remaining egg yolk in a bowl with the remaining ginger syrup and orange and lemon rinds. Bring the cream to just below boiling point and gradually stir it into the yolk. Pour the mixture back into the milk saucepan and set it on a low heat. Stir the sauce until it thickens, without letting it boil. Pour it into a jug. Serve the soufflé straight from the dish and let everyone help themselves to the sauce.

Preparation: 35 minutes
Cooking: 30 minutes

Cheese scone with nut and date topping

Rich breads and scones are made soft and moist if you add curd cheese to the mixture. This one has a light, nutty topping. It can be served hot or cold, with cream, as a pudding, or just plain for tea.

SCONE:
12 oz (350 g) wholemeal flour
½ teaspoon (2·5 ml) sea salt
2 teaspoons (10 ml) ground
    cinnamon
6 oz (175 g) butter
6 oz (175 g) curd cheese
½ pint (275 ml) milk
butter for greasing
TOPPING:
8 oz (225 g) mixed walnuts,
    hazelnuts and Brazil nuts

4 oz (125 g) pressed dates
6 fl oz (175 ml) soured cream
4 oz (125 g) clear honey

Heat the oven to Reg 4/350°F/ 180°C. Put the flour into a bowl with the salt and cinnamon and rub in the butter. Make a well in the centre, put in the cheese and pour in the milk. Gradually beat them into the flour with a wooden spoon, bringing the flour from the sides of the bowl to the centre. When it is well mixed, the mixture should have the consistency of a slightly thick cake mixture. Thickly butter a sponge tin 8 by 11–12 inches (20 by 28–30 cm) and 2 inches (5 cm) deep. Put in the scone mixture and spread it out in an even layer.

To make the topping, grind the nuts in a blender or electric mill (a clean coffee grinder or one kept specially for nuts and spices) and finely chop the dates. Mix them with the soured cream and honey. Spread the nut mixture over the scone. Bake the scone for 1 hour so the top is a rich brown. Cut the scone into slices and serve it hot or cold with cream.

Preparation: 30 minutes
Cooking: 1 hour

Beestings

Beestings is the first milk that the cow produces after calving. It is very rich and yellow, like a creamy custard, and makes delicious puddings and tarts that need neither eggs nor cream. Most of the beestings should go to the calf to build it up and make it strong but there is always a little left over. On farms where a house cow was kept the beestings would be given as a present to a friend and for good luck the jug always had to be returned unwashed. We made the recipes below with beestings from a neighbouring house cow.

We realise that not many people are able to obtain beestings but we decided to include all these recipes for the benefit of farmers' wives who would like to keep the old recipes going and also for the increasing number of people who are now keeping just one cow to provide milk for the family.

Beestings pudding

Beestings makes a delicious, golden, light batter pudding without the aid of eggs that tastes almost creamy. Serve it hot, either for dessert with jam, syrup or honey, or, like Yorkshire pudding, with roast meat and gravy.

4 oz (125 g) flour
1 teaspoon (5 ml) salt
4 fl oz (120 ml) beestings
from the second or third
milking
$\frac{1}{4}$ pint (150 ml) water
$\frac{1}{4}$ pint (150 ml) milk
1$\frac{1}{2}$ oz (45 g) dripping

Heat the oven to Reg 7/425°F/ 220°C. Put the flour and salt into a bowl and make a well in the centre. Gradually beat in the beestings and water and then the milk. Beat until bubbles appear on the surface. Put the dripping into a roasting tin 8 by 12 inches (20 by 30 cm) and put it into the oven to melt. When the dripping is smoking hot, take it out and pour in the batter. Bake the pudding for 25 minutes so it is risen and golden brown.

Preparation: 20 minutes
Cooking: 25 minutes

Beestings custard tart

Beestings will make a rich, golden, custard tart.

shortcrust pastry made with

6 oz (175 g) wholemeal
flour
$\frac{1}{4}$ pint (150 ml) beestings
$\frac{1}{2}$ pint (275 ml) milk
3 oz (75 g) currants
$\frac{1}{8}$ nutmeg, grated

Heat the oven to Reg 3/325°F/ 170°C. Make the pastry and use it to line an 8-inch (20-cm) diameter flan ring or tin. Mix the beestings with the milk. Scatter the currants in the bottom of the tart and pour in the beestings mixture. Grate the nutmeg over the top and bake the tart for 1 hour or until the custard is risen and a beautiful yellow-brown. Eat it straight away or leave it to get completely cold. As it cools it will sink slightly but this won't spoil the texture or flavour.

Preparation: 25 minutes
Cooking: 1 hour

Beestings cheese

This isn't really a cheese, but a rich, creamy custard. Eat it hot or let it cool completely.

1 pint (575 ml) milk from the
second milking after
calving
2 tablespoons (30 ml) honey
$\frac{1}{4}$ pint (150 ml) cream from
the first milking
butter for greasing an 8-inch
(20-cm) diameter flan dish

Heat the oven to Reg 3/375°F/ 160°C. Put the second milk into a bowl. Gently warm the honey over a low heat and when it has melted, stir it into the milk. Pour the mixture into the buttered dish and pour the cream over the top. Leave the custard to stand for 15 minutes so the cream comes to the surface in an even layer. Bake it for 1 hour so it is set and slightly risen and a beautiful golden colour.

Preparation: 30 minutes
Cooking: 1 hour

VEGETABLES

While goody neath the cottage shade
Sits wi a baskett tween her knees
Ready for supper shelling peas.

(John Clare)

ALL THROUGH the year, and changing with the seasons, vegetables come tumbling in colourful heaps onto market stalls and shop counters. We are very lucky in Britain as our climate is neither too hot nor too cold, and it enables us to grow a wide and interesting variety, from the sun-loving sweetcorn to the winter roots and hardy cabbages.

Commercial vegetable growing first started in earnest during the industrial revolution when market gardens began to appear all round London and the other main towns and cities, providing fresh vegetables for the new urban populations who had no means of growing their own. It is hard to imagine now places like Deptford and Battersea being covered with plots of vegetables, but that was the case. The vegetables were picked early in the morning and carted into Greenwich market. Some were sold from costermongers' barrows and some, like watercress, were cried individually through the streets.

Large-scale vegetable growing has since become an important part of British agriculture. Vegetables are grown all over the country, but most come from the flat, fertile lands of the east. Lincolnshire has the greatest acreage, followed by Norfolk, Humberside, Cambridgeshire, Essex and Kent. Vegetables are grown on contract for the large supermarkets and chainstores, for the wholesaler and for direct supply to local shops and markets. Some are sold at the farm gate and others by 'Pick-Your-Own'. They come from farms of all sizes and from small market gardens, and the people involved in their production may be a staff of twenty or more or just one or two, and they are mostly women. The work is always hard as they are out in all weathers, getting wet and dirty in the winter and hot and dusty in summer, yet wherever we have visited we have never seen a dismal face. There is something about working with vegetables that is very satisfying.

This commercial aspect is, however, only one side of vegetable growing. Large country houses have always had their kitchen garden, presided over by the lady of the house but with the gardener doing the hard work. From it came a succession of vegetables, both ordinary and exotic, to feed the family and the often large number of guests. The

FOOD FROM THE COUNTRY

farmer also had his vegetable patch, usually looked after by his wife, and so did every other country dweller. They concentrated mainly on the good cropping vegetables that would make substantial everyday meals: the roots, cabbages, beans and peas, together with large areas of potatoes, strings of runner beans, Brussels sprouts and marrows.

It is always a great pleasure to drive through the country and see well-stocked gardens, particularly in summer when the peas are hanging from their sticks in fat pods, the feathery tops of the carrots are thick and tall, the marrows are swelling and the bright red flowers of the runner beans are at the tops of their strings. There may be someone hoeing or harvesting, raking or planting, or simply wandering down the path to see how everything is growing.

I have always been fascinated by allotments. Behind our garden in Aylesbury, where I lived until I was nine, there were what seemed then to be acres and acres of allotments. I used to wake in the morning to the sound of whistling. It was not birds, but the man in the allotment nearest the garden gate, who was always digging or planting from very early in the morning. He whistled happily away to himself all day and at the end rode away with cabbages and onions overflowing from the top of his bicycle basket. The allotments are still there; there is even probably someone still whistling on that same plot.

My father had one of those allotments as well as a large garden vegetable patch, and there I learned the basics of vegetable growing by just watching people, reading the seed packets and picking caterpillars off the cabbages, one penny for ten! The first garden that Mick and I had together was tiny and so all we grew were herbs and wild strawberries, but then we moved to our own acre. It was wild and overgrown and all through the first winter we hacked and cleared and finally dug, and the following summer our vegetable patch was just like those we had always admired. Growing vegetables is not just a hobby, it gradually takes you over. Every bit of spare time is spent lovingly caring for them and each year another part of the lawn is dug up to provide extra room for that new variety which you hadn't room to try last season.

The gardener's year begins just after Christmas when the seed catalogues arrive. These have tempting, full-colour pictures of the best specimens and glowing reports of their large crops and superb flavour. We go through marking the ones we want and realise at the end that it would have been easier to mark the ones we didn't want because the list is so long! Then it is time to be realistic; after all, we have only one acre, not ten. The list is whittled down. The old favourites are always there: Green Windsor broad beans, Musselburgh leeks, Density lettuces, Savoy cabbages and Roodnerf Brussels sprouts; but as well as these we always try something new like asparagus peas or a new variety of pepper and, if they are successful, we add them to the list.

As soon as the snow has gone and the frosts are only very light, it is time to start digging. It is a very satisfying job, as you can stand

Most people spoil garden things by over-boiling them. All things that are green should have a little crispness, for if they are over-boiled, they neither have any sweetness nor beauty.
(Hannah Glasse, *The Art of Cookery Made Plain and Easy*)

**RAW EGG AND
POTATO:** *On a very hot
plate beat a raw egg with a
knife. Into it bruise two or
three potatoes. Add a piece of
butter and seasonings.
Note: – This is a very common
dinner for country children,
eaten with a glass of
buttermilk or new milk, and
acknowledged by dieticians as
being a perfect meal.*
(Florence Irwin, speaking
of life in Northern Ireland
in *The Cookin' Women*)

and look at your progress at the end of the day. The earth smells sweet
and fresh and the friendly robin hops about looking for worms on the
upturned clods. When the seeds that we have ordered arrive, we try
to get them into some sort of order and make a chart of which to plant
in which month, leaving spaces for writing in the actual dates of sewing
and planting out. Then in March, everything happens. We are finish-
ing digging and getting the greenhouse ready, sowing seeds in pots,
in the cold-frame and directly into the garden, finding pea sticks and
stringing beans. This chaos seems to go on until the end of May when
most things should be in. The main job after that is hoeing, and waiting
for the first of the early summer vegetables.

The first to be ready are the broad beans and when you taste them,
young and tender and freshly picked, you realise all the sore knees
and aching backs are more than worth it. Tiny early potatoes are next
and later come sweet, tender young carrots and the early peas, and
everyone in the area is giving away lettuces. Courgettes come first in
ones and twos but once you have started picking, they won't let you
stop. The first marrows are soft and melting, the summer crop of white
turnips always tastes more delicate than the late-sown ones, and the
beetroots are small, round and sweet. There will be rows of glossy
green, large-leaved spinach and round, pale summer cabbages.

In July our village, like many others, holds its annual flower and
vegetable show. The largest, cleanest and most presentable vegetables
are taken on a Saturday morning to the village hall and entered in their
respective classes. Even if you think you have no chance of winning,
you still enter for the fun of it and to show your support. Bursting
pea pods are laid in sixes on plates and goodness knows how many

**We can highly recommend
this way of dealing with
freshly gathered mushrooms.
It really does make the most
of their delicate flavour:**

*When the mushrooms were
brought into the kitchen they
were peeled at once and the
tips cut from their stalks, and
then they were put convex side
down into a saucer or two of
cream. Salt and pepper was
sprinkled over them and the
saucers were placed at once in
the hot oven. They were cooked
and were ready for the early
breakfast. They were poured
over hot buttered toast and
they made a 'dish fit for a
king'. We never ate them with
bacon and we never fried them,*
*for then the delicate flavour
would be lost. We had
mushrooms for tea, from an
afternoon's picking, but they
were always cooked in china
saucers to retain flavour. At*
*tea-time we ate them with
bread and butter straight from
the saucers in which they were
cooked.*
(Alison Uttley,
Recipes from an Old Farmhouse)

roots of potatoes have been dug up to provide you with the required number of large, even-sized ones! The cup for the most points is always won by the same person, but we all try again next year. If ever you want to buy really good vegetables, then go to village fêtes. Ours is held on the same afternoon as the show and we all contribute to the produce stall. The arrangement may not be as attractive as the one in the supermarket and the paper bags may all be second hand, but you will never taste vegetables as good.

In August, small, waxy French beans crop regularly and always seem to yield the right amount. The runners that come later are often over-generous, and just as you have finished your own, you may come home to find that someone else has left a bag by your front gate! They are, however, everyone's favourite, and as their season is such a short one, you never seem to mind eating them every day. In late summer there is Florence fennel and, provided, of course, there has been enough sun, the changing colour of the tufts on the sweetcorn will tell you that the corns have swelled to a bright golden yellow. The calabrese, a green autumn broccoli, will be ready for its first picking, there will be still more lettuces and the cabbages will be greener and more robust. It is time to lift the garlic and onions and hang them up in strings and dig and store the remaining potatoes.

We always grow pumpkins. They are a delight to watch as the stems get longer and longer and the tiny, pale orange golf ball gradually becomes a huge golden coach. Our pumpkins will never reach the size of those in pumpkin-growing competitions in the North but when we pick them in October, we always take them up to the bathroom scales to weigh them. After the pumpkin has been picked, the garden settles down and produces hardy, slow-growing winter vegetables. The heads of the crinkly-leaved Savoy cabbages get larger and harder, and the January Kings grow tough, purple outer leaves that protect the green inner hearts from the worst of the weather. We never pick Brussels sprouts until after the first frost. This is partly because we have always been told they will then be nuttier and partly because they seem to represent winter. Picking them too soon would be hastening the seasons. Sweet, yellow parsnips and firm round swedes are always left until at least November, and just in time for Christmas salads come the firm, crisp, red and white cabbages.

All these winter vegetables continue until March when the last to be cleared are the leeks, which are as good then as they were in December. Then the last stumps are pulled out for the land to be cleared and dug. To clear it completely, though, you have to enjoy several weeks of broccoli and cauliflowers. Then, if the pigeons kept away last autumn, the fresh, conical-shaped spring cabbages should tide you round to the first of the broad beans.

A barrowload of tomatoes from a Kent smallholding

Recipes for Vegetables

Artichoke, mustard and yoghurt soup

Jerusalem artichokes make translucent, creamy white soups with a delicate, earthy flavour. This one has mustard for a dry savouriness and yoghurt for lightness.

1 lb (450 g) Jerusalem
   artichokes
1 oz (25 g) butter
1 large onion, thinly sliced
2 teaspoons (10 ml) mustard
   powder
1½ pints (850 ml) stock
1 bouquet garni
6 tablespoons (90 ml) natural
   yoghurt

Peel the artichokes whilst holding them under water. Slice them thinly. Melt the butter in a saucepan on a low heat. Stir in the artichokes, onion and mustard powder, cover them and cook them gently for 10 minutes. Stir in the stock and bring it to the boil. Add the bouquet garni, cover and simmer for 30 minutes. Work the soup in a blender or rub it through the fine blade of a vegetable mill. Return it to the pan, stir in the yoghurt and parsley and reheat it gently without letting it boil.

Preparation: 25 minutes
Cooking: 30 minutes

Cauliflower and ham soup

This thick and tasty soup is good as a first course before a light meal and substantial enough to be a lunch or supper on its own.

1 large cauliflower
1½ pints (850 ml) ham stock

2 medium onions, thinly
   sliced
1 bayleaf
freshly ground black pepper
1 oz (25 g) butter
1 tablespoon (15 ml) flour
¼ pint (150 ml) milk
4 oz (125 g) ham
2 tablespoons (30 ml)
   chopped parsley

Break the cauliflower into florets. Put the stock into a saucepan and bring it to the boil. Add the cauliflower, onions and bayleaf and season them with the pepper. Cover and simmer for 20 minutes. Remove the bayleaf and rub the soup through the fine blade of a vegetable mill (or work it in a blender until it is smooth). Melt the butter in a saucepan on a moderate heat. Stir in the flour and cook it for 1 minute, stirring. Take the pan from the heat and stir in the milk. Replace the pan on the heat and bring the sauce to the boil, continuing to stir. Simmer for 1 minute and stir in the cauliflower and stock. Bring everything to the boil, then simmer for 1 minute. Chop the ham very finely and add it to the soup with the parsley just before serving.

Preparation: 20 minutes
Cooking: 40 minutes

Mushrooms with sorrel and bacon topping

This dish works best with large, freshly gathered field mushrooms. It can be served with bread and butter for lunch or as a first course.

4 really large, flat
   mushrooms about 4 inches
   (10 cm) in diameter

½ oz (15 g) butter, softened
2 collar rashers bacon
8 large radishes
8 sorrel leaves
4 thin slices Farmhouse
   Cheddar cheese,
   approximately the same
   size as the mushrooms

Remove the stalks from the mushrooms and spread the dark side of the caps with a very little butter. Chop the bacon and mushroom stalks and slice the radishes. Remove the ribs from the sorrel leaves and finely chop the leaves. Heat the remaining butter in a small frying-pan on a low heat. Put in the bacon pieces and radishes and brown them. Raise the heat and put in the mushroom stalks and sorrel. Stir them about for 1 minute. Grill the buttered mushrooms under a high heat, dark side up, for 2 minutes. Pile the bacon mixture onto each one and place a slice of cheese on top. Put the mushrooms back under the grill for the cheese to melt.

Preparation: 25 minutes
Cooking: 5 minutes

Savoury stuffed tomatoes

The most enormous tomatoes, particularly the Spanish ones, are very good stuffed. Use best quality butcher's sausage-meat for this recipe and you will have a delicious and cheap main meal.

4 extra large tomatoes, each
   weighing about 8 oz (225 g)
1 lb (450 g) sausage-meat
2 medium onions, finely
   chopped
2 oz (50 g) fine oatmeal
¼ pint (150 ml) stock

1 tablespoon (15 ml) chopped
  marjoram
1 tablespoon (15 ml) chopped
  thyme
2 teaspoons (10 ml) chopped
  savory
2 chopped sage leaves
little butter or dripping for
  lightly greasing a large,
  flat, ovenproof dish

Heat the oven to Reg 6/400°F/
200°C. Scald and skin the tomatoes. Cut them in half lengthways
and scoop out all the seeds and
pith. Save these for a soup or casserole – they will be much too
good to throw away. Heat a large,
heavy frying-pan on a high heat
with no fat. Put in the sausage-
meat and break it up well. Stir it
around until it is cooked through
and beginning to brown. Add the
onions and keep stirring for 2
minutes. Lower the heat and stir
in the oatmeal. Cook, still stirring, for 1 minute. Pour in the
stock and bring it to the boil. Add
the herbs and simmer very gently
for 10 minutes. Take the pan
from the heat. Put the tomato
halves into a large, flat, lightly
greased ovenproof dish and fill
them with the stuffing. Pile it up
high if necessary. Put the tomatoes into the oven for 30 minutes
so the top of the stuffing browns.

Preparation: 30 minutes
Cooking: 30 minutes

Marrow filled with cheesy vegetables

A freshly picked marrow that
melts in your mouth when it is
cooked makes an ideal container
for a selection of summer
vegetables in a cheese sauce.
The wheatgerm and cheese on
top finish off the dish with a
crispy golden crust. It will
make a light lunch or supper
for four or a very substantial
main meal for two.

1 small marrow, weighing 1–
  1½ lbs (450–675 g)
1 lb (450 g) new carrots
1 lb (450 g) peas, weighed
  before shelling
2 lbs (900 g) broad beans,
  weighed before shelling
3 sprigs mint
butter for greasing a large,
  flat, ovenproof dish
½ oz (15 g) butter
8 spring onions, finely
  chopped
1 tablespoon (15 ml)
  wholemeal flour
¼ pint (150 ml) milk
4 oz (125 g) grated
  Farmhouse Cheddar
  cheese
1 tablespoon (15 ml) chopped
  savory
1 tablespoon (15 ml) chopped
  chervil or parsley
2 tablespoons (30 ml)
  wheatgerm

Heat the oven to Reg 6/400°F/
200°C. Cut the marrow in half
lengthways, scoop out the seeds
and peel each half. If the carrots
are small, leave them whole, if
larger, cut them into ¾-inch (2-
cm) lengths. Shell the beans and
peas. Put a mint sprig into each
marrow half and steam the halves
for 15 minutes. (A colander
covered with foil will be more
suitable than a vegetable steamer
as it is larger.) Boil the other
vegetables together with a mint
sprig for 10 minutes.

Drain the marrow halves, in
which water will have collected,
and drain the other vegetables.
Melt the butter in a saucepan on
a low heat. Mix in the onions and
cook them for 2 minutes. Raise
the heat to moderate and stir in
the flour. Stir it for 1 minute and
stir in the milk. Bring the sauce
to the boil and stir it for about 2
minutes until it is thick and bubbling. Take the pan from the heat
and beat in the herbs and three
quarters of the cheese. Then fold

in the carrots, beans and peas.
Butter a large, flat, ovenproof
dish and put in the two marrow
halves. Fill them with the vegetables in their cheese sauce. Scatter first the wheatgerm and then
the cheese over the top. Put the
marrow into the oven for 20
minutes so the cheese topping
turns a golden brown.

Preparation: 40 minutes
Cooking: 20 minutes

Beef and swede pudding

This is a low calorie pudding,
but none the less delicious for
that. Swede and beef always
make hearty, savoury winter
meals.

1½ lbs (675 g) good quality
  stewing steak
2 tablespoons (30 ml)
  seasoned wholemeal flour
12 oz (350 g) small swede
½ oz (15 g) beef dripping
2 teaspoons (10 ml) grated
  horseradish
2 tablespoons (30 ml)
  chopped parsley
1 large onion, quartered and
  thinly sliced
¼ pint (150 ml) strong light
  ale
1 tablespoon (15 ml) tomato
  purée

Cut the beef into ¾-inch (2-cm)
dice and toss it with the seasoned
flour. Slice the swede into rounds
⅛ inch (3 mm) thick. Grease a 2-
pint (1·150-l) pudding basin with
about three quarters of the dripping. Line the basin with the
slices of swede. (This is a bit
tricky and it is easier to do the
lower half, put in some of the filling to hold the swede in place
and then carry on with the top
half.) Put in one third of the meat,
sprinkle over 1 teaspoon (5 ml) of
the horseradish and 1 tablespoon
(15 ml) of the parsley. Put in half
the onion. Repeat the process and

A farm shop in late summer – all the vegetables and other produce come from the farm
(overleaf) *Marrow stuffed with cheesy vegetables and Savoury stuffed tomatoes*

finish with the remaining beef. Mix the tomato purée with the beer and pour it into the basin. Cover the top with more thin slices of swede and dot with the remaining dripping. Cover the pudding with a layer of grease-proof paper and foil and tie them down with string. Bring a sauce-pan of water to the boil, lower in the pudding and steam it for 2 hours, topping up the water when necessary. Turn the pudding into a high-sided dish, being careful not to break it, and take it to the table as it stands.

Preparation: 40 minutes
Cooking: 2 hours

Cheese and cabbage casserole

This cabbage casserole is lightened in flavour by the apple. It is cheap and easy to prepare and makes a substantial autumn or winter meal for four.

1 large Savoy cabbage
6 oz (175 g) streaky bacon
2 medium-sized cooking apples
1 large onion, quartered and thinly sliced
2 tablespoons (30 ml) wholemeal flour
$\frac{1}{2}$ pint (275 ml) stock
6 chopped sage leaves
8 oz (225 g) grated Farmhouse Cheddar cheese

Heat the oven to Reg 6/400°F/200°C. Finely shred the cabbage and cut the bacon into small dice. Peel, core and thinly slice the apples. Put the bacon into a large, flameproof casserole and set it on a low heat. When the fat begins to run, mix in the onion. Cook them until the onion is soft. Mix in the cabbage and then the flour. Pour in the stock and bring it to the boil. Mix in the sage leaves and two thirds of the cheese. Cover the casserole and put it into the oven for 30 minutes. Remove the lid and scatter the remaining cheese over the top of the cabbage. Put the casserole back into the oven for a further 15 minutes for the cheese to melt and just begin to brown. Serve the cabbage straight from the dish.

Preparation: 20 minutes
Cooking: 45 minutes

Potato and herb roll

Cooked mashed potatoes can be mixed with flour and made into pastries or cakes. This savoury roll is best served hot. It is good at lunch time with cheese or can be served instead of plain potatoes with a main meal.

1½ lbs (675 g) old potatoes
1 small onion, thinly sliced
4 oz (125 g) good beef or pork dripping
6 oz (175 g) 81% or 85% wheatmeal flour
sea salt and freshly ground black pepper
1 egg yolk
4 tablespoons (60 ml) mixed chopped parsley, thyme, marjoram and sage
1 egg, beaten

Cut the potatoes into chunks and cook them with the onion in lightly salted water until they are tender. Drain and skin the potatoes and mash them with the onion. While they are still hot, work in the dripping. If you are using pork, it will be soft and melt well. Beef dripping, which is harder, needs to be chopped first and worked well in with a potato masher. When all the dripping has melted, work in the flour, egg yolk, and seasonings, again using the potato masher. Leave the mixture to get cold and firm.

Heat the oven to Reg 4/350°F/180°C. Grease a large baking tray. The mixture will be too wet to be rolled out but it is quite manageable by hand. Make an oblong of it on the baking tray about 12 inches by 5 inches (20 cm by 12 cm) and about ½ inch (1·5 cm) thick. Strew the herbs in a line down the centre. Fold over each side of the mixture with a palette knife and then smooth over the surface making it look like a long sausage roll. Brush the roll with beaten egg. This will not only glaze it but make the surface smooth. Bake the roll for 1 hour, then turn up the heat to Reg 6/400°F/200°C and continue cooking for a further 15 minutes so it becomes really brown. It will change shape as it cooks, puffing up at first and then flattening and spreading. Serve the roll very hot, cut into slices.

Preparation: 1 hour
Cooking: 1 hour 15 minutes

Sweet potato cakes

Savoury cakes aren't the only thing you can make with mashed potatoes. There are many recipes for sweet potato puddings and cakes which make hearty everyday lunchbox fare.

8 oz (225 g) floury potatoes
3 oz (75 g) butter
3 eggs, beaten
8 oz (225 g) wholemeal flour
2 teaspoons (10 ml) baking powder
6 oz (175 g) Barbados sugar
1 teaspoon (5 ml) mixed spice
2 teaspoons (10 ml) caraway seeds
6 oz (175 g) currants
butter for greasing a shallow 8-inch by 12-inch (20- by 30-cm) cake tin.

Heat the oven to Reg 5/375°F/190°C. Boil the potatoes in their skins until they are tender. Drain and skin them and mash them with the butter. Gradually beat in the eggs, alternately with the flour and baking powder. Beat in the sugar, spice and caraway seeds and fold in the currants. Put the mixture into the prepared tin and smooth the top. Bake it for 30 minutes or until a skewer inserted in the centre comes out clean. Turn the cake onto a wire rack and let it cool completely. Cut it into small squares for serving.

Preparation: 45 minutes
Cooking: 30 minutes

Mixed English salad

The English salad unfortunately consists of lettuce, tomatoes and beetroot arranged unappetisingly on a plate with a bottle of salad cream for dressing – or does it? Using the same ingredients but with a homemade mayonnaise, you can make a very attractive and very appetising salad. Served alone it is a side salad, but add some halved or quartered hard-boiled eggs and some curls of ham, and it can be a light main meal.

**6 small inner sticks from a
  head of celery
celery root and a few leaves
3 medium-sized carrots
2 medium-sized beetroot,
  cooked until they are just
  tender**

**2 small Cox's apples
8 oz (225 g) firm tomatoes
1 very small onion
1 tablespoon (15 ml) chopped
  capers
$\frac{1}{4}$ pint (150 ml) mayonnaise
1 small round lettuce**

Finely chop the celery. Coarsely grate the carrots. Finely chop the beetroot and quarter, core and finely chop the apples. Finely chop the tomatoes. Cut the onion into lengthways quarters and slice it as thinly as you possibly can. Mix all these in a bowl with the capers and fold in the mayonnaise. Line a salad bowl attractively with the lettuce leaves, the stalk ends towards the base and the rounded edges coming up towards the edge. Pile the salad in the middle.

Preparation: 20 minutes

Mixed summer salad

This is a light salad for summer meals with an Elizabethan flavour. Don't be afraid of using the lemon if you haven't any of the other fruits. It adds

hints of interesting sharpness here and there, but isn't overpowering and the salad certainly wouldn't be the same without it.

**1 small lettuce
$\frac{1}{2}$ cucumber
1 lemon or 4 oz (125 g)
  redcurrants or raspberries
4 chopped spring onions
2 tablespoons (30 ml)
  chopped mint
1 tablespoon (25 ml) chopped
  tarragon
10 chopped sage leaves
4 tablespoons (60 ml) olive
  oil
2 tablespoons (30 ml)
  tarragon vinegar
freshly ground black pepper**

Shred the lettuce. Cut the cucumber in half lengthways and thinly slice the two halves. Cut the rind from the lemon and chop all the flesh; or string the redcurrants. The raspberries are used whole. Put the lettuce, cucumber and fruit into a bowl with the onions, mint, tarragon and sage. Mix the oil and vinegar together and season them with the pepper. Fold them into the salad.

Preparation: 15 minutes

FRUITS and NUTS

To bend with apples the moss'd cottage-trees,
And fill all fruit with ripeness to the core;
To swell the gourd, and plump the hazel shells
With a sweet kernel.

(John Keats)

A BOWL of crimson strawberries to be eaten with cream, raspberries for a trifle, blackcurrants for a tart, apples for pies and for serving with pork: all these, and many more, are provided every year by British fruit farms and, as a bonus, you can go out in the autumn to hedgerows and woods and take your pick of wild fruits and fresh, sweet nuts.

You always know that summer is here when the first strawberries arrive. Different counties start at different times, but the earliest is probably Hampshire where they are ready in May. All the way down the road through Hampshire to the West Country in the strawberry season you come across stalls heaped with full punnets. You know they are going to be there because of the big red strawberry sign further up the road and maybe a white sunshade with a strawberry emblazoned in the middle. We can never resist stopping, especially if our Kentish strawberries are not yet ready. We eat some of them there and then. On a long and thirsty journey it is more refreshing than drinking a pint of beer to sink your teeth into a luscious sweet strawberry.

It was with strawberries that the pick-your-own boom first started. Paying pickers, buying punnets and transporting strawberries to market or to local shops is expensive for the producer and puts the price up for the customer. What better than to sell them direct and let the customer do the picking? A few farmers started the idea in an experimental way and, although their fellow growers looked at it with suspicion, the system worked. There were a few people who just came in for a good feed whilst they were picking and actually only bought half a pound, but the majority only nibbled at a few strawberries, did no damage, did not trespass on other parts of the farm and bought pounds and pounds of fruit. Everyone was pleased. The farmer cleared his strawberry fields easily and his customers had the benefit of fruit at half the price of that in the shops. The next year, more fields were opened to the public and more farmers copied the idea. They went from strawberries to raspberries and now there are pick-your-own red and black currants, gooseberries, loganberries, apples, pears, plums and cherries. Now, in summer, country districts have a new road sign –

101

FOOD FROM THE COUNTRY

PYO plus an arrow; and the NFU produces a yearly booklet listing all the pick-your-own farms in the country, together with the crops they have available and facilities such as car parking or picnic areas.

It is not just the price that makes picking your own so attractive. You also know that the fruit you are buying is as fresh as it possibly can be. And more than this, since the fruit is so cheap and so good that you can't stop picking it, you tend to pick more than you originally wanted. When you take it home you must do something with it, particularly if it is soft fruit that deteriorates fairly quickly. So you have to get to work in the kitchen. Never, since before the last war, have so many pots of homemade jam and jelly lined the store cupboard, and never has such an interest been taken in fruit. Many a recipe or useful tip can be picked up on the strawberry fields and some farmers have recipe leaflets printed. Another aspect of picking your own is that it gives people an opportunity of a few hours or, in some cases, the whole day out in the country, seeing something of farming life. Children love it. They learn far more by actually seeing things grow than by learning about them in books, and it is a good idea for them to know something of where their food comes from, apart from the supermarket shelf.

It is difficult to say which of the soft fruits is best. Strawberries are dripping with fresh sweetness, but some say raspberries have more flavour. Both these fruits, together with loganberries, are really best eaten raw. Redcurrants are made into their traditional jelly and are also good cooked with rich meats or put into savoury salads. The flavour of blackcurrants is always better when they are cooked and put into a tart or made into jam. Gooseberries are best cooked as well. Put a sprig of elderflowers with them to make them taste like muscat grapes.

The first of the tree fruits to ripen are the cherries. There are white ones, which are really a blushing yellow, and reds and blacks. The whites are sweet and generally stronger flavoured, the reds can be on the tart side, but the blacks are sweet and so juicy that you stain your fingers just picking them. Cherries are getting very scarce now and most of the trees are over thirty years old. When the fruits are ripe the trees look as though someone has hung them with thousands of small, round decorations that shine in the sun. They have been made into cherry batters, cherry puddings, cherry bumpers (turnovers), cherry tarts and a cherry ale, and the sharp, almond-flavoured Morello cherries are still made into cherry brandy.

The plum that most people know by name is the large, pinky-red Victoria, which is juicy and sweet enough to be eaten raw and yet makes the most delicious of compotes if it is simmered gently with wine and honey. The others are often just asked for as 'plums', which is a pity, as you may not get the right one for your particular purpose. The first that we get are the deep purple Early Rivers, small and quite sharp and best for cooking. Next come the Czar, which always look unripe as their purple skins can be tinged with green. They can be sweet

We have a good many fine Sweet Chestnut trees, and they ripen more or less well every year. We cook them in a great many ways: boil them and shell them, and warm them up in butter or with a little stock, as a vegetable. They are very good made into a purée with butter and cream, to eat with cutlets; or boiled and rubbed through a wire sieve, to serve round whipped cream well flavoured with sugar and vanilla.

(Mrs C. W. Earle, *Pot Pourri From a Surrey Garden*)

FRUITS AND NUTS

(top) Boxes of Crispin apples
waiting to go to the packhouse

(below) Chestnuts amongst the
autumn leaves

enough to eat raw and are good for all types of cooking. Golden-coloured early Laxtons can be put into pies, preserved whole or made into jam or wine, and when they are ripe they are a sweet dessert plum. Crimson Burbanks, round purple Monarchs and the egg-shaped red Warwickshire Drooper are all multi-purpose plums; and the golden Yellow Egg Plums and oval Purple Pershores are best for preserving and making wine. Damsons should always be cooked and are best in late September and early October when their flesh has turned translucent yellow.

One of the treats of autumn is to go out into the garden in the chill mist of early morning and pick an apple from the tree. Bite into it, and it will be cool and crisp and the refreshing juice will splash all over your tongue. It makes a perfect breakfast. The first English apples to ripen in August are the more unfamiliar ones that stay in the shops for only a short time. Grenadiers are the first cookers, bright green and smaller than Bramleys; and for eating there are George Caves, James Grieves, Millers and the tiny Beauty of Bath. Later on there are Discovery, Crispin, Laxtons, Worcester Pearmains and the celebrated, sweet Cox; but best of all, with a skin the colour of autumn leaves and a smooth, creamy flesh, are the Egremont Russets, an old variety that, because of popular demand, is still being grown. There is so much flavour in an English apple and so much variety in colour and texture that it is inconceivable that anyone should even want to look at an anaemic green French Golden Delicious which tastes as though it is made of solidified water.

Pears are the last fruit to be ready. In October comes the Conference, long and slender, crisp and firm but, when ripe, very sweet. They are superb with cheese or chopped into savoury salads, and as they get

softer and riper they can be mixed with other fruits in fruit salads. They are also a good cooking pear. You can poach them whole or in thin slices, bake them in wine, put them in a pie, or pickle them whole in sweet, spiced vinegar. For a real treat, wait until November for the sweet Comice. It is the sweetest, juiciest pear you will ever taste and should always be eaten raw. When it is fully ripe, you may need a spoon!

Quinces are an old-fashioned fruit that is not grown commercially but which occasionally reaches country shops through someone who has several trees and more fruit than they can cope with. Quinces are yellow-gold in colour and shaped like a pear. The pink-tinged flesh is very hard and granular, but when it is cooked it softens to a golden, apple-like purée. Eaten raw, quinces will make your tongue wrinkle, but when cooked they are sweeter than apples and have a pungent, almost perfumed flavour. They are rarely used by themselves unless they are to be mixed with something bland such as the cream in the recipe below, and are most often mixed with apples in pies. They go superbly with pork, they make a golden jelly and a delicious, light, dry wine.

We have a friend who raises fruit trees on his smallholding and every year he brings us the tiny fruits of his crab-apple trees. Of the cultivated crab-apples, John Downy are the best for cooking. They look like large red and yellow marbles and, when cooked, make a beautiful orangey-pink purée or jelly. They are best left for a few days after you have picked them so that the skin becomes almost translucent. Then they will be sweet and mellow and you can even eat them raw. When they are cooked, their flavour is richer than that of an ordinary

Plum picking
There is an art in moving a long ladder, the hands have to catch hold of the right rungs and the balance has to be perfect. And the ladder has to be correctly placed against the tree, almost upright (to take the weight), and in such a way that, should it fall, it would fall into the centre of the tree.
(Humphrey Phelps,
Just across the Fields)

Jelly of quince: Mrs Green's Receipt

(This method of making fruit jellies has been the same for years and it is still the one that most people use. Only hard fruits like apples and quinces need so much water, but the one pound to one pint is the best sugar-liquid proportion.)

Take quinces pare and quarter them and put a pound of quince to a quart of water, and let it boyle apasse till it comes to a pinte, keepe it stiring that it may looke payle and clare, strayne it and let it stand till next day then put to a pint of liquer a pound of fine sugar. Let it boyle halfe an howre then strayne it through a jelly bag.

(Rebecca Price, *The Compleat Cook*)

FRUITS AND NUTS

cooking apple and it has a slightly effervescent, sherbert-like quality which always makes crab-apple dishes so special. Other cultivated crab-apples are the bright yellow Golden Hornet and Oldenham Ensis, which is an amazing, deep purple.

Everyone loves picking blackberries. At the beginning of September we make expeditions to our favourite bushes, carrying with us baskets of varying shapes and sizes and walking sticks to pull the bramble arches towards us. We pick for hours and return home with scratched and very stained hands, but it is worth it in order to see the bubbling wine and bottles of cordial and to taste the fruit in pies, puddings and cakes.

If you want enough elderberries for cooking you generally have to race against the birds, for as soon as those deep purple clusters hang downwards, they too know that the berries are sweet and ripe. The best use of elderberries is for wine, but if you only find a few, don't leave them behind. You can use them like blackberries and mix them into apple tarts, or coat them in honey and fill baked apples with them, or make them into tiny, triangular pastry turnovers. After the first two frosts of winter we also go out for rosehips, to make syrup, and rowan-berries, which, with windfall apples, make a bitter-sweet, dark orange jelly that is delicious with game and pork.

We are lucky enough to live in a county famous for its nuts. The Kent Cob was first raised in 1830 by Mr Lambert of Goudhurst and was grown mainly on a three-mile-wide strip of greensand that stretches from Charing to Ightham (and on which we now live). The acreage is very small now but nuts still reach shops all over the country. Kent Cobs are not actually a true cob, but a filbert. True cob nuts are round, like the wild hazels, with a casing that does not quite cover the nut. Kent cobs are elongated and the long, shaggy-ended casing covers each one completely. They hang in clusters on the trees and slowly ripen from pale green to russet brown. Then they are harvested simply by shaking the trees and picking the fallen nuts from the ground. A fresh Kent Cob is crisp and milky. You can put them into salads or eat them with cheese, or just sit down and crack your way through a bowlful. Wild hazels grow in the woods and we sometimes go out and pick a few of these, but with Kent Cobs so close, we prefer to leave most of them for the squirrels.

There are a few walnut trees to be found growing wild, but most of them grow in gardens and are closely guarded by their owners. If you ever want to pickle walnuts, use them green and prick them with a pin first to make sure they are really soft; and, unless you want hands stained brown like a gypsy's, it is best to wear polythene gloves!

The best time to gather chestnuts is November, and the best way to do it is to stamp on the prickly cases where they lie on the woodland floor to expose the shiny brown nuts inside. English chestnuts are smaller than the Italian ones and the bitter inner skin fits round more cracks and crevices in the nut, but once cooked they are sweeter; they are delicious roasted and served, as Mrs Beeton recommends, in a napkin and accompanied by butter.

Recipes for Fruits and Nuts

Elderberry-stuffed apples

Just a small amount of elderberries, mixed with demerara sugar, makes a rich and fruity filling for baked apples.

4 medium to large cooking apples
½ oz (15 g) butter
3 oz (175 g) elderberries (weighed on the stems)
2 oz (50 g) demerara sugar
½ teaspoon (2·5 ml) ground cinnamon or a pinch of ground cloves

Heat the oven to Reg 6/400°F/ 200°C. Core the apples and cut a shallow slit in the skins all the way round, about half-way down. Grease a flat, ovenproof dish with the butter and put in the apples. Remove the elderberries from the stems and mix them with the sugar, cinnamon or cloves. Stuff them into the middles of the apples. Push them in well and make sure they heap up a little on top. Bake the apples for 20 minutes and, just before serving, spoon the rich, dark syrup that has gathered in the dish over the top of them.

Preparation: 15 minutes
Cooking: 20 minutes

Trembling crab-apples

A light, pink purée of crab-apples mixed with a little arrowroot makes a wobbling, trembling light pudding. Serve it plain or with single cream.

1½ lbs (675 g) crab-apples
8 tablespoons (120 ml) dry cider
2 teaspoons (10 ml) arrowroot
4 tablespoons (60 ml) water
4 tablespoons (60 ml) honey

Chop the apples and put them into a saucepan with the cider. Cover them, set them on a low heat and simmer them until they are soft and pulpy (15–20 minutes). Take them from the heat and rub them through a sieve. Mix the arrowroot with the water. Return the apple purée to the rinsed-out pan and stir in the arrowroot and honey. Bring the apples to the boil, stirring, and boil until they thicken (about 3 minutes). Pour the mixture into a bowl and cool it. Chill it until it sets.

Preparation: 30 minutes
Cooking: 20 minutes
Cooling and chilling: 2 hours

Syllabub of quinces

This light, creamy-gold dessert is similar to the eighteenth-century fruit creams and syllabubs.

2 medium to large quinces
2 tablespoons (30 ml) water
1 egg, separated
2 tablespoons (30 ml) honey
3 fl oz (90 ml) double cream

Peel, quarter, core and chop the quinces. Put them into a saucepan with the water. Cover them and set them on a low heat. Cook them until they are reduced to a thick purée and then rub them through a sieve. Return the purée to the pan and beat in the egg yolk. Set the pan on a low heat and stir the mixture with a wooden spoon until it begins to thicken, without letting it boil. Take the pan from the heat and mix in the honey. Let the mixture get quite cool. Lightly whip the cream and stiffly whip the egg white. Fold first the cream and then the egg white into the quince purée. Pile the syllabub into a serving bowl and chill it for 1 hour.

Preparation: 45 minutes
Chilling: 1 hour

Gingered pear flan

Spiced, glazed pears make an attractive filling for a sponge base that is flavoured to match with the same spices. Cook the base in a 7-inch (18-cm) diameter flan mould which has a raised base so that when you turn out the sponge, it has a hollow in the centre for the fruit.

BASE:
4 oz (125 g) butter
4 oz (125 g) demerara sugar
4 oz (125 g) wholemeal flour
1 teaspoon (5 ml) ground ginger
½ teaspoon (2·5 ml) ground cinnamon
2 eggs, beaten

FILLING:
3 firm Conference pears
2 oz (50 g) demerara sugar
2 tablespoons (30 ml) cold water
pinch ground ginger
½ teaspoon (2·5 ml) ground cinnamon

Heat the oven to Reg 4/350°F/ 180°C. Beat the butter until it is creamy and beat in the sugar so the mixture becomes fluffy. Toss the flour with the spices and beat it into the butter and sugar alternately with the eggs. Put the mixture into a 7-inch (18-cm) flan mould and smooth the top. Bake the sponge for 25 minutes so it is firm and has shrunk from the sides of the tin. Turn it onto a wire rack to cool completely.

Peel, quarter and core the pears, and cut them in half cross-ways. Then cut the pieces into thin, lengthways slices. Put the sugar and water into a saucepan and stir them over a low heat until the sugar has melted. Fold in the pears and spices. Bring them to simmering point, cover them and cook them very gently for 15 minutes or until the pears are translucent and tender but still in shape. Take off the lid and raise the heat. Cook fairly briskly until the syrup has reduced to a sticky glaze. Turn the pears onto a plate to cool completely. When both the pears and the base are cool, put the one into the other. Serve with whipped cream.

Preparation: 45 minutes
Cooking: 25 minutes

Upside down plum seedcake

This is a harvest-time cake. Plums and corn are always gathered at the same time and seed cakes are traditional harvest-time fare. It is a delicious sweet cake with a sharp, fruity contrast.

8 oz (225 g) Early River or other cooking plums
4 oz (125 g) butter
8 oz (225 g) Barbados sugar
12 oz (350 g) wholemeal flour
2 teaspoons (10 ml) caraway seeds
4 eggs, beaten
butter for greasing a 9-inch (25-cm) diameter cake tin

Heat the oven to Reg 4/350°F/180°C. Halve and stone the plums and put them in a single layer in the bottom of the pre-pared tin, cut side up. Cream the butter in a bowl and beat in the sugar until the mixture is light and fluffy. Toss the flour with the

caraway seeds and beat it into the butter and sugar, alternately with the eggs. Put the mixture on top of the plums and smooth the top. Bake the cake for 1 hour. A skewer stuck in the centre should come out clean and the cake should have shrunk slightly from the sides of the tin. Cool the cake in the tin for 10 minutes and then carefully turn it onto a cooling rack. The plums should all be on what is now the top of the cake. (If the cake has risen too much, cut a slice of the risen part off.) Eat the cake cold for a harvest-time tea.

Preparation: 30 minutes
Cooking: 1 hour

Layered damson pudding

This is a warming autumn pudding, just right for eating after a hard day spent sweeping up the leaves or digging. The layers of sweet, juicy damsons make it lighter than a solid suet pudding.

6 oz (175 g) wholemeal flour
2 teaspoons (10 ml) baking powder
pinch salt
3 oz (100 g) freshly grated suet
$\frac{1}{4}$ pint (150 ml) cold water
12 oz (350 g) damsons
2 oz (50 g) raisins
4 oz (125 g) demerara sugar
$\frac{1}{2}$ teaspoon (2·5 ml) ground ginger
butter for greasing a $1\frac{1}{2}$-pint (850-ml) pudding basin

Mix the flour, baking powder, salt and suet in a bowl, and mix them to a dough with the water. Halve and stone the damsons and mix them in another bowl with the raisins, sugar and ginger. Set aside one third of the dough and divide the remaining piece into three equal pieces. Roll out one piece

to a size just bigger than the base of the pudding basin and then put it into the basin. Put in one third of the damsons, the next small piece of dough, rolled out to size, damsons again, and the last small piece of dough. Put in the remaining damsons and top the pudding with the large piece of dough rolled out to fit the top of the basin. Cover the basin with a layer of buttered greaseproof paper and one of foil and tie them down. Bring a large sauce-pan of water to the boil and lower in the pudding. Steam it, covered, for 2 hours, never let-ting it come off the boil and topping it up with boiling water when necessary. Turn the pud-ding onto a plate and serve it hot, plain or with single cream.

Preparation: 30 minutes
Cooking: 2 hours

Gooseberry fool

A soft, pale green mixture of gooseberries, eggs and cream is cool and refreshing and easy to eat on a hot summer night. It is not set completely but is like a thick custard and looks very pretty served in chilled glass dishes.

1 lb (450 g) gooseberries
4 tablespoons (60 ml) dry white wine
1 sprig elderflowers (if available)
4 tablespoons (60 ml) honey
2 egg yolks
1 egg white
$\frac{1}{4}$ pint (150 ml) double cream

Top and tail the gooseberries and put them into a saucepan with the wine and elderflower sprig. Cover them and set them on a low heat for 20 minutes, or until they can be beaten to a thick pulp. Rub them through a sieve and put them into a double saucepan or a basin standing in a saucepan of water.

Set the pan on a low heat and stir in the honey. When it has dissolved, beat the egg yolks and white together. Stir them into the gooseberries and keep stirring over a low heat until the mixture becomes really thick. Remove it from the heat and leave it in a cool place until it is on the point of setting. Stiffly whip the cream and fold it into the gooseberries. Put the mixture into a serving bowl and chill it for about 1 hour.

Preparation: 1 hour
Cooking: 20 minutes
Chilling: 1 hour

Raspberry and blackcurrant tart

The rich, sweet crumbly pastry for this tart contrasts superbly with the slightly sharp and refreshing fruit.

PASTRY:
7 oz (200 g) wholemeal flour
pinch sea salt
1 egg, separated
4 oz (125 g) butter, softened
1 tablespoon (15 ml) clear honey
FILLING:
8 oz (225 g) raspberries
8 oz (225 g) blackcurrants
4 oz (125 g) clear honey

Heat the oven to Reg 6/400°F/ 200°C. Put the flour onto a work top with the salt and make a well in the centre. Put in the egg yolk, butter and honey, and work everything with your finger tips to make a smooth dough. For the filling, put the honey into a saucepan and melt it gently. Take the pan from the heat and fold in the fruit. Line an 8-inch (20-cm) diameter tart tin with about three quarters of the pastry and fill it with the fruit. Make a lattice pattern on the fruit with the remaining pastry

and brush the lattice and the sides of the tart with the egg white. Bake the tart for 25 minutes so the pastry is golden brown. Eat it hot or cold, with single cream.

Preparation: 30 minutes
Cooking: 25 minutes

Blackberry mousse

This is a light, fluffy mousse, gently spiced and a soft purple colour. It is superb accompanied by a glass of blackberry wine.

1 lb (450 g) blackberries
2 tablespoons (30 ml) blackberry wine, or ordinary red wine, or water
one 2-inch (5-cm) piece cinnamon stick
6 cloves
4 allspice berries
4 tablespoons (60 ml) honey
$\frac{1}{2}$ oz (15 g) gelatine
juice $\frac{1}{2}$ lemon
1 egg, separated
4 fl oz (120 ml) double cream

Put the blackberries into a saucepan with the wine or water, cinnamon, allspice and cloves. Cover them and set them on a very low heat until the blackberries are soft and pulpy (about 15 minutes). Rub them through a sieve. Return the purée to the rinsed-out saucepan, add the honey and set on a low heat until it is dissolved. Reserve 4 teaspoons of the purée. Soak the gelatine in the lemon juice. Stir it into the blackberries and stir on a low heat until it has dissolved. Beat in the egg yolk and keep stirring, without boiling, until the mixture thickens. Take it from the heat and cool it until it is on the point of setting. Lightly whip the cream and stiffly whip the egg white. Fold first the

cream and then the white into the blackberry purée. Pour the mousse into small pots or glasses, and leave in a cool place for 2 hours to set. Just before serving, decorate each glass with 1 teaspoon (5 ml) of the deep purple reserved purée.

Preparation: 1 hour
Cooling: 2 hours

Strawberry or raspberry vinegar

Fruit vinegars are thick, sweet-sharp syrups and make deliciously refreshing drinks diluted with soda or sparkling mineral water. They were once used as sauces for sweet fruit puddings and you can also use them to top ice-cream and milk puddings. The vinegars have the distinct flavours of the original fruits. The strawberry one is a deep, clear crimson and the raspberry vinegar is a much deeper red.

$1\frac{1}{2}$ lbs (675 g) strawberries or raspberries (preferably 8 oz (225 g) picked fresh once every four days)
one 13 fl oz (369 ml) bottle white wine vinegar
equal weight of strained vinegar in sugar or honey (8–12 oz (225–350 g)

Put 8 oz (225 g) of strawberries or raspberries into a bowl with the vinegar. Cover them with kitchen paper or a cloth and leave them in a cool larder for four days. Strain the vinegar and put in a further 8 oz (225 g) fruit. Leave for a further four days and repeat the process again. Strain the vinegar through a jelly bag. Put it into a saucepan and weigh it (having first weighed the saucepan). Add the weight of the vinegar in sugar or honey. Bring the vinegar to the boil on a low heat, stirring until the sugar or honey has dissolved. Boil for 5 minutes, skimming well. Pour the vinegar into an earthenware jug and cover it with a linen tea cloth, folded into four. Tie the cloth down securely and leave the vinegar for 24 hours. Pour the vinegar back into the original bottle (you will find you will have exactly the amount that you started with) and screw on the top. The vinegar will keep for up to a year, but can be used immediately.

Preparation: 13 days

Pear and cobnut salad

When the first pears are ready, the cobnuts should be fresh and sweet. Together they make a simple autumn first course.

4 firm Conference or
　Comice pears
4 tablespoons (60 ml) soured
　cream
1 tablespoon (15 ml) cider
　vinegar
freshly ground black pepper
48 fresh Kent Cobs

Quarter and core the pears and chop them into $\frac{1}{2}$-inch (1·5-cm) dice. Mix the sour cream with the vinegar and season with the pepper. Fold it into the pears. Divide the pears between four small dishes. Shell the nuts and scatter them over the top.

Preparation: 25 minutes

A russet salad for a Sunday evening

Salads are the best meal for a Sunday evening, especially if you have had a large lunch. We first had this one on an autumn evening with local russet apples and fresh 'wet' walnuts.

2 large russet apples
6 large sticks celery

8 oz (225 g) streaky bacon
6 oz (175 g) Farmhouse
　Cheshire cheese
1 small onion, very thinly
　sliced
4 chopped sage leaves
4 tablespoons (60 ml) olive
　oil
2 tablespoons (30 ml) cider
　vinegar
1 teaspoon (5 ml) mustard
　powder
8 oz (225 g) fresh 'wet'
　walnuts, weighed before
　shelling, or 2 oz (50 g)
　chopped ready-shelled
　walnuts
1 bunch watercress

Quarter, core and chop the apples and finely chop the celery. Grill the bacon until it is crisp, and crumble it. Cut the cheese into small dice. Mix all these with the onion and sage leaves in a bowl. Beat the oil, vinegar and mustard powder together and fold them into the salad. Either arrange the salad in a serving bowl or divide it between four individual plates. Shell the walnuts and scatter them over the top. Decorate the salad with watercress.

Preparation: 30 minutes

Chestnut stuffing

A purée of chestnuts mixed with bacon makes a smooth and savoury stuffing. This amount will pack nicely into a medium-sized roasting chicken or a large pheasant or guinea fowl.

4 oz (125 g) chestnuts
1 small onion
1 stick celery
3 oz (75 g) streaky bacon
$\frac{1}{2}$ oz (15 g) butter
1 tablespoon (15 ml) mixed
　chopped marjoram and
　thyme

Nick the tops off the chestnuts. Put them into a saucepan of cold water, bring them to the boil and simmer for 15 minutes. Peel

them, keeping them immersed until you get to them. Chop them finely. Finely chop the onion and celery and dice the bacon. Melt the butter in a frying-pan on a low heat. Mix in the onion, celery and bacon and cook them until the onion is soft. Work in the chestnuts and herbs with the pan still on the heat. When everything is well mixed, cool the mixture slightly and stuff the bird.

Preparation: 40 minutes

Lamb chops stuffed with redcurrants

Redcurrants make a jelly that goes superbly with lamb, but when fresh ones are in season, you can use these instead.

8 small best end neck chops
　with long tails
4 oz (125 g) redcurrants
1 oz (25 g) butter
1 medium onion, finely
　chopped
1 clove garlic, finely chopped
3 oz (75 g) granary or
　wholemeal breadcrumbs
1 tablespoon (15 ml) mixed
　chopped thyme and
　marjoram
1 tablespoon (15 ml) chopped
　mint

Carefully remove all the bones from the chops. String the redcurrants. Melt the butter in a frying-pan on a low heat. Mix in the onion and garlic and cook them until they are soft. Mix in the redcurrants and cook them for 1 minute so they release their juices. Take the pan from the heat and mix in the breadcrumbs and herbs. Lay the chops on a flat surface and put a portion of stuffing under the tail of each one. Fold the tails round and tie the chops with fine cotton string. Leave them in a cool place for 30 minutes to 1 hour to set into shape. When you are ready to cook, heat the grill to high and if you have an open wire rack, cover it with foil. Grill the chops as close to the heat as possible until they are done to your liking.

Preparation: 45 minutes
Cooling: 30 minutes–1 hour
Cooking: approximately 15 minutes

Apple sauces for pork

Where would roast pork be without apple sauce? Here are three different variations that are all cooked in the oven beside the pork and require the minimum amount of preparation. You don't even have to peel the apples as the peel seems to melt away in the cooking. The apple sauce with quince has a lovely pungent flavour and the crab-apple sauce is a pretty pink.

Quince and apple sauce

1 medium-sized quince
2 large Bramley apples
1 oz (25 g) butter
1 tablespoon (15 ml) clear honey

Peel, core and chop the quince. Quarter, core and chop the apples, but don't peel them. Put the butter into the bottom of a small earthenware casserole and put the fruit on top. Mix in the honey, cover, and put the casserole into the oven beside the pork for 45 minutes. Mix everything together and serve it hot.

Crab-apple sauce

8 oz (225 g) crab-apples
$\frac{1}{2}$ oz (15 g) butter
1 tablespoon (15 ml) honey

Quarter and core the crab-apples and proceed as for the quince and apple sauce.

Traditional apple sauce

2 large Bramley apples
1 oz (25 g) butter
2 teaspoons (10 ml) honey

Quarter, core and chop the apples and proceed as for the quince and apple sauce.

FOR EACH SAUCE:
Preparation: 15 minutes
Cooking: 45 minutes

All through the fruit season, country housewives are busy making jams and jellies; they seem to make just as much now as they ever did. Here are two for the store cupboard, one to make in early summer and the other in the autumn.

Gooseberry and elderflower jam

Elderflowers give this gooseberry jam a delicate flavour of Muscat grapes. It makes about 7 lbs (3 kg).

4 lbs (1·8 kg) green gooseberries
$\frac{1}{4}$ pint (150 ml) water
6 elderflower sprigs, tied in a bunch
4 lb (1·8 kg) demerara sugar

Top and tail the gooseberries and put them into a preserving pan with the water and elderflowers. Set them on a low heat and cook them, stirring occasionally, until they are soft and broken. Remove the elderflowers. Pour in the sugar and stir until it dissolves. Raise the heat and boil rapidly, stirring, until a blob of jam sets on a cold plate. Pour the jam into warmed jars and cover it with circles of waxed paper. Cover it completely when it is cool.

Preparation: 30 minutes
Cooking: approximately 30 minutes

Mixed fruit jelly

You can make jelly with almost any spare autumn fruits. It is rather extravagant as you need a lot of fruit to fill so few jars, but ideal when you have so much fruit that you don't know what else to do with it. If you haven't enough of one fruit, then use a mixture, adding plenty of windfall apples to help it set. This is just one example of a mixed fruit jelly. You could just as easily have equal quantities of plums and damsons, more plums or just one of the fruits. This particular jelly is very dark and very fruity and superb with scones or toasted muffins. It makes about $4\frac{1}{2}$ lbs (2 kg).

2 lbs (900 g) dark purple cooking plums
4 lbs (3·6 kg) windfall eating apples
1 lb (450 g) windfall cooking apples
4 lbs (3·6 kg) damsons
2 pints (1·150 l) water
1 lb (450 g) sugar per pint (575 ml) strained liquid (about 3 lbs (1·350 kg) altogether)

Halve and stone the plums. Wipe and chop the apples, including the cores. Cut slits round the damsons but only remove the stones if it is easy. Put the fruits into a preserving pan with the water. Bring them to the boil and simmer gently until they are very soft ($1\frac{1}{2}$–2 hours). Skim off as many of the damson stones as you can while it is cooking. Strain everything through a jelly bag and measure the liquid. Return it to the saucepan. Weigh out the required amount of sugar and warm it in a low oven for 5 minutes. Bring the liquid to the boil. Stir in the sugar and keep stirring until it has dissolved. Boil until setting point is reached. Pour the jelly into warm jars and cover it with circles of waxed paper. Cover it completely when it is cold and has set.

Cooking: $1\frac{1}{2}$–2 hours
Preparation: 1 hour 15 minutes

HERBS and FLOWERS

Here's flowers for you;
Hot lavender, mints, savory, marjoram;
The marigold, that goes to bed wi' the sun
And with him rises weeping: these are flowers
Of middle summer, and I think they are given
To men of middle age.

(William Shakespeare)

THE TRADITIONAL cottage garden that one always imagines, with its neat herbaceous borders and old-fashioned flowers, was never cultivated merely to look pretty. Nearly every plant in the garden could work its magic in the kitchen and round the house. The addition of a subtle blend of herbs can make the plainest dish more interesting, and herbs or flower petals scattered over the top of a cooked dish or a salad add to flavour and to appearance. Both herbs and flowers can be dried and made into refreshing tisanes, they can be used to flavour beer or be made into wine. Preserves and candies can be made from flowers, and pickles from herbs and from flower buds and seeds. Around the house, bunches of dried herbs keep flies away and perfume linen, and the scent of summer flowers can last all winter in a pot pourri. The country housewife, who had very few medicines, also used herbs for curing aches and pains and illnesses. The housewife who did not know about herbs was not a very good housewife.

In this century, however, people lost interest in herbs. Plainer cooking was enforced by rationing (although a few home-grown herbs would have improved many a war-time economy dish) and tea and coffee became very much cheaper; patent medicines flooded the market, and ready-flavoured convenience foods appeared on supermarket shelves alongside aerosol sprays of synthetic air freshener. Herbs were now for the gourmet and the professional cook and only the most adventurous used them at home.

When did the turn around happen? It is difficult to say, but in the past few years, herbs have once again been welcomed into many British kitchens and people are eagerly relearning the old skills of making lavender bags and pots pourris. Herbal medicines are considered by many to be safer than drugs for minor ailments and you are no longer considered odd if you drink herb tea. Most people with gardens have set aside at least a small plot for culinary herbs, and to supply them with seeds and plants there are herb farms, many of which have started up only over the past few years and all of which are flourishing.

FOOD FROM THE COUNTRY

Growing herbs is an absolute pleasure. You can start off with a few culinary varieties but as you learn more about them you become fascinated and plant more and more for the sheer joy of watching them grow and flower and being able to walk down the plot taking in the different scents. Working with them is very therapeutic. If ever we come home tired after a day's travelling or running round London, or have spent too long getting frustrated in the studio or at the typewriter, an hour or so working quietly in the herb garden, weeding or trimming or planting out seedlings, will soon restore sanity. So let us take a walk round the garden and see what we can find.

We try to grow the tallest plants at the back of the herb garden. Fennel completely disappears during the winter but in March the feathery leaves begin to show and gradually the stems grow to about six feet high. In late July and August it has yellow, umbrella-like clusters of flowers. Fennel is the traditional herb to use with fish and it is excellent with pork and in mixed summer salads, especially those which contain tomatoes and cucumber. We dry the seeds and the stems at the end of the summer. The seeds we use in salads and sparingly to flavour fish dishes and sometimes to flavour bread. You can also use them for a herb tea. When grilling meat, put some dried fennel stalks on the grill rack first and put the meat on top of them so it acquires a smoky, aromatic flavour.

Lovage has a similar cycle to fennel in that it disappears soon after the first frost. Its red shoots appear in March and, like fennel, by the end of the summer it is about six feet high. I had a German landlady once, who called it 'Magikraut' as it magically gives its celery-like flavour to stocks and stews. It can also be used to flavour chicken and to make a soup with potatoes. Use it only sparingly, for it can be quite overpowering. Angelica grows tall and has a large flower head which, when the tiny green flowers are fully out, looks like a floral ball. The main use of angelica is to candy the stem for cake decorations. You can also chop the leaves and cook them with sharp fruits such as apples or rhubarb. It sweetens them and you will not need so much sugar. We grow elecampane for its big, shaggy yellow flower. It is a medicinal plant so we just walk past and admire it. We made a mistake with the catmint and put it at the front of the herb garden. It should really be towards the back as it grew surprisingly tall. We grew it for the cats, who sit in it for hours, roll about in it and chew the stems.

The borage is uncontrollable in our herb garden. It readily seeds itself every year and even when we think we have only left a few plants at the back, they spring up all over the place. To judge by the big, furry, slightly prickly leaves, you would suppose it to be the most inedible of plants, but catch them young and chop them into salads and you will have the flavour of cucumber before the real cucumbers are ready in the greenhouse. The flowers are weird and remind you of witches and spells. They are blue, with five pointed petals, pink tinged in the middle, with black stamens in the centre. Float them in wine

Unsalted butter should be used for this recipe, and the strongest smelling rose petals:

ROSE BUTTER *Put into a stone jar ¼ pound of butter and cover it entirely with Rose petals above and below and leave overnight in a cool place with the lid on. This butter can be used for spreading on very thin bread and after a few Rose petals have been placed on the top the bread should be delicately rolled, the Rose petals being allowed to protrude at either end.*

(Mrs C. F. Leyel, *Herbal Delights*)

cups with summer fruits (see page 149) and you have a drink with a fairy-tale quality.

Next tallest are the mints. We have spearmint and apple mint for cooking with lamb, putting into salads and scattering over potatoes and young peas and carrots, and peppermint, with which I make my morning tea.

Our garden produces the thickest sage bushes I have ever seen, and in late June they have large spikes of purple flowers which can be picked and put in a vase, or dried and used in winter flower arrangements. Probably the flavour most used by country cooks is sage and onion. In stuffing it is used for pork, goose, chicken and duck, and sausages smothered with onions that have been fried with chopped sage are absolutely delicious. We also crush chopped sage leaves with garlic, allspice, black peppercorns and sea salt, and rub the mixture either over a joint of pork before it goes into the oven or into the surface of pork chops before grilling them. Sage used sparingly also goes well with beef and one leaf chopped very finely improves a lettuce salad.

Lemon balm grows in a low bush and has yellowy-green leaves that slightly resemble dead nettles. With its light, lemony scent, it can be used in salads and also makes a delicious tea. There are two types of tarragon, French and Russian. We originally made the mistake of buying Russian; it ran amok over everything else and had a very bland, sweet flavour. So we have since replaced it with French, which grows in smaller clumps and is infinitely better for culinary purposes as it has a nice, fiery bite to it. Use it in salads, especially with chicken or avocados, and for making vinegar (see left). Bergamot is a fairly tall plant with shaggy red flowers that bloom in August. It is mostly used for making a herb tea which is refreshing and reviving. For the opposite effect, to calm and relax, there are the daisy-like flowers of the sweet-smelling chamomile.

We have four sorrel bushes and they keep us well supplied with fleshy, spinach-like leaves which are sharp and refreshing and ideal for soups, sauces and salads. With sugar and dried fruits they also make a delicious sweet pie (see below). Good King Henry has a more spinach-like flavour and if you have enough plants it makes a delicious spring vegetable on its own; if you only have one or two plants, mix the leaves with other vegetables such as leeks or spring greens.

Thyme grows in gradually spreading bushy clumps and has heads of tiny purple flowers that first appear in June and only disappear from the later flowering bushes at the end of August. We add it to salads, cook vegetables with a sprinkling of thyme in the pot, put it into casseroles and stews, tie it into bouquets garnis and lay sprigs all over roasting meats. Lemon thyme we use a lot with fish, and herba-barona, or caraway thyme, is a good flavouring for beef casseroles. In medieval times it was used to tenderise tough meats. Marjoram is soft and sweet. It is a very good herb for lamb and is delicious with carrots. Put it into stuffings for chicken, tie it into a bouquet garni, add it to casseroles or use it, with sage, for pork.

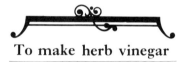

To make herb vinegar

By the end of the summer we have bottles of different flavoured herb vinegars on the larder shelf. It is a way of preserving the flavours of summer herbs to use in winter salads. You can use any herb for vinegar that you like.

1 bottle white wine vinegar or good quality cider vinegar

2 large or 4 small sprigs herbs

Pour out a little vinegar from the bottle and push in one large or two small herb sprigs. Screw the lid back on and leave the bottle on a sunny windowsill for three weeks. Change the herb sprig for a fresh one. You can start using the vinegar straight away but it will keep for up to a year.

FOOD FROM THE COUNTRY

We grow winter savory and summer savory. The winter variety is more robust and best for winter casseroles and stocks. The leaves of summer savory are more delicate and can be used in summer salads and to flavour lightly cooked, young vegetables, including broad beans, for which it is particularly famous. A sprig is also beneficial when put into the pot with a poaching chicken. Garlic is grown in the vegetable patch in an attempt to keep the root fly away from the carrots, but in the herb garden are chives, whose purple flowers make a lovely decoration for summer salads and first courses, and Welsh onions, or scallions, which stay in their tight clumps all winter and can even be picked in the snow. You use only their green parts leaving the ends to grow again to supply you with the flavour of extra strong spring onions all through the year.

The parsley plot is a large one as the herb is so universal. Chervil is related to parsley but has a more delicate flavour. We like it best of all with eggs and, if you can time it right, cook it with carrots. It springs up very early in May, disappears at the end of June, and then a second crop comes in September. Dill is small and delicate with thin stems and feathery leaves and small, umbrella clusters of yellow flowers. It has a rounded, pungent flavour and is best of all with fish. In Scandinavia it is used in a salting mixture for salmon to make Gravlax, and it is particularly good with fresh salmon or in a smoked salmon salad. Put it into cucumber salads, pickle cucumbers with it, or gently simmer peeled cucumbers in butter with chopped dill to be served as a hot vegetable. Basil has to be raised indoors and planted out in early summer. Tomatoes would never be the same without it.

Our favourite flowers in the herb garden are marigolds and nasturtiums. With their bright, splashy flowers of orange and yellow they are true flowers of high summer. We put marigold petals into beef stews, scatter them into glazed vegetables, put them into cheese sauce and use them to decorate both cooked dishes and salads. You can chop nasturtium leaves into salads and casseroles and use the flowers for decoration. We like them filled with cream cheese as a summer first course (see recipe below).

In complete contrast, in another plot are the soft mauves, pinks and blues of lavender and hyssop. The hyssop we grow principally to attract bees, but also to use as a hot poultice for sprains and bruises. The lavender is there mainly for its scent, but also to be added very sparingly to a mixture of herbs in a casserole. We have just planted an Apothecary's Rose, the oldest rose and one of the most sweet smelling; so when it grows there will be rose petal tea, butter and jam.

On the kitchen windowsill there are pots of scented geraniums: Attar of Roses with a faint rose scent, Denticulatum which smells of lemon, and Tomentosum which has the aroma of mint. As well as making the kitchen smell sweet, the leaves can be used in cooking, infused in the milk for a custard or a sweet sauce, or in the water for making a jelly.

If you have never grown herbs before, start now, for they will give you constant joy.

Picked a bunch of deep orange marigolds this morning. They had soft, velvet brown eyes. I felt that the millionaires were quite welcome to all the orchids in the world. I could be perfectly happy with my marigolds.
(Elvira, *Kentish Yesterdays*)

HERBS AND FLOWERS

Oak Cottage Herb Farm, Nesscliff, Shropshire
(overleaf) Flower and tomato salad

Recipes for Herbs and Flowers

Flower and tomato salad

The basil makes all the difference to the flavour in this delightfully colourful summer first course.

4 very large or 8 medium-sized tomatoes
2 tablespoons (30 ml) olive oil
2 tablespoons (30 ml) chopped basil
freshly ground black pepper
4 nasturtium flowers
2 oz (50 g) sweet cream cheese
petals from 2 marigold heads

Slice the tomatoes into rounds $\frac{1}{4}$ inch (6 mm) thick and arrange them on four small plates. Sprinkle the tomatoes with the oil, basil and a little pepper. Fill the nasturtium flowers with the cheese and place one on each plate of tomato slices. Press a few marigold petals into the cheese to look like long yellow stamens and scatter the rest over the tomatoes.

Preparation: 15 minutes

Cauliflower and marigold cheese

This is a soft, creamy purée of cauliflower and cheese given colour and a delicate flavour by the marigold petals. It is a first course again and should be eaten with a small spoon.

1 medium to large cauliflower
$\frac{1}{2}$ oz (15 g) butter
$\frac{1}{4}$ pint (150 ml) stock
1 tablespoon (15 ml) chopped thyme
petals from 6 marigold heads
4 oz (125 g) grated Farmhouse Cheddar cheese

Break the cauliflower into florets and put them into a saucepan with the butter, stock and thyme. Cover, and set it on a moderate heat for 15 minutes so the cauliflower is tender and the liquid has reduced to a glaze. Put the cauliflower into a blender with any liquid that is left and the thyme. Work it to a purée. Put the purée into a bowl and mix in the marigold petals and half the cheese. Divide the mixture between four small heatproof ramekins or soufflé dishes and top it with the remaining cheese. Put the dishes under a high grill for the cheese to melt.

Preparation: 15 minutes
Cooking: 15 minutes

Pickled mackerel

Fresh herbs added to a pickle mixture make a light and tasty dish of mackerel.

4 small or 2 large mackerel
freshly ground black pepper
sea salt
$\frac{1}{2}$ teaspoon (2·5 ml) ground mace
$\frac{1}{2}$ nutmeg, grated
4 tablespoons (60 ml) olive oil
$\frac{1}{4}$ pint (150 ml) white wine vinegar
1 tablespoon (15 ml) chopped parsley
1 tablespoon (15 ml) chopped lemon thyme or common thyme
1 tablespoon (15 ml) chopped fennel
1 bayleaf, torn in half
1 small onion, thinly sliced
lettuce, tomatoes and watercress for serving

Fillet the mackerel and cut each fillet crossways into serving pieces (the small mackerel in half and the larger ones in three or four pieces). Lay the pieces in a flat dish, cut side up. Grind over plenty of pepper and a little salt and sprinkle them with the mace and nutmeg. Leave the mackerel to stand for 1 hour.

Heat the oil in a heavy frying-pan on a moderate heat. Fry the pieces of mackerel, cut side down first, until they are cooked through (about $1\frac{1}{2}$ minutes on each side). When they are done, put them back into the dish. Keeping the heat at moderate, pour the vinegar into the pan and add the herbs and onion. Stir well to blend in any oil that is left in the pan. Simmer for 1 minute and then pour the contents of the pan over the mackerel. Leave the mackerel to get quite cold before serving. The longer they stand, the better they seem to be, so you can very easily make this dish the day before you need it. Remove the bayleaf before serving. The onion slices can either be left or removed, but the herbs must definitely stay clinging to the mackerel. Arrange the mackerel on a bed of lettuce and decorate it with tomatoes and watercress.

Marinade: 1 hour
Preparation and cooking: 45 minutes
Cooling: at least 3 hours

117

Braised beef with herbs

It looks as though there are an awful lot of herbs in this dish but their flavours mellow together as they cook and the chopped herbs themselves thicken the sauce to make the dish very satisfying but at the same time very light.

2 lbs (900 g) braising steak
1 oz (25 g) butter
1 large onion, finely chopped
$\frac{3}{4}$ pint (425 ml) bitter beer
$\frac{1}{4}$ teaspoon (1·5 ml) ground
    mace
6 chopped sorrel leaves
2 tablespoons (30 ml)
    chopped parsley
1 tablespoon (15 ml) chopped
    chervil
1 tablespoon (15 ml) chopped
    thyme
1 tablespoon (15 ml) chopped
    marjoram
1 tablespoon (15 ml) chopped
    savory
4 chopped sage leaves
2 anchovy fillets, crushed to
    a paste
freshly ground black pepper

Heat the oven to Reg 4/350°F/ 180°C. Trim the beef of any fat and cut it into pieces 2 inches by 1 inch (5 cm by 2·5 cm). Melt the butter in a flameproof casserole on a high heat. Put in the pieces of beef, in two batches if necessary, and brown them. Remove them, lower the heat and put in the onion. Cook it until it is soft. Pour in the beer and bring it to the boil. Add the mace, all the herbs and the anchovies, and season with the pepper. Replace the beef. Cover the casserole and put it into the oven for 1 hour 30 minutes.

Preparation: 30 minutes
Cooking: 1 hour 30 minutes

Lamb and herbs in a parcel

If herbs are wrapped up with meat, their flavours will gently penetrate it as it cooks. This parcel method also makes the meat very tender and moist.

$\frac{1}{2}$ shoulder of lamb
sea salt and freshly ground
    black pepper
butter for greasing
as many sprigs of thyme
    and mint as will cover the
    top and bottom surfaces
    of the lamb

Heat the oven to Reg 4/350°F/ 180°C. Season the lamb well. Thickly butter a large sheet of greaseproof paper. Lay as many sprigs of thyme and mint in the centre as will cover the underside of the lamb. Set the lamb on top and cover it with more sprigs of herbs. Wrap the greaseproof securely round the lamb. Wrap it again with an ungreased piece, just as large. Tie up the parcel with string and put it into a roasting tin. Put it into the oven for 2 hours.

Lift the parcel onto a plate and unwrap it carefully to save all the juices. Discard the herbs and carve the lamb. Moisten it just a little with the juices but otherwise serve it quite plain, with lightly cooked vegetables and either boiled new potatoes or, if it is winter, jacket potatoes.

Preparation: 15 minutes
Cooking: 2 hours

Herbed roast chicken with yoghurt sauce

This is a light roast chicken dish with a herby yoghurt sauce. Again, roasting the meat in a parcel of herbs flavours it gently as it cooks.

1 roasting chicken weighing
    3–3$\frac{1}{2}$ lbs (1·350–1·575 kg)
3 sprigs tarragon
3 sprigs thyme
3 sprigs marjoram
3 sprigs parsley
6 large sorrel leaves
$\frac{1}{2}$ lemon, thinly sliced
2 cloves garlic
1 oz (25 g) butter, softened
1 tablespoon (15 ml)
    wholemeal flour
$\frac{1}{2}$ pint (575 ml) stock, made
    from the giblets
1 carton natural yoghurt
2 tablespoons (30 ml) mixed
    chopped tarragon, thyme,
    marjoram and parsley

Heat the oven to Reg 6/400°F/ 200°C. Inside the chicken put one sprig each of the tarragon, thyme, marjoram and parsley, two sorrel leaves, the lemon and one of the garlic cloves, finely chopped. Truss the chicken and spread it with the butter. Cover it with the remaining herb sprigs. Place it in a roasting tin, cover it with foil and put it into the oven for 1 hour. Remove the foil and continue roasting for 30 minutes so the skin is a good golden brown. Take out the chicken, put it on a serving dish and keep it warm. Crush the remaining clove of garlic and chop the remaining four sorrel leaves. Set the roasting tin on top of the stove on a moderate heat. Stir in the chopped herbs and sorrel and cook them for $\frac{1}{2}$ minute. Stir in the flour and let it bubble. Pour in the stock and bring it to the boil, stirring. Add the garlic and simmer for 2 minutes, then take the pan from the heat and stir in the yoghurt. Pour the sauce into a warm sauceboat and take the chicken to the table separately.

Preparation: 30 minutes
Cooking: 1 hour 30 minutes

Pork chops with rosemary stuffing

Rosemary used in a stuffing for pork makes a delicious change from sage. The chops are not actually stuffed with the mixture but given a moist topping that becomes crisped and browned on the outside.

4 pork chops
4 sprigs rosemary
1 teaspoon (5 ml) chopped rosemary
1 small onion, finely chopped
1 teaspoon (5 ml) mustard powder
3 tablespoons dry cider, apple wine, apple juice or stock
2 oz (50 g) wholemeal breadcrumbs
freshly ground black pepper

Heat the oven to Reg 6/400°F/ 200°C. Cut the rind from the chops. Put them on a rack in a roasting tin with a sprig of rosemary on each one and place the rind underneath to render down. Put the chops into the oven for 40 minutes. Half-way through the cooking time spoon 2 tablespoons (30 ml) fat from the roasting tin into a small frying-pan. Set it on a low heat, mix in the onion and cook it until it is soft. Scatter in the mustard powder and cook it for 1 minute. Pour in the cider (or other liquid) and bring it to the boil. Take the pan from the heat and mix in the breadcrumbs and chopped rosemary. Season with the pepper. Press the stuffing onto the meat part only of the chops and put them back into the oven for a further 15 minutes for the top of the stuffing to brown. Serve them quite plain, with no gravy, and with crisp roast potatoes.

Preparation: 20 minutes
Cooking: 55 minutes

Sorrel pie

This is a dish from an old Sussex manuscript. The pie has a mellow flavour with a slight apple-like sharpness. The sorrel leaves are not distinguishable but melt into the rest of the ingredients. Cook it on one of those flat, enamel pie plates so it looks as though it has come from a country kitchen.

shortcrust pastry made with 8 oz (225 g) wholemeal flour
4 oz (125 g) sorrel leaves
2 oz (50 g) sultanas
2 oz (50 g) raisins
2 oz (50 g) Barbados sugar
½ teaspoon (2·5 ml) ground cinnamon
little freshly grated nutmeg
beaten egg or milk for glaze

Heat the oven to Reg 6/400°F/ 200°C. Make the pastry and chill it. Remove the stems from the sorrel and finely chop the leaves. Mix them with the rest of the ingredients. Use about half the pastry to line an 8-inch (20-cm) enamel pie plate. Put the sorrel filling on top, cover it with the remaining pastry and seal the edges. Brush the top of the pie with beaten egg or milk and put it into the oven for 25 minutes so the top is well browned. Serve the pie hot with single cream or cold with double cream.

Preparation: 30 minutes
Cooking: 25 minutes

Pickled nasturtium seeds

Pickled nasturtium seeds can always be used instead of the now vastly expensive capers. They are very similar in flavour but slightly hotter and spicier and are particularly delicious in a black butter sauce.

1 lb (450 g) nasturtium seeds
6 oz (150 g) salt
3 pints (1·725 ml) water
1 pint (575 ml) white wine vinegar
1 shallot, thinly sliced
½ oz (15 g) salt
1 tablespoon (15 ml) white peppercorns
1 teaspoon (5 ml) blade mace
2 chips nutmeg
approximately 4 sprigs tarragon
approximately 2 tablespoons (30 ml) grated horseradish

Pick the nasturtium seeds as soon as the flowers have dropped. If you leave it too long, they will be unpleasantly hard and no pickle will be able to soften them adequately. Wash the seeds and put them into a bowl. Dissolve 2 oz (50 g) salt in 1 pint (575 ml) water and pour the resulting brine over the seeds. Leave them for 24 hours, drain them and put them into fresh brine. Repeat this process twice more, so that the seeds have been left in brine for a total of three days. Drain the seeds again and dry them in a tea cloth. Put the vinegar into a saucepan with the shallot, salt, peppercorns, mace and nutmeg chips. Bring it to the boil, simmer it, covered, for 10 minutes, then allow to cool. Pack the seeds into jars, layering them between tarragon leaves and grated horseradish. Strain the vinegar and pour it over the seeds. Cover the jars and keep them for two weeks before opening.

Brining: 3 days
Preparation: 1 hour

HONEY

Nine bean rows will I have there,
a hive for the honey bee,
And live alone in the bee-loud glade.

(W. B. Yeats)

IT IS TEA-TIME on a summer's afternoon and the table is laid outside. There is new, crusty bread and golden butter and flower-scented honey to be scooped thickly out of the pot. There is the sweet, delicate flavour of honey in the cakes and it enriches the filling of the fruit tart. Foxgloves and delphiniums show their colours in the gentle breeze; and all around is the busy hum of the worker bees as they visit flower after flower, their back legs becoming heavier and heavier with yellow pollen. Not every afternoon is as idyllic as that, but close your eyes when you eat honey and you might just be transported into that sunny garden.

A long time before sugar became the cheap and readily available commodity that it is now, honey was the only sweetener that was used in the country and beekeeping played just as important a part in rural life as growing vegetables and baking bread. Honey was used for sweetening cakes, biscuits and cooked fruit; it was stirred into herbal teas or into hot milk or mulled ale; it was made into mead and used in sweet brines for curing bacon and ham. In the eighteenth century, sugar became more readily obtainable and beekeeping began to lose its importance; but even at the end of the nineteenth century, honey was still of use to the country cook and hives could be found in many cottage gardens.

The first world war was responsible for hastening the decline of many of our country crafts and, as the twentieth century wore on, another war and later the increase in sugar production and the availability of cheap, imported honey caused beekeeping to become just another of those quaint country pastimes that was practised by the few. In recent years, however, the situation has changed again. People want natural foods produced by traditional methods and the increasing number of tourists want edible souvenirs to take home. Locally made honey has never been more sought after. To match these demands, there has been a boom in self-sufficiency and beekeeping is once again becoming an important hobby and, for some, a full-time occupation. Local honey is sold in wholefood shops, delicatessens and country tea shops; jars are stacked up beside country crafts and souvenirs; you

HONEY

(*above*) *Smoking the bees so the comb can be taken from the hive*

(*below*) *A frame full of dripping honeycomb is taken from the hive*

can also buy honey directly from the producer who advertises it for sale outside his house.

The basic craft of the beekeeper has changed very little over the years: he still cares for them and respects them, feeds them when necessary during the winter and catches them when they swarm. The hives, however, have changed quite considerably. At the turn of the century they were dome-shaped and made of plaited rye-straw and these were still in children's picture books at the end of the 1940s. The bees filled up the inside of the hives with their wax comb and no attempt was made by the keeper to separate the workers from the queen and her attendant drones.

Wood is the material used to make beehives now. There is a stout wooden exterior, usually painted white, and inside is a set of eleven rectangular frames made from a lighter wood. The bees build the comb within these. To start them off, a very thin beeswax plan is inserted on which they build the rest, but if it becomes damaged, they can very easily repair the structure themselves. The queen and the drones are separated from the rest of the hive so that no eggs mix with the honey, and the workers gradually fill the smaller cells in the frames above with their sweet, pure syrup.

FOOD FROM THE COUNTRY

The hives are put in a sheltered spot away from contamination by sprays. All through the spring and summer, the bees collect pollen from country flowers. Some are taken up into heather-covered moorlands and others are put by clover fields, but most visit a mixture of flowers, starting with the early fruit blossoms and trees such as lime and chestnut, then moving on through the season with the clovers and wild roses to the rosebay willowherb and blackberry flowers of late summer.

By late July, the wax comb stands above both edges of the frames and the cells are heavy with dripping honey. The beekeeper lifts them out of the hives and takes them back to the extracting shed. Inside, it smells sweet, but very fresh, not at all sticky as you might expect. First of all, the cappings (the parts of the comb that come over the level of the frames) are sliced off the top and bottom. These consist of pollen, wax and honey. If you chew them they are slightly crunchy at first, then the sweet honey oozes over your tongue and finally you are left with a fresh-tasting beeswax 'chewing-gum'. These cappings are sometimes put into jars just as they are or they are heated very gently so the wax and pollen float to the top and the honey can be run off.

On the honey farm where we buy all our supplies of honey, the main frames full of honeycomb, after capping, are put into an electric extractor which works in a similar way to a spin drier. It takes twenty trays, all radiating from the centre, and when it is turned on and the drum starts to spin you can hear the honey hitting the sides and trickling down into a container underneath. It is strained through wire and put into tins, then gently warmed and strained again through muslin. It is stored in large containers until it is finally put into the familiar squat, screw-topped jars. All honey, when it is first extracted, is like a clear syrup which varies in colour from a pale yellow to a deep amber, depending on the type of flowers that the bees visited. If it is left to stand, particularly if the weather is cold, it will granulate naturally, but the granules may be large and you will certainly have to wait for some time. To make a smooth, thick honey with small granules in a short time, the beekeeper stirs together a mixture of half granulated and half clear honey and leaves it for only a few days. Again it varies in colour, from almost white to light brown.

Granulated honey is the one to spread on bread. You can put it on as thickly as you like without there being any fear of its running over the edges. Honey, however, has many more uses than this. In our own kitchen it is used far more often than sugar. Honey cakes are light, but with a slight touch of delicious stickiness and a fragrant flavour. Honey can be used to sweeten fruit for pies and can also be mixed instead of sugar into rich pastries, such as a pâte brisée (see the fruit tart on page 108). Stewed fruit, fruit compotes and purées of fruit for mousses and creams can all be sweetened with honey, and instead of making a sugar syrup for a fresh fruit salad, spoon on a little clear honey and leave it to stand for a while so the natural juices of the fruits

*Now dames oft bustle from
  their wheels
Wi childern scampering at
  their heels
To watch the bees that hang
  and swive
In clumps about each
  thronging hive
And flit and thicken in the
  light
While the old dame enjoys
  the sight
And raps the while their
  warming pans
A spell that superstition
  plans
To coax them in the garden
  bounds
As if they lovd the tinkling
  sounds.*
(John Clare, 'The Shepherd's
  Calendar')

HONEY

Each kind of honey makes a different kind of mead. Honey that is light in colour – clover honey – makes a most beautifully clear, amber mead. Dark honey makes a dark, thick mead. Honey varies greatly in quality depending on the plants of the region, the weather, the apiarist even, and the time of year when the honey is taken from the hive. All this affects the making of mead.
(André Launay, *The Merrydown Book of Country Wines*)

are drawn out. Add honey and spices to whipped cream and you have a honey syllabub, and if you add it to plainer puddings such as a junket, it will provide flavour as well as sweetness.

Honey can also be used in savoury cookery. Use it instead of sugar when glazing vegetables such as carrots or button onions and spoon a little over roasting ham or pork, or over a duck as its browns. You can mix it with mustard powder to spread over pork, or add it to a plainly mixed English mustard for serving with plainly roasted meats. Honey in a marinade will help to tenderise meat and it is particularly good mixed with dry cider as a marinade for streaky pork rashers which can then be grilled. Put into brines or dry salting mixtures for hams or pickled beef, honey helps the salt penetrate the meats and the final results will be tasty and moist.

Herb teas can be sweetened and flavoured with honey; milk and honey is a favourite bedtime drink; and honey and cider vinegar, diluted with hot water, is refreshing and supposedly very healthy. Mulled ales and wine punches taste far better if sweetened only with honey instead of with sugar. Mead has been made with honey for centuries. True mead is made only with honey, but there have been some fine country recipes produced using spices, raisins and other ingredients. There are many meads on sale today that are made with honey and grape concentrate, but wc have found several made only with honey. They are generally lighter in colour than the grape ones, so thick that they cling to the sides of your glass and, although they have a distinct honey flavour, are often pleasantly dry. They improve with age and some are five or more years old when they are sold. We had a mountain of surplus apples one year and decided to make an apple mead. It turned out a rich amber colour. At the time of writing it is two years old and just beginning to be deliciously mellow, dry and roundly flavoured. In another two years, it will be perfect.

Recipes for Honey

Honeyed pork and apples

Honey and apples cooked with pork make it meltingly tender.

1 piece lean end of belly of pork, weighing about 2½ lbs (1 kg)
1 tablespoon (15 ml) mustard powder
3 tablespoons (45 ml) cider vinegar
1 tablespoon (15 ml) honey
1 large Bramley apple
1 large onion, thinly sliced
1 teaspoon (5 ml) cloves

Heat the oven to Reg 3/325°F/170°C. Bone the pork and cut off the rind. Put the mustard powder into a small bowl and mix in 1 tablespoon (15 ml) vinegar and the honey. Spread a little of the mixture over the underside of the pork. Roll up the pork and tie it with fine cotton string. Quarter, core and chop the apple, without peeling it. Put it into the bottom of a casserole with the onion, cloves and remaining cider vinegar. Put the pork on top and spread it with the rest of the honey and mustard. Cover the casserole and put it into the oven for 2 hours. Remove the pork and keep it warm. Rub the apples and all the juices in the casserole through a sieve and skim them if necessary. Put the sauce into a small pan and reheat gently. Carve the pork, arrange it on a serving dish and spoon the apple sauce down the centre.

Preparation: 40 minutes
Cooking: 2 hours

Honeyed spiced beef

Honey instead of sugar in a salting mixture makes the juiciest, tastiest salt beef.

8 lbs (3·6 kg) brisket, weighed on the bone
1 tablespoon (15 ml) black peppercorns
1 teaspoon (5 ml) cloves
3 tablespoons (45 ml) coarse sea salt
2 bayleaves
3 tablespoons (45 ml) honey
FOR BOILING:
1 small onion, cut in half but not peeled
1 large carrot, cut in half lengthways
1 stick celery, broken, and few celery leaves
water to cover

Remove the bone and any excess fat from the brisket. Crush the peppercorns and cloves together and mix them in a small bowl with the salt. Crumble the bay-leaves into the bowl and stir in the honey. Lay the meat out flat on a large pyrex or earthenware dish and rub it all over with the honey mixture. Cover it with grease-proof paper and leave it for three days in a cool place, turning it and rubbing it with the brine every day. Just before you are ready to cook it, wash it under cold water and pat it dry with kitchen paper. Roll it up and tie it with fine cotton string. Put the meat into a large saucepan or flameproof casserole with the boiling in-gredients. Cover them with water and bring them to the boil. Cover and simmer for 2 hours. Lift out the meat and let it get quite cold before carving. It is best left over-night. Serve it with salads, with hot vegetables, with brown bread and butter, or in sandwiches.

Preparation: 40 minutes
Salting: 3 days
Cooking: 2 hours
Cooling: 12 hours

Honeyed button onions with rosemary

Use honey instead of sugar for glazing vegetables. These button onions with rosemary are particularly good with lamb.

12 oz (350 g) button onions
1 oz (25 g) butter
¼ pint (150 ml) stock
1 teaspoon (5 ml) honey
2 teaspoons (10 ml) chopped rosemary
15 black peppercorns, crushed

Peel the onions and leave them whole. Melt the butter in a heavy frying-pan on a low heat. Put in the onions and cook them until they look transparent and are beginning to brown (about 15 minutes). Raise the heat to moderate, pour in the stock and bring it to the boil. Stir in the honey, rosemary and crushed peppercorns. Cover the pan and keep it on a moderate heat for 10 minutes.

Preparation: 30 minutes
Cooking: 10 minutes

Honey junket

Just a tablespoon of honey will add sweetness and flavour to an old-fashioned creamy junket.

1 pint (575 ml) full cream milk (preferably Gold Top)
1 teaspoon (5 ml) junket rennet
1 tablespoon (15 ml) honey
a little freshly grated nutmeg

Warm the milk to blood heat. Stir in the rennet and honey. When they have dissolved, pour the milk into a flat dish. Put the junket in a warm place to set, grating some nutmeg over the top after about 30 minutes. The junket should stand for about 2 hours before it is ready.

Preparation: 10 minutes
Setting: 2 hours

Honey cream

Honey, milk, eggs and cream make a soft and delicate flavoured dessert which, surprisingly enough, isn't at all rich.

$\frac{1}{2}$ **pint (275 ml) milk**
$\frac{1}{2}$ **oz (15 g) gelatine**
2 tablespoons (30 ml) honey
2 eggs, separated
$\frac{1}{4}$ **pint (150 ml) double cream**
2 tablespoons (30 ml) brandy

Soak the gelatine in 4 tablespoons (60 ml) of the milk. Put the rest of the milk into a saucepan. Set it on a low heat, add the honey and stir until it has dissolved. Stir in the gelatine and let it melt. Stir in the egg yolks and keep stirring until the mixture thickens, never letting it come to the boil. Take the pan off the heat. Pour the mixture into a large bowl and put it in a cool place until it is on the point of setting (about 30 minutes). Whip the cream with the brandy and stiffly whip the egg whites. Fold first the cream and then the egg whites into the milk and honey mixture. Pour the cream into a pretty serving bowl and put it in a cool place to set (about 1 hour). For a special occasion, decorate the top with crystallised violets and candied angelica.

Preparation: 30 minutes
Chilling: 1 hour 30 minutes

Strawberry and honey cheese

Cream cheese beaten with wine and honey makes a light but creamy coating for fresh strawberries.

6 oz (175 g) cream cheese
3 tablespoons (45 ml) dry white wine
2 tablespoons (30 ml) honey
1 lb (450 g) strawberries

Put the cheese into a bowl. Gradually beat first the wine and then the honey into the cheese. Quarter the strawberries and stir them into the cheese. Chill the mixture for 30 minutes and serve it in chilled glasses with their rims dipped in caster sugar.

Preparation: 30 minutes
Chilling: 30 minutes

Cherry and honey pudding

This light steamed pudding has a delicious topping of cherries and honey which drips down the sides as it is turned out.

1 lb (450 g) white cherries
6 oz (175 g) butter
6 tablespoons (90 ml) honey
2 eggs, beaten
8 oz (225 g) wholemeal flour
4 tablespoons (60 ml) milk
a little butter for greasing a 2-pint (1·150-l) pudding basin

Stone and slice the cherries. Cream the butter in a mixing bowl and gradually beat in 4 tablespoons (60 ml) of the honey. Add alternately a little beaten egg and a little flour to the mixture until they are both well mixed in. Beat in the milk and fold in half the cherries. Lightly butter the pudding basin and put the remaining cherries in the bottom. Spoon in the rest of the honey. Add all the pudding mixture to the basin and smooth the top. Cover the top of the pudding with a layer of buttered greaseproof paper and a layer of foil

and tie them down. Bring a large saucepan of water to the boil and lower in the pudding. Cover it and steam it for 2 hours 30 minutes, not letting it come off the boil and topping the water up if necessary. Turn the pudding out onto a flat plate and serve it plain or with cream.

Preparation: 45 minutes
Cooking: 2 hours 30 minutes

Dark ginger and honey cake

Honey cakes are always very moist and tasty and this one is made dark and extra rich by the molasses.

4 oz (125 g) butter
4 oz (125 g) honey
10 oz (275 g) molasses
2 eggs, beaten
8 oz (225 g) wholemeal flour
2 teaspoons (10 ml) ground ginger
1 teaspoon (5 ml) ground cinnamon
$\frac{1}{2}$ **teaspoon (2·5 ml) fine sea salt**
$\frac{1}{2}$ **teaspoon (2·5 ml) bicarbonate of soda**
2 tablespoons (30 ml) black coffee
2 oz (50 g) sultanas
2 oz (50 g) raisins
butter for greasing a 7-inch (18-cm) cake tin

Heat the oven to Reg 3/325°F/170°C. Beat the butter until it is fluffy. Beat in the honey and then the molasses. Beat in the eggs, a little at a time. Mix the flour, ginger, cinnamon, salt and bicarbonate of soda together and fold them into the butter mixture with a wooden spoon. Fold in the coffee and the fruit. Put the mixture into the prepared tin and bake it for 1 hour. Turn down the heat to Reg 2/300°F/150°C and cook the cake for a further hour.

Turn the cake onto a wire rack and let it cool completely.

Preparation: 30 minutes
Cooking: 2 hours

Apple, honey and clotted cream pie

This pie is best served hot. It needs no accompaniment as it has its own thick, creamy sauce oozing out from beneath the pastry.

shortcrust pastry made with 6 oz (175 g) wholemeal flour
beaten egg or milk to glaze
FILLING:
1 lb (450 g) Bramley apples
2 tablespoons (30 ml) honey
1 teaspoon (5 ml) ground cinnamon
freshly grated nutmeg
2 oz (50 g) Cornish clotted cream

Heat the oven to Reg 6/400°F/ 200°C. Make the pastry and set it aside to chill. Peel, core and thinly slice the apples. Put them into a bowl and mix in the honey and spices. Roll out two thirds of the pastry and line an 8-inch (20-cm) diameter pie plate. Put in all the apple filling and cover the surface with small blobs of cream. Cover the apples with the remaining pastry. Seal the edges and brush the top with beaten egg or milk. Bake the pie for 30 minutes.

Preparation: 30 minutes
Cooking: 30 minutes

Honey and almond slices

These nut-topped slices are light and golden. Serve them for tea or after dinner.

4 oz (125 g) butter, plus extra for greasing
4 oz (125 g) honey
4 oz (125 g) wholemeal flour
1 teaspoon (5 ml) baking powder
1 tablespoon (15 ml) poppy seeds
2 eggs, beaten
TOPPING:
4 oz (125 g) almonds, blanched and split
3 tablespoons (45 ml) clear honey or melted thick honey

Heat the oven to Reg 4/350°F/ 180°C. Cream the butter in a bowl and gradually beat in the honey. Mix together the flour, baking powder and poppy seeds. Beat the egg and flour into the butter mixture alternately. Butter a shallow baking tin measuring 8 inches by 10 inches (20 cm by 25 cm). Spread the honey for the topping evenly in the base and put in the almonds in a single layer. Put the cake mixture on top and smooth it over. Bake the cake for 20 minutes or until it is set and golden. Let it cool for about 10 minutes in the tin and then cut it into slices. Carefully lift them out with a fish slice or palette knife and turn them over, making sure that all the almonds are now sticking to the top. Leave them to cool before serving.

Preparation: 30 minutes
Cooking: 20 minutes

Honey bread

This moist, slightly sweet bread has a delicate honey flavour.

1 oz (25 g) fresh or ½ oz (15 g) dried yeast
3 tablespoons (45 ml) plus 1 teaspoon (5 ml) clear honey
7 fl oz (200 ml) warm water
1 lb (450 g) wholemeal flour
2 teaspoons (10 ml) sea salt
2 oz (50 g) butter
3 oz (75 g) raisins
3 oz (75 g) sultanas
2 eggs beaten

If you are using fresh yeast, crumble it into a bowl and mix in the honey and water. If dried, dissolve the honey in the water and sprinkle the yeast on top. Leave the yeast in a warm place to froth. Put the flour and salt into a bowl and rub in the butter. Toss in the dried fruits with your fingers. Make a well in the centre and pour in the yeast mixture and the eggs. Mix everything to a moist dough, turn it onto a floured board and knead it. Return it to the bowl, make a cross cut in the top, cover it with a clean tea cloth and put it in a warm place for 1 hour to rise.

Heat the oven to Reg 6/400°F/ 200°C. Knead the dough again and lightly press it into a greased 2-lb (900-g) loaf tin. Put it on top of the stove, cover it with the cloth again and leave it for 20 minutes or until it has risen about ½ inch (1 cm) above the top of the tin. Bake the loaf for 50 minutes and turn it onto a wire rack to cool.

Preparation: 1 hour 50 minutes
Cooking: 50 minutes

Honey punch

Honey and fresh fruits turn red wine into a simple but heady and warming fruit punch.

1 large orange
12 cloves
2 crisp eating apples
1 lemon
3 bottles dry red wine (not too cheap)
2 pieces cinnamon stick about 3 inches (7 cm) long
12 oz (350 g) honey

Stick the orange evenly with the cloves and bake it in a moderate oven for 20 minutes. Cut it into twelve pieces, each with a clove. Core and thinly slice the apples. Thinly slice the lemon. Put the wine into a large saucepan with the fruits and cinnamon. Add the honey and stir on a low heat until the honey has dissolved. Bring the punch to just below boiling point and keep it there for 5 minutes for all the flavours to infuse. Pour the punch into a special punchbowl or large mixing bowl, and serve it hot, in mugs.

Preparation: 35 minutes

Honey beer

Adding honey instead of sugar or malt extract to beer gives it an underlying fresh flavour.

1 gallon (4·6 l) water
1 oz (25 g) hops
thinly pared rind and juice 1 lemon
1 lb (450 g) clear honey
1 lb (450 g) plus 8 teaspoons (40 ml) Barbados sugar
1 teaspoon (5 ml) dried brewer's yeast

Put the water into a large pan with the hops, thinly pared lemon rind, honey and sugar. Bring it to the boil and keep it on a good boil for 20 minutes. Strain the liquid into a large container and add the lemon juice. Cool the liquid to luke-warm and stir in the yeast. Leave the brew in a warm place until it has stopped working, skimming off any yeast that comes dangerously near the top. When it stops working (in about eight days) strain and bottle it, putting 1 teaspoon (5 ml) Barbados sugar into each bottle.

Apple mead

One year the apple tree in the garden produced pounds and pounds more fruit than we could eat or even give away. We made apple jelly and ordinary apple jam and still there were some left, so we hit on the idea of this apple mead.

It is a light golden wine with the distinct flavour of honey and needs to be kept for at least two years before opening. Judging by other meads that we have bought, it will probably be at its best after another two years, but we haven't had long enough yet to find out.

14 lbs (6 kg) apples
7 lbs honey
2 cups strong, cold, black tea
yeast
yeast nutrient
pectolase

Crush the apples well and put them into a large container with the honey. Pour on 3 gallons (13·8 l) boiling water, stir and add the tea. Let the mixture cool to lukewarm and add yeast, yeast nutrient and pectolase. Cover the mixture and leave it for six days, stirring every day. Strain it into gallon (4·6 l) jars and fit a fermentation lock. Rack it as it clears and bottle it.

CEREALS

See! The wide cornfields are shining like gold;
Heavy the ears with the grain that they hold.
(Lucy Diamond)

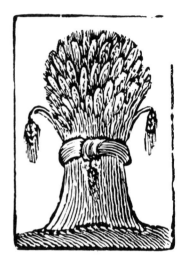

IT IS BAKING DAY, and the warm, yeasty smell of new bread fills the house. Standing on trays to cool are puffy scones, slabs of currant cake to take out into the fields, rich sponges full of butter and cream, and tiny, light buns. There are sweet pies full of hedgerow and garden fruits, meat pies with a light shortcrust that crumbles into the rich, brown gravy, and solid standing pies waiting to be filled with savoury jelly. There are crusty cottage loaves, round cobs topped with cracked wheat, and small, soft, round baps that must be wrapped in a thick cloth to cool. Beside them are crisp biscuits, light and sweet, or plain for eating with cheese; and oatcakes and bannocks are cooking gently on the griddle. The flour to make them all came from the miller, who bought grains from the farmer, who in autumn reaped the fields that were sown in winter or spring. It is a pattern that has been the same for centuries and that is unlikely to change.

In Britain most of our cereals are grown in the south, the middle and the east of the country, where the weather is mild and the soil flat and fertile. The main areas are East Anglia, Essex, Bedfordshire, Cambridgeshire and Northamptonshire and, further north, Lincolnshire and Humberside. Oats are grown mainly in Scotland; and a certain amount of cereals are grown in varying degrees throughout the country. The most widely grown of all cereals is barley, but very little is actually milled for flour. Some is sold as pearl or pot barley, some is malted for brewing beer and whisky, but most is used to make feed for cattle and other farm animals. Wheat is the next most commonly grown and it is the most popular cereal for the miller, as well as providing animal feed. Oats are milled into oatmeal and rolled into oatflakes and some are fed to horses. We grow very little rye. Some is milled into flour, some is used for feed and the straw is used for thatching.

Cereals can be either winter or spring sown. When they first appear above the earth they look almost indistinguishable from grass. Winter-sown barley grows in thick tufts and wheat looks thin and more sparse. By the beginning of May, they are beginning to grow tall and all the fields look green. At the end of June the landscape begins to turn golden and the ears of corn get larger. The long-whiskered barley is yellow

CEREALS

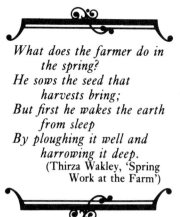

*What does the farmer do in
the spring?
He sows the seed that
harvests bring;
But first he wakes the earth
from sleep
By ploughing it well and
harrowing it deep.*
(Thirza Wakley, 'Spring
Work at the Farm')

at first, and the ears are streaked with thin, maroon lines, but as it ripens, these disappear and the ear and the straw become very pale. Oats are delicate and golden with the small grains hanging separately in golden coats. They are very susceptible to the wind and the rain, and in bad weather half your crop can be lost overnight. Wheat turns a pale yellow-brown and when it is fully ripe the compact ears turn downwards and rattle very quietly in the wind. Rye is soft brown, with short whiskers.

Harvest is the farmer's busiest time and when you drive through our part of the world in August, you would think that the whole world is harvesting. Work begins in the morning as soon as the dew has dried and it is not uncommon to come home late at night and find the combine and tractors with full headlights on working in the dark. Until the last war, combine harvesters were virtually unknown in British fields. The corn was cut by hand, either with a binding knife or with a mechanical cutter, and then stacked up in stooks in the field. It was left for a few days to dry and then pitched onto a cart and taken back to the farmyard. Here it was made into stacks with thatched tops and threshed at regular intervals throughout the winter. Combine harvesters were first introduced on the 'War Ag' (Ministry of War Agriculture) farms but were looked on by most other farmers as an expensive and rather unnecessary gimmick. Soon, however, labour became expensive and time more important, and now one combine can do in a day what twenty men once did in five.

The older harvesters are smaller with no driving cab, but the new ones can have a reel in front up to twelve feet across and are very high with a closed-in cab that has foot pedals and various levers and dials. The day we went to photograph the harvest, it was hot and dry and the huge harvester was just starting to open up the field. It set off down one side in a cloud of dust while we waited by the grain trailer with the tractor driver. 'They say all the time there's dust, it goes well,' he said; so it must have been going very well! The combine turned and reversed round the tight corners of the field and came back towards us. Sticking forward on one side was a sharp metal pointer which isolated the rows of corn that the combine would take in. The big, spindly reel in front turned inwards making the corn bend and dance towards the cutters. The ears were drawn into the machine by the auger (like a giant screw) and, once they were inside and out of sight, the grain was threshed from them and sieved and passed into a tank. The straw was left in a long heap parallel with the edge of the field and the short dry stubble that remained made hollow, cracking sounds as we walked on it. When the grain tank was full, the tractor pulled the grain trailer alongside the combine and for a short distance they went slowly along together. Then the driver of the combine pulled a lever in the cab and the threshed wheat grains poured out of a funnel and into the trailer in a yellow-brown heap. The combine continued round the field and the tractor took its load back to the farm.

It has been the practice in recent years to burn the stubble. This can be a smoky nuisance or it can be quite spectacular. One night we came across a field of burning stubble just as it was getting dark. The air was still and warm and the fires were all the same size and burning softly with gentle, barely audible crackles. As there was hardly any wind, the farmer had thought it safe to leave the field alone and there was a tremendous atmosphere of peace. The fires were in a ring and so at one point, when all the smoke seemed to be curling into the centre, they looked like bright performers in a timeless ritual dance who, the harvest being over and successful, were giving thanks for its completion.

On the farm the grain is stored in huge silos until it is sold to the miller. The milling industry is largely controlled by big companies but it is good to see that small, family firms are flourishing and old water-mills are being lovingly restored to working order. It is the smaller miller who produces most of the wholemeal flour that is now in increasing demand. The best flavoured, nutrition-packed flour is milled slowly, either on a water-powered roller system or stoneground between two millstones. Some of the independent millers have now become household names (Allinsons and Prewetts, for example, who produce stoneground flour, and Jordans, who use a roller mill powered by the River Ivel), but many of the smaller ones sell only in their own area. Some have opened their mills to the public and added museums

SCOTCH BARLEY BROTH is considered best when made with a sheep's head, the wool from which has been singed off with a red-hot iron.... When singed the head should be soaked in water all night. In the morning it is scraped and washed, and then it is split open, and the brains taken out.... When properly prepared it is put into a kettle with some turnips and carrots, cut small, some onions and some salt; and a gallon of water should be added, in which a teacupful of Scotch or pearl barley has been boiled slowly for half an hour. The whole should then be boiled very gently for two or three hours, or

longer, in a close kettle. When served the soup should not be strained, but only the head taken out and served on a separate dish, and the broth should be sent to the table with the barley and vegetables in it.... If the taste of the **head be disliked, the soup may be made by adding to the barley the vegetables, and three pounds of the lean end of a neck of mutton, instead of the head.**

(Mrs Loudon,
The Lady's Country Companion)

... There is no cleaner work for man than this business of grain gathering. It seems to me it is the one business left in this imperfect world that does the least harm to anyone, from the sowing to the reaping. After this, of course, the grain, the flour, the bread, is turned into £.s.d., and one cannot vouch for its cleanliness any more! But up to its storing, at least, it is as sweet as the pure country air that grows it.
(Elvira, *Kentish Yesterdays*)

of old milling equipment and exhibitions of paintings or photographs of mills in years gone by. So you can have a guided tour, a walk in the usually picturesque gardens, and afterwards go to the tearooms where you can sample cakes and pastries made from the home-produced flour. You can buy a bag of flour and very often a recipe leaflet from the mill, so you go away well equipped and full of enthusiasm to try some home baking.

Although the larger proportion of our bread in this country is plant baked, there are still about five thousand independent bakers who produce superb quality bread using yeast and traditional methods. Many small, country bakers still have their original brick ovens, although most have gone over from coal to oil-fired heat. They start very early in the morning and by six o'clock the first batch of loaves is ready to be lifted out of the oven with a long-handled peel. There are round loaves on trays, loaves in sandwich tins with lids to make them square, and oval-topped loaves in open tins. One swift knock on the base and they fall onto the table, golden brown all over, to contrast with the unbaked ones that have been set aside to prove. The master baker works with admirable skill. When he makes a cottage loaf he kneads the large piece with his right hand and the small piece with his left, both at the same time, quickly fits them together and slashes a pattern on the top. Tiny rolls are kneaded one in each hand in a swift, circular motion and others are shaped into tins and rapidly glazed and patterned. By eight o'clock the second batch is in the oven, the first customers are knocking on the door for their orders and the delivery van is loading up to take the loaves and rolls to local shops and pubs.

We seem to get through quantities of flour in our household. We buy English wheat direct from the farmer and mill it ourselves on an electric, stone-grinding mill. We always use it wholemeal, with perfect results. Barley, rye and oat groats we buy in smaller quantities from a wholefood shop and mill them as we need them.

Baking is always immensely satisfying. Even if I am only making a plain household loaf with nothing but flour, yeast, salt and water, I always like to glaze the top with beaten egg and slash a pattern on it with a sharp knife, and perhaps scatter it with cracked wheat or poppy or sesame seeds. For a very nutty-textured loaf, probably the one we like the best of all, I mix in 6 oz (175 g) cracked wheat with 3 lbs (1·35 kg) wholemeal flour, with a little extra water to make up for it, and always scatter more cracked wheat on the top. Different types of flour make different textured loaves. Rye flour mixed with half wheat will make a slightly heavier loaf with a rich, nutty, flavour. Barley in the same proportions produces a crumbly-textured loaf, light in colour with a slightly sweet flavour. Oatmeal should be used in smaller proportions, one quarter to three quarters wheat, and the loaf will be very soft. Add herbs, spices, cheese, nuts, chopped cooked bacon or dried fruits to breads; mix them partly with eggs or milk; or rub in a little butter or lard. You can have an infinite number of textures and flavours.

Our cakes, pastry and biscuits are always the same familiar wholemeal brown. We think they taste better that way and they are certainly more nutritious. Oatmeal added to cakes makes them soft and crumbly and it is particularly good in ginger or honey cakes. Flat, crisp, biscuit-type oatcakes are superb with cheese or spread with butter and honey; and if you haven't a griddle to make them on, just use a large, heavy frying-pan.

Dumplings are made by mixing two thirds flour and one third suet; always try to use freshly grated beef suet. Dumplings can be added to soups and stews to fill them out. You can also use the same mixture to enclose completely a joint of salt beef. Then wrap it in a pudding cloth and boil it so all the juices are enclosed in the crust. This, my father informs us, was called a 'toad' in his grandmother's house, and any small pieces of dough that were left over were wrapped round a teaspoonful of sugar or syrup and boiled in the same pot. They were called 'swimmers' and were served for pudding with more syrup. You can also cook whole grains. Oat groats and pot barley (the whole barley grain) can be made into substantial savoury casseroles and wheat grains form the base of that most traditional of celebratory dishes – frumenty.

The fields of bearded barley,
The graceful hanging oats,
And ears of wheat packed
closely,
The cheerful reaper notes.

He sees the cornfields waving,
Yellow and ripe and strong,
And so, his heart rejoicing,
He sings his harvest song.
(K. Fisher, 'Story of the Corn')

CEREALS

(*top*) *Holme Mills, Biggleswade – and the River Ivel that provides the power*

(*above*) *A field of golden oats waiting for the combine*

(*right*) *Stubble burning at night*

FOOD FROM THE COUNTRY

The harvester's lunch – Fourses cake, Saffron bread and buns, Sausage scones, Wheat and oatmeal biscuits

Recipes for Cereals

Frumenty

This is our own recipe for frumenty, the old English dish of slowly simmered wheat enriched with cream and fruits and laced with brandy. It was served on high days and holidays and we always have it for breakfast on Christmas morning. This amount will serve eight to ten people. You can halve all the ingredients if it is too much, or eat it cold on Boxing Day (if you can face it, with all the other rich leftovers there are around). It is, in fact, almost as good cold as it is hot.

1 lb (450 g) whole wheat
    grains
water to cover
1 pint (575 ml) milk
4 oz (125 g) sultanas
4 oz (125 g) raisins
4 tablespoons (60 ml) honey
$\frac{1}{4}$ nutmeg, grated
1 teaspoon (5 ml) ground
    cinnamon
4 tablespoons (60 ml) brandy
4 tablespoons (60 ml) double
    cream

Heat the oven to Reg $\frac{1}{4}$/225°F/110°C. Put the wheat into a large casserole and fill it to the brim with water. Cover it and put it into the oven for 12 hours. Take it out and let it stand until it is completely cool. Drain it in a colander in several batches. The grains will be soft, round and puffy.

Put the wheat into a saucepan with the milk, sultanas, raisins, honey, nutmeg and cinnamon. Set it on a low heat, bring to the boil and simmer, stirring frequently, until nearly all the liquid is absorbed. It will take 30–45 minutes. (If you want to prepare frumenty in advance on Christmas Eve, you can do so up to this stage, which will give you more time for present unwrapping and all the excitement of Christmas morning.) Take the pan from the heat and stir in the cream and brandy; or, if you have prepared it in advance, reheat it gently first. Serve immediately.

Preliminary cooking: 12
    hours
Preparation: 1 hour

Wheat and oatmeal biscuits

These little oatmeal biscuits are crisp and light and best of all eaten with cheese.

4 oz (125 g) wholemeal flour
4 oz (125 g) fine oatmeal
1 teaspoon (5 ml) salt
$\frac{1}{2}$ teaspoon (2·5 ml) baking
    powder
2 oz (50 g) lard
4 fl oz (120 ml) sour milk, or
    yoghurt, or buttermilk

Heat the oven to Reg 4/350°F/180°C. Put the flour and oatmeal into a bowl with the salt and baking powder. Rub in the lard. Make a well in the centre and pour in the sour milk. Mix everything to a dough. Turn it onto a floured board and roll it out to about $\frac{1}{8}$ inch (3 mm) thick. Stamp it into rounds or other shapes with a biscuit cutter. Lay them on a floured baking sheet and prick them all over with a fork. Bake the biscuits for 25 minutes so they are crisp but not coloured. Lift them onto a wire rack to cool.

Preparation: 20 minutes
Cooking: 25 minutes

Rich simnel cake

This is the traditional Mothering Sunday simnel. It is dark, rich and moist, with a layer of sticky almonds in the middle.

8 oz (225 g) almonds
2 tablespoons (30 ml) honey
1 tablespoon (15 ml)
    orangeflower water
12 oz (350 g) butter
1 lb (450 g) molasses sugar
1 lb (450 g) wholemeal flour
1 nutmeg, grated
8 oz (225 g) raisins
4 oz (125 g) currants
4 oz (125 g) sultanas
5 eggs, beaten
$\frac{1}{4}$ pint (150 ml) double cream
$\frac{1}{4}$ pint (150 ml) brandy
butter for greasing an 8-inch
    (20-cm) diameter cake tin

Blanch the almonds and grind them in a blender. Put them into a bowl and mix them with the orangeflower water and honey. Heat the oven to Reg 3/325°F/170°C. Beat the butter to a cream and beat in the sugar. Toss the flour with the nutmeg and fold one quarter of it into the fruit. Beat the rest of the flour into the butter, alternately with the eggs, cream and brandy. Fold in the fruit. Put half the mixture into the prepared cake tin and on top put half the almond paste in an even layer, coming to within $\frac{3}{4}$ inch (2 cm) of the edges. Put in the remaining cake mixture, smooth the top and very lightly brush it with water (fingers are better than a pastry brush). Put the cake into the oven for 1 hour 30 minutes. Meanwhile, form the remaining almond paste into twelve small balls. Take the cake from the oven and gently press the balls around the edge, flattening them so they touch. Turn the heat down to Reg 2/300°F/160°C and put the cake back into the oven for 30 minutes. Cool the cake in the tin for 30 minutes and carefully turn it onto a cake rack.

Preparation: 45 minutes
Cooking: 2 hours

Oatmeal gingerbread

This is a real ginger bread, as opposed to the cake varieties. The oatmeal gives it a soft, light, close texture and the molasses makes it semi-sweet. It is delicious buttered for tea or breakfast.

1 oz (25 g) fresh yeast or $\frac{1}{2}$ oz (15 g) dried
4 tablespoons (60 ml) molasses
$\frac{1}{4}$ pint (150 ml) warm water
12 oz (350 g) wholemeal flour
4 oz (125 g) fine oatmeal
2 teaspoons (10 ml) sea salt
1 teaspoon (5 ml) ground ginger
4 crushed allspice berries
$1\frac{1}{2}$ oz (40 g) butter
3 oz (75 g) sultanas
3 oz (75 g) raisins
$\frac{1}{4}$ pint (150 ml) warm milk

If you are using fresh yeast, cream it with 1 teaspoon (5 ml) of the molasses and the water; if dried, dissolve the molasses in the water and sprinkle the yeast on top. Leave the yeast in a warm place to froth. Put the flour and oatmeal into a bowl with the salt, ginger and all-spice, and rub in the butter. Toss in the sultanas and raisins. Make a well in the centre and pour in the yeast mixture and the milk and add the remaining molasses. Mix everything to a dough. Turn it onto a floured

board and knead it well. Return the dough to the bowl, cover it with a cloth and leave it in a warm place for 1 hour to double in size.

Heat the oven to Reg 6/400°F/200°C. Knead the dough again and press it lightly into a 2-lb (900-g) loaf tin. Put it on top of the stove, cover it with the cloth again and leave it for 20 minutes or until it has risen about $\frac{1}{2}$ inch (1 cm) above the top of the tin. Bake the loaf for 50 minutes and turn it onto a wire rack to cool.

Preparation: 1 hour 40 minutes
Cooking: 50 minutes

Fourses cake

This cake was made in Suffolk for the harvest workers' four o'clock break. It is a good idea to make extra dough when you are making a batch of bread rather than making it specially for this cake. It is a moist, light, semi-sweet cake that doesn't need butter. It is excellent with cheese.

plain bread dough made with 1 lb (450 g) flour
4 oz (125 g) lard, softened
2 teaspoons (10 ml) ground mixed spice
3 oz (75 g) currants
2 oz (50 g) Barbados sugar
extra lard for greasing a 7-inch (18-cm) square cake tin

Let the dough rise in the bowl once. Heat the oven to Reg 6/400°F/200°C. Knead the dough and roll it out to about $\frac{1}{4}$ inch (6 mm) thick. Spread it lightly with all the lard and sprinkle it with 1 teaspoon (5 ml) of the spice. Roll it up fairly tightly. Knead the dough well so the lard becomes incorporated into it and it becomes fairly moist but not sticky. Roll it out again and cover it with the currants, sugar and the

remaining spice. Knead the dough again so these latest in-gredients become well mixed in. Lightly knock it down into the greased tin and put it on top of the stove, covered with a cloth, to prove for 20 minutes. Bake the cake for 40 minutes and turn it onto a wire rack to cool.

Preparation: 35 minutes (excluding making bread dough)
Cooking: 40 minutes

Granary malt loaf

This is a fairly light loaf tasting beautifully of malt but with a bread-like texture, not moist and sticky like bought malt loaves. It is lovely with honey or just plainly buttered.

$\frac{3}{4}$ oz (20 g) fresh yeast or 2 teaspoons (10 ml) dried
3 tablespoons (45 ml) malt extract
6 tablespoons (90 ml) warm water
12 oz (350 g) granary bread meal
1 teaspoon (5 ml) sea salt
$1\frac{1}{2}$ oz (40 g) sultanas
$1\frac{1}{2}$ oz (40 g) raisins
1 oz (25 g) butter
1 egg, beaten
butter for greasing a 1-lb (450-g) loaf tin

If you are using fresh yeast, cream it with 1 teaspoon (5 ml) of the malt extract and the water; if dried, dissolve the malt extract in the water and scatter the yeast on top. Put the yeast in a warm place to froth. Put the bread meal into a bowl with the salt and fruit. Put the remaining malt extract into a saucepan with the butter and melt them together on a low heat. Cool them a little. Make a well in the centre of the flour. Pour in the yeast mixture, butter and malt, and the egg. Mix everything to a dough. Turn it onto a floured board and knead it well. Return it to the bowl, make a crosscut in the top and cover it with a clean tea cloth. Put it in a warm place for 1 hour to double in size.

Heat the oven to Reg 6/400°F/200°C. Knead the dough again and press it lightly into the prepared tin. Cover it with a cloth again and put it on top of the stove for 20 minutes or until it has risen about $\frac{1}{2}$ inch (1 cm) above the top of the tin. Bake the loaf for 40 minutes and turn it onto a wire rack to cool.

Preparation: 1 hour 50 minutes
Cooking: 40 minutes

Saffron bread and buns

Although sugar is put into saffron cakes today, this was not always the case. This is the more traditional way, and you will find the currants and candied peel make them quite sweet enough. They are delicious, yellow buns that can be eaten either plain or buttered.

1 oz (25 g) fresh yeast or $\frac{1}{2}$ oz (15 g) dried
1 teaspoon (5 ml) Barbados sugar
$\frac{1}{4}$ pint (150 ml) warm water
1 lb (450 g) 81% or 85% wheatmeal flour
pinch sea salt
freshly grated nutmeg
3 oz (75 g) butter
2 oz (50 g) lard
8 oz (225 g) currants
1 oz (25 g) candied peel, finely chopped
$\frac{1}{4}$ pint (150 ml) warm milk
pinch saffron infused in 2 tablespoons boiling water

If you are using fresh yeast, cream it in a bowl with the sugar and water; if dried, dis-

solve the sugar in the water and sprinkle the yeast on the top. Leave the yeast in a warm place to froth. Put the flour and salt into a bowl and grate in about $\frac{1}{4}$ of a nutmeg. Rub in the butter and lard and toss in the currants and peel. Make a well in the centre and pour in the yeast mixture, milk and infused saffron together with its water. Knead the mixture with your hand in the bowl, taking it from the sides to the middle. Cover it with a cloth and leave it in a warm place for 1 hour to double in size.

Heat the oven to Reg 4/350°F/180°C. Knead the dough with your hands again. Either divide it into two and put it into two buttered, 1-lb (450-g) loaf tins, or make it into sixteen small buns and put them on a floured baking sheet, (or make one loaf and eight buns). Cover them with a cloth and leave them on top of the stove to prove for 10 minutes. Bake the loaf for 1 hour and the buns for 30 minutes. Cool them on a wire rack.

Preparation: 1 hour 50 minutes
Cooking: 30 minutes or 1 hour

Sausage scones

A good quality sausage-meat rolled up in a scone mixture can be made into attractive little rounds which cook very cleanly and aren't over-fatty as pastry sausage rolls often can be. Instead, they are very moist and herby.

8 oz (225 g) wholemeal flour
$\frac{1}{2}$ teaspoon (2·5 ml) sea salt
$\frac{1}{2}$ teaspoon (2·5 ml) bicarbonate of soda
2 teaspoons (10 ml) mustard powder
6 chopped sage leaves
1 tablespoon (15 ml) chopped savory

1 oz (25 g) lard
$\frac{1}{4}$ pint (150 ml) natural yoghurt, or buttermilk, or sour milk
8 oz (225 g) sausage-meat

Heat the oven to Reg 6/400°F/200°C. Put the flour into a mixing bowl with the salt, soda, mustard powder and herbs. Rub in the lard and mix everything to a dough with the yoghurt, buttermilk or sour milk. Knead it lightly and roll it out into an oblong about $\frac{1}{4}$ inch (6 mm) thick. Spread the sausage-meat evenly over the surface. Roll the dough up like a Swiss roll and cut it into rounds $\frac{3}{4}$ inch (2 cm) thick. You should get twelve to fourteen rounds. Lay them on a floured baking sheet and bake them for 30 minutes. Eat them hot or lift them onto a plate to cool. They are ideal for packed lunches and picnics.

Preparation: 25 minutes
Cooking: 30 minutes

Mustard and spring onion bread

This is a lovely savoury loaf that is excellent with cheese.

$\frac{1}{2}$ oz (15 g) fresh yeast or 2 teaspoons (10 ml) dried
1 teaspoon (5 ml) honey
$\frac{1}{4}$ pint (150 ml) warm milk, preferably skimmed
8 oz (225 g) wholemeal flour
6 medium-sized spring onions, finely chopped
2 teaspoons (10 ml) mustard powder
1 teaspoon (5 ml) sea salt

If you are using fresh yeast, cream it in a bowl with the honey and milk; if dried, dissolve the honey in the milk and scatter the yeast on top. Leave the yeast in a warm place to froth. Put the flour into a mixing bowl with the onions, mustard powder and salt. Make a well in the centre and pour in the yeast mixture. Mix everything to a dough and turn it onto a floured board. Knead it well. Return it to the bowl, make a cross cut in the top and cover the bowl with a clean tea towel. Put the dough into a warm place to double in size for 1 hour.

Heat the oven to Reg 6/400°F/ 200°C. Knead the dough again, place it on a floured baking sheet and form it into a flattish round. Put it on top of the stove, cover it with the cloth again and let it prove for 20 minutes. Bake the loaf for 25 minutes, so it is golden, and lift it onto a wire rack to cool.

Preparation: 1 hour 50 minutes
Cooking: 35 minutes

Sally Lunn with cheese

This light-textured loaf has a dark brown crispy top. It is excellent for lunch, supper or Sunday tea. Cut it into long slices to serve it, not in wedges like a cake.

5 oz (150 g) wholemeal flour
1 oz (25 g) bran
pinch sea salt
3 fl oz (90 ml) milk
½ oz (15 g) butter
½ oz (15 g) fresh yeast or 2 teaspoons (10 ml) dried
1 egg, beaten
4 oz (125 g) grated Farmhouse Cheddar cheese
a little butter for greasing a 6-inch (15-cm) diameter, high-sided cake tin

Heat the oven to Reg 7/425°F/ 210°C. Put the flour, bran and salt into a bowl. Put the milk and butter into a saucepan and set them on a low heat for the butter to dissolve. Cool them so they are just tepid. Mix the

yeast with the honey and mix in the milk and butter. If the yeast is dried, leave it for 10 minutes. Stir the egg into the yeast mixture. Toss half the cheese into the flour and bran, and make a well in the centre. Mix in the yeast mixture so that you have a fairly moist dough. Turn it onto a floured board and knead it lightly. Put the dough into the greased cake tin. Cover it with a cloth and put it on top of the stove for 30 minutes to double in size. Bake the loaf for 20 minutes. Turn it out of the tin and split it in half crossways. Scatter the remaining cheese on the bottom half and replace the top. Put the loaf onto a heatproof plate and return it to the oven for 5 minutes. Serve it hot.

Preparation: 1 hour
Cooking: 25 minutes

Carrot dumplings

Suet dumplings have always been a country favourite for adding body to soups and stews and for filling you up when there isn't much meat to go round. Freshly grated suet gives the best texture in dumplings and they will be much more interesting if you can flavour them with herbs or spices. These carrot dumplings are very good in an Irish stew or with boiled beef and carrots.

8 oz (225 g) wholemeal flour
1 teaspoon (5 ml) baking powder
4 oz (125 g) freshly grated suet
4 oz (125 g) finely grated carrot
2 tablespoons (30 ml) chopped parsley
salt and pepper
cold water to mix

Mix the flour, baking powder,

suet, carrot, parsley and seasonings together and mix them to a stiff dough with water. Form the dough into sixteen small balls. You can simmer them separately in salted boiling water or stock, or drop them straight into your soup or stew. They need to cook for 30 minutes.

Preparation: 20 minutes
Cooking: 30 minutes

Spiced dumpling roll

This spiced dumpling goes best with beef stews and beef dishes with rich sauces.

8 oz (225 g) wholemeal flour
1 teaspoon (5 ml) baking powder
pinch sea salt
4 oz (125 g) freshly grated suet
¼ pint (150 ml) water
1 teaspoon (5 ml) ground cinnamon
a little freshly grated nutmeg
1 medium onion, very finely chopped

Put the flour into a bowl with the baking powder, salt and suet, and mix them to a stiff dough with the water. Divide the dough into two. Roll both pieces out to ½-inch (1·5-cm) oblongs and scatter them with the spices and the onion. Roll them up and seal the ends. Wrap each one in butter papers or buttered greaseproof paper and then tie them both together in a piece of muslin or an old linen tea towel. Put them into a saucepan of boiling water, cover them and simmer them for 1 hour.

Preparation: 25 minutes
Cooking: 1 hour

WINE

*Now and then it is a joy to have
one's table red with wine and roses.*
(Oscar Wilde)

TAKE THE MANY colours of the countryside and the sun sparkling on the dew; take the fragrant scents of its flowers and the luscious sweetness of its fruits; mix them in a glass with warmth and hospitality, and you have country wine.

Various alcoholic brews have been made in the country for centuries. At first there was no sugar, so people mostly made ale or sometimes mead. In the eighteenth century, supplies of sugar increased and the art of country wine making became an essential accomplishment of every country housewife. In the stillroom of the manor house, the wines were not the same as those in the cottages, for the lady had at her disposal imported fruits such as oranges or lemons. She could buy raisins and currants and take her pick from the spice cupboard, mix in bottles of French wine or Madeira, or even fortify her brews with brandy. In Victorian times the making and bottling of wines in farmhouses were often turned into special occasions, especially the bottling, when not all that was made actually found its way into the bottles!

In the cottages, all that was available were the flowers, fruits and berries of the hedgerows and the vegetables and fruits of the garden. Smaller quantities were made at one time, according to the availability of ingredients, and wine making was fitted into the everyday running of the home. Some of the wines produced could not be bettered whilst others were good enough only for the family, but there was always something in the cellar to offer the unexpected guest or the friend who dropped in for a gossip.

My grandmother, at the beginning of this century, used to make her wines in a large, earthenware crock. She would pulp the fruit, put it into the crock, add sugar and boiling water and the juice of a lemon. The yeast she used was ordinary fresh baker's yeast, spread on a piece of toast and floated on the top. The brew would be covered with several layers of old net curtains, and as the yeast frothed and bubbled its way up to the edge of the crock it was skimmed off. When the bubbling stopped, my grandmother strained the wine into bottles and stood them on a tray. One bottle was set aside, and as the others frothed over, it was used to top them up. When all the frothing stopped, the

FOOD FROM THE COUNTRY

The wine shop at Biddenden Vineyards

WINE

BALM WINE

Boil forty pounds of sugar and nine gallons of water for two hours, skim it well gently, and put it into a tub to cool. Bruise two pounds and a half of the tops of balm, and put them into a barrel with a little new yeast; and when the liquor is cold, pour it on the balm. Stir it well together, let it stand.

bottles were corked. It was a very hit-and-miss method but, apparently, she was nearly always successful. Only very rarely did the vinegar bug get in to turn it all sour.

In the towns, interest in home brewing waned between the wars and later sugar rationing made wine making in the country virtually impossible for a time. But the fruits and berries still grew, and people still went out with their baskets at the right time of the year and friends were still asked round to try the latest bottling. Wine making never really stopped being a natural part of country life. A country wine section was always included in the competitions held at the local flower show and the skills of making it were taught at Women's Institute meetings. In 1963, the restrictions on the home brewing of beer were lifted and this revived the interest in homemade wine as well. Country wines went up in everybody's estimation from being something rather awful that granny used to make, to being a very drinkable commodity that people wanted to learn about.

It seems that as long as you have the necessary skill, you can make country wine from almost anything, from spinach and pea pods to oak leaves, and even in winter, when there are few fresh ingredients available, you can work magic with a bag of wheat or barley. In spring there are the flowers and the first are the sunny golden dandelions that are traditionally picked on St George's Day to make a fragrant golden wine. Broom flowers make a paler, pungent wine, and May blossom one that is light and delicate. You can make a sparkling champagne with elderflowers, and later pick red clover, marigolds or the old, sweet-smelling varieties of roses. From the herb garden you can gather parsley or balm, which makes a softly lemon-scented wine.

Any surplus fruits from the garden were always made into wine, and nearly everybody made rhubarb wine since the plant was so prolific. Gooseberry wine is golden and often sparkling, strawberry soft and delicate and redcurrant light and dry and a superb table wine. Plums, greengages and damsons make rich wines and apple can be light and pale or enriched, and tawny-brown, with raisins. Quince wine is yellow and dry and distinctly flavoured; pear is sparkling and soft; and deep red morello cherry has an underlying taste of almonds. The wines made from the hedgerow fruits are best of all. Blackberry and elderberry wines are rich and dark, hawthornberry, red-brown and smoky, and rosehip made with raisins can be like a medium sherry. The best vegetable wine by far is parsnip. It is rich and golden but it does need a long time to mature. When first bottled it tastes a little like raw parsnips but after two years it becomes mellow and rounded and the parsnip flavour is completely disguised. Carrot wine, as long as you keep it dry, can resemble a malt whisky in flavour, and artichoke wine is soft and rich. All year round in country kitchens, buckets of working, frothing, newly made wine stand in the warm, and gallon jars with fermenting locks (so much more efficient than lace curtains!) give out their regular 'blip' from the corner. The art of the country wine maker is flourishing.

Something else that is flourishing is the English vineyard. To everyone's surprise, we have finally proved that we can grow grapes and make wines as good as many from Germany and France. The first person to risk putting his wine on the market was a Mr Pettigrew of Glamorgan in 1875. Although few people seem to have heard of him, he actually found it sold very well and would have carried on increasing the amount that he made had it not been for the first world war which, for a time, brought an end to such luxurious experimental ventures. There were no further significant developments until 1945 when the Viticultural Research Station was set up at Oxted in Surrey by Mr R. Barrington-Brock and Mr Edward Hyams. They finally discovered that there was no reason at all why grapes should not ripen in British vineyards. Basically, if we can grow red apples we should be able to grow good wine-making grapes.

In 1952 Major General Sir Guy Salisbury Jones planted a vineyard at Hambledon in Hampshire. Ten years later, a second was planted by Margaret Gore Brown, and in 1963, Jack Ward and Ian Howie of the Merrydown Wine Company, who had hitherto made only country wines, planted their first commercial grapevines at Horam. In 1967 there were fifteen productive vineyards covering only ten acres, but it was enough to see the formation of the English Vineyards Association, which was set up under the chairmanship of Jack Ward. There are now, in 1980, two hundred and thirty vineyards in Britain, they cover seven hundred and fifty acres and are spread over twenty-seven counties. The most northerly, at the time of writing, is Renishaw in Derbyshire, but plans are being made for one even further north than that. There is one in Dyfed in Wales and one in Cornwall, but the majority are in the east and south of England. They have replaced fields

Parsnip Wine

To every four pounds of parsnips, cleaned and quartered, put a gallon of water. Boil till they are quite soft, and strain the liquor clear off without crushing the parsnips. To every gallon of the liquor put three pounds of loaf-sugar, and a half ounce of crude tartar. When nearly cold, put fresh yeast to it. Let it stand four days in a warm room, and then bung it up.

N.B. *Parsnip wine is said to surpass all the other homemade wines as much as*

East-India Madeira does that of the Cape. So much is said for it, and on good authority, that it certainly deserves a trial.

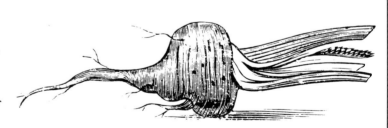

(Cook and Housewife's Manual, 1829)

WINE

Grape harvesting traditionally requires a strong back

of soft fruits and orchards of apples and pears and in many cases are proving to be more successful. Many growers have their own wine presses and some will also press for those who do not have their own facilities.

The grapes are picked in October when the vineyards are lit by a low, yellow sun, the shadows are long and the mornings are chill. The number of pickers and the methods they use depends on the size of the vineyard. At Biddenden, which is our nearest commercial vineyard, the pickers each take a bucket and work down the rows of vines. The full buckets are emptied into a tub which a man carries strapped to his back (which is the same shape as the baskets used in French vineyards) and when that is full, the grapes are tipped into a sixteen-bushel wooden apple bin and taken to the pressing shed. The grapes go first into a pulper which detaches them from the stalks and splits the skins. From there they go down a big plastic pipe to splash down into the drum of the press. Even before the press is switched on, the sweet juice pours down into the trough underneath and when the drum starts to revolve it is syphoned off into a vat. The juice is left overnight so that all the sediment sinks to the bottom, the clear juice is then taken off into another vat and the wine-making process begins.

One of the nicest things about British wine is that you can quite easily go and see it being made for yourself. A hundred and twenty-nine of the vineyards are open to the public, so you can go and buy your wine directly from them and perhaps have a guided tour of the vines and the winery. Some even provide snacks and wine-tasting facilities so you can turn the visit into an enjoyable evening out. Most British wines are light and dry and vary in their degree of richness. There is one champagne-type wine being produced at the moment, some rosé, and very soon there should be a red. Compared with the cheap 'plonks' they may seem expensive, but most of them are estate bottled and we can honestly say that we have enjoyed every one that we have tasted. British wines are no longer something to be laughed at – they can hold their own with the best.

Some Notes on Wine Making

We have to admit that the person who makes the wines in our family is my father. We help him pick the fruit and prepare it (and are always on hand to sample!) but the rest we leave to him as he does it so well. It is he who has given us all our recipes. He is very difficult to pin down as he works completely instinctively, throwing in a handful of this and a spoonful of that, and he has some inner knowledge that enables him to get the perfect balance between dryness and strength. However, these hints should help to explain the recipes.

Country fruits and country wines have a range and subtlety rivalling grape wines

WINE

Equipment

Depending on the amount of wine that you intend to make, you will need some sort of container with a lid, such as a large bucket or a lightweight plastic dustbin, both of which must withstand boiling water.

One of the most useful implements is the homemade masher for pulping the fruit. This is made with a long, stout piece of wood with a thick knob on the end which you pound up and down on the fruit.

Gallon jars are necessary when the wine is fermenting; and you need a fermenting lock for each one (although we have a friend who simply fits a balloon over the neck of the jar!).

A syphon is also essential.

Yeast and yeast nutrient

The strengths of these vary from brand to brand, so it is best to follow the directions on the packet. Two teaspoons (10 ml) of dried brewer's yeast, and one tablet of nutrient per gallon is about normal.

Pectolase

This breaks down the fruit cells to release more juice and it also helps to make the wine clear and bright. Again, the amount will be on the packet. It comes in powder or tablet form. Two dessertspoonfuls (20 ml) per gallon is usually the right amount.

Racking and bottling

The recipes tell you to strain, rack and bottle, but what is racking? All the time that the yeast is working, it reproduces itself and forms a sediment in the bottom of the jar. About three weeks to a month after the wine first went into the jar, this sediment will be thick (if you have used bananas, it will be sooner), so syphon off the clear liquid into another jar. Make a sugar syrup by boiling 4 lbs (1·8 kg) sugar with 2 pints (1·15 l) water for 15 minutes. When it is made, add $\frac{1}{4}$ oz (7 g) tartaric acid. This will make the sugar easy for the yeast to digest. Cool the syrup and top the wine up with it, so that it again measures one gallon. This will feed the yeast and make the wine stronger without adding to the sweetness. Wait until another layer of thick sediment forms (it will take longer the second time) and rack again, adding more syrup. Leave again until more sediment forms. Rack off for the last time into a jar with no lock. Add two campden tablets per gallon. Leave the wine until it is completely clear and bottle it. Depending on the strength of your wine this whole process could take three months or longer, and even up to one year.

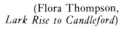

All kinds of home-made wines were brewed by all but the poorest. Sloes and blackberries and elderberries could be picked from the hedgerows, dandelions and coltsfoot and cowslips from the fields, and the garden provided rhubarb, currants and gooseberries and parsnips.

(Flora Thompson, *Lark Rise to Candleford*)

Recipes for Wine

First of all, here are three recipes which all contain English white wine.

Mustard and cress soup

Adding white wine to a soup just before serving will give it richness and flavour. Ham and mustard is a favourite combination. The hotness of the mustard seed used in this soup cooks out, leaving only the savoury flavour.

1 oz (25 g) butter
1 large onion, finely chopped
1 tablespoon (15 ml) flour
1½ pints (850 ml) ham stock
2 teaspoons (10 ml) mustard seed
¼ pint (150 ml) dry white wine
2 boxes mustard and cress

Melt the butter in a saucepan on a low heat. Put in the onion, cover it and cook it gently for 10 minutes. Stir in the flour and cook it for 1 minute. Stir in the stock and add the mustard seed. Bring the soup to the boil and simmer it, uncovered, for 15 minutes. Pour in the wine and cut in the cress. Reheat the soup without letting it boil.

Preparation: 20 minutes
Cooking: 15 minutes

Spiced cabbage in wine

This is a good, savoury dish of cabbage that is excellent with pork.

1 green cabbage
1 large Bramley apple
1 large onion
1 oz (25 g) butter
¼ teaspoon (1·5 ml) ground cloves
a little freshly grated nutmeg
¼ pint (150 ml) dry white wine

Heat the oven to Reg 4/350°F/180°C. Shred the cabbage, peel, core and slice the apple and thinly slice the onion. Melt the butter in a flameproof casserole on a low heat. Mix in the onion and let it soften, adding the apple for the last minute of cooking. Stir in the cabbage and spices. Pour in the wine and bring it to the boil. Cover the casserole and put it into the oven for 50 minutes.

Preparation: 20 minutes
Cooking: 50 minutes

Roast chicken with green grapes

The sharp freshness of the grapes and the light flavour of white wine in this recipe contrast beautifully with the rich stuffing.

1 roasting chicken weighing 3½ lb (1·575 kg)
1 teaspoon (5 ml) ground cinnamon
1 oz (25 g) butter, softened
STUFFING:
½ oz (15 g) butter
1 small onion, finely chopped
2 oz (50 g) fresh wholemeal breadcrumbs
2 oz (50 g) curd cheese
1 tablespoon (15 ml) mixed chopped thyme and marjoram
2 tablespoons (30 ml) dry white wine
2 oz (50 g) green grapes, halved and seeded
SAUCE:
1 tablespoon (15 ml) flour
¼ pint (150 ml) dry white wine
¼ pint (150 ml) stock
1 tablespoon (15 ml) mixed chopped marjoram and parsley
4 oz (125 g) green grapes, halved and seeded

Heat the oven to Reg 6/400°F/200°C. For the stuffing, melt the butter in a frying-pan on a low heat. Put in the onion and soften it. Off the heat work in the crumbs, cheese, herbs and wine. Carefully mix in the grapes, taking care not to break them. Stuff and truss the chicken. Put it on a rack in a roasting tin and cover it completely with foil. Put it into the oven for 1 hour. Remove the foil and continue cooking for 30 minutes so the skin turns crisp and golden. Remove the chicken and joint or carve it. Arrange the chicken on a serving dish, put the stuffing into a separate small dish and keep them both warm. Pour off all but 1 tablespoon (15 ml) fat from the roasting tin and set the tin on top of the stove on a moderate heat. Stir in the flour and cook it for 1 minute. Stir in the stock and wine, and bring to the boil, stirring. Add the herbs and simmer the sauce for 2 minutes. Add the grapes and heat them through. Pour the sauce over the chicken.

Preparation: 45 minutes
Cooking: 1 hour 30 minutes

Morello wine

Morello cherry trees are quite scarce now and you can seldom buy the fruits in the shops. However, if you happen to have a tree in the garden you will be able to make a deep crimson, full-bodied dry wine with the cherries.

5 lbs (2·5 kg) morello cherries
4½ lbs (2·25 kg) sugar
1 gallon (4·6 l) water
1 cup strong, cold black tea
yeast
yeast nutrient

Mash the fruit in a bucket, without crushing the stones. Put the sugar on top and pour on the boiling water and the tea. Add the yeast and yeast nutrient. Leave the cherries to ferment in the bucket for four days and then strain them. Put the liquid into a glass jar and fit a fermentation lock. Rack the wine until it is clear. Bottle it and keep it for at least six months before opening.

Hawthorn blossom wine

This is a lovely light and delicate wine, best kept for drinking in the summer.

3 pints (1·725 l) hawthorn
   blossoms
8 oz (225 g) raisins
8 oz (225 g) sultanas
2 lemons
1 large orange
1 gallon (4·6 l) water
3 lbs (1·350 kg) sugar
pectolase
yeast
yeast nutrient

Pick the blossoms on a dry, sunny day, after the dew has dried but before the sun is too hot. Finely chop or mince the raisins and sultanas. Thinly pare the orange and lemon rinds and squeeze the juices. Put the water and thinly pared rinds into a large pan and bring them to the boil. Add the sugar and simmer for 3 minutes. Put the blossoms and dried fruits into a large container and pour on the boiling liquid. Stir well

and cover. When the mixture is cool, add the juices of the oranges and lemons, the pectolase, yeast and yeast nutrient. Cover and leave in a warm place for a week, remembering to stir every day. Strain the wine into a gallon (4·6 l) jar and fit a fermentation lock. Rack off until the wine is clear. Bottle it and don't open it until six months are up. It is really best kept until the following summer.

Apple and raisin wine

This makes five gallons of a golden apple wine, slightly richer in flavour and body than a plain apple wine.

14 lbs (6·3 kg) apples
2 lbs raisins
4 gallons boiling water
7½ lbs (3·375 kg) sugar
4 cups strong, cold black tea
yeast
yeast nutrient
pectolase

Crush the apples and mince the raisins. Put them into a large container and pour on the boiling water. Add the cold tea. Cool the mixture to lukewarm and add the yeast, yeast nutrient and pectolase. Cover and leave the wine for five days, stirring every day. Strain it into gallon (4·6 l) jars and fit fermentation locks. Rack it as it clears and bottle it when it stops working.

Damson wine

This is a rich, but quite dry red wine that can, if it is kept for long enough, be similar in flavour to port.

6 lbs (2·7 kg) damsons
3½ lbs (1·575 kg) sugar
1 gallon (4·6 l) boiling water
pectolase
1 cup strong, cold black tea
yeast
yeast nutrient

Wash the damsons, remove the stalks and put them into a large container with 2 lbs (900 g) of the sugar. Pour on the water, add the pectolase and tea, and stir well. When the mixture is cool, add the yeast and yeast nutrient. After a day, the damsons will be soft, so squeeze them with your hands to remove the pips. Let most of the pips sink to the bottom but take out ten, crack them open and put back just the kernels. This will give an underlying almondy flavour. Leave everything for five days and then strain off the liquid through muslin onto a further 1½ lbs (675 g) sugar, squeezing very gently but being very careful not to let the liquid go cloudy. Stir well and put the liquid into a jar. Fit a fermentation lock. Rack the wine as it clears and bottle it when it has finished working. Use dark-coloured bottles so the wine keeps its rich colour and leave it for at least nine months before opening.

Light redcurrant wine

This makes a dry, very light, pinky-red wine that is superb with chicken and pork.

5 lbs (2·25 kg) redcurrants
1 lb (450 g) raisins
4 lbs (1·8 kg) sugar
1 gallon (4·6 l) boiling water
1 cup strong, cold black tea
pectolase
yeast
yeast nutrient

String the redcurrants, wash them and thoroughly crush them. Mince the raisins. Put the redcurrants and raisins into a large container with the sugar. Pour on the boiling water and wait until it cools to 75°–85°F. Add the tea, yeast, yeast nutrient and pectolase. Cover the container with a thick cloth and leave everything for five days, stirring twice a day. Strain the liquid into a gallon (4·6 l) jar and fit a fermentation lock. Rack the wine as necessary, and when it is clear and has stopped working, bottle it. The wine will be ready to drink in three months but it improves with age, so, after sampling, leave the rest for a further three to six months.

Blackberry wine

Blackberry wine, made with a Bordeaux yeast, turns out very like a rich French wine. It is a beautiful ruby colour and, as it should be with a well-made wine, you cannot guess at the fruit from which it was made.

3 lbs (1·35 kg) blackberries
8 oz (225 g) raisins
4 lbs (1·8 kg) sugar
1 gallon (4·6 l) boiling water
Bordeaux yeast
yeast nutrient
pectolase

Remove any stalks from the blackberries, wash them well and drain them. Put them into a container and pound them to a thick pulp. Chop the raisins and add them to the blackberries with the sugar. Pour the boiling water over them. Cool everything to lukewarm and add the yeast, yeast nutrient and pectolase. Cover the brew and leave it in a warm place, stirring twice a day. Strain it after five days and put the liquid into a gallon jar. Fit a fermentation lock. Rack the wine until it is clear and, when it is ready, put it into dark bottles. You can drink it in six months, but if you can wait three years, so much the better.

Gooseberry wine

This is a light, dry white wine.

5 lbs (2·25 kg) gooseberries
3 lbs (1·35 kg) sugar

1 gallon (4·6 kg) boiling water
yeast
yeast nutrient
pectolase

Mash the gooseberries and put them into a large container with the sugar. Pour the boiling water over them and let them cool to lukewarm. Add yeast, yeast nutrient and pectolase and let the brew ferment for five days, stirring it every day. Strain the wine into a gallon (4·6 l) jar and fit a fermentation lock. Rack the wine about once a month, until it is clear, and bottle it when it has completely stopped fermenting. It was the belief in most country households that if the wine was bottled the following year at the time when the gooseberry bushes were in bloom, the wine would turn out to be sparkling and you would have a gooseberry champagne. This happened for us once, and the wine had all the life and flavour (and effect) of a true champagne.

Ginger wine

During the winter months, when there is no fruit about, the cook must turn to the store cupboard to make her wines. Ginger wine is a way of laying down warmth for the following year. This is a golden-brown wine, dry and very gingery and it is superb in a Whisky Mac.

2 oranges
2 lemons
8 oz (225 g) raisins
1 gallon (4·6 l) water
3 oz (75 g) ginger root, well bruised
$\frac{1}{2}$ oz (15 g) essence of cayenne or $\frac{1}{2}$ oz (15 g) dried red chillies
1 cup strong, cold black tea
$\frac{1}{2}$ oz (15 g) tartaric acid
yeast
yeast nutrient
pectolase

Thinly pare off the rinds of the oranges and lemons. Chop the raisins. Put these into a large container with the squeezed juices from the oranges and lemons. Bring the water to the boil and add the sugar and root ginger (and also the dried chillies if you are using these). Boil for 30 minutes and cool the liquid to 65°–75°F. Pour it into the container with the juices and add the essence of cayenne, tea, tartaric acid, yeast, yeast nutrient and pectolase. Cover the mixture and leave it to ferment for ten days. Strain it and put it into a gallon (4·6 l) jar. Fit a fermentation lock. Rack the wine as necessary and bottle it when it is clear and has stopped working. It will be ready to drink in six months but is better kept until the following winter, when you will really need it.

Rosehip and raisin wine

This rich, tawny brown wine is similar in flavour to a medium dry sherry. When you go out to pick rosehips, always wait until there have been two sharp frosts to mellow and soften them.

3$\frac{1}{2}$ lbs (1·575 kg) rosehips
8 oz (225 g) raisins
3 lbs (1·35 kg) sugar
1 gallon (4·6 l) boiling water
sherry yeast
yeast nutrient
juice 1 lemon
cold boiled water, if necessary

Wash and mince the rosehips. Mince the raisins. Put them into a large polythene container with the sugar. Pour on the boiling water, give everything a stir and let the mixture cool to lukewarm. Add the yeast, yeast nutrient and lemon juice. Cover the mixture and let it stand for eight days, stirring every day. Strain the liquid into a gallon (4·6 l) jar and if it does not come to just above the shoulders of the jar, top it up with cold, boiled water. Fit the fermentation lock and rack when the wine clears. Leave it for three months before bottling, and don't open the bottles for nine months.

Elderberry enchant

This is a rich, full-bodied wine with a deep maroon colour. It is excellent with beef or lamb and the best wine of all for mulling at Christmas.

4 lbs (1·8 kg) elderberries
1 lb (450 g) malt extract or
**   black malt grains**
1 gallon (4·6 l) boiling water
juice 4 lemons
3 lbs (1·350 kg) sugar
½ pint (275 ml) water

Strip the elderberries from the stalks. Put them into a container and crush them. Add the malt extract or malt grains and pour on the boiling water. Cool everything to lukewarm and add the yeast, yeast nutrient and lemon juice. Cover and ferment the mixture for five days, stirring every day. Make a syrup with the sugar and water and strain the liquid onto it. Mix well and pour the liquid into a gallon (4·61) jar. Fit a fermentation lock. Rack it when necessary and put the wine into dark green bottles. Keep the

wine for at least nine months. It improves with age, so resist the temptation to drink it all at once. Instead, keep some of the bottles for three years before you open them.

Summer wine cup

This is a delightfully attractive summer punch. The fruits stain it a gentle pink colour and the blue borage flowers float prettily on the top. The borage leaves give it a very refreshing flavour.

4 oz (125 g) raspberries or
**   small strawberries**
3 fl oz (120 ml) brandy
1 bottle English white wine
**   or a light homemade wine**
**   such as elderflower or**
**   hawthorn blossom**
20 borage flowers
4 borage leaves
ice cubes (optional)

Put the raspberries or strawberries into a large glass or pyrex bowl and pour in the brandy. Leave them for 30 minutes. Pour in the wine and float the borage flowers and leaves on top. Leave for 10 minutes. If it is a very hot day, add ice cubes just before serving.

Preparation: 10 minutes
Marinade: 40 minutes

Mulled elderberry wine

This is John Clare's 'eldernberry wine',

'Which, bottled up, becomes a rousing charm,
To kindle winter's icy bosom warm,
And, with its merry partner, nut-brown beer,
Makes up the peasant's Christmas-keeping cheer.'

In total contrast to the summer cup, it is rich and very warming and perfect for welcoming the carol singers.

1 bottle elderberry wine
1 piece bruised ginger root
one 2-inch (5-cm) piece
**   cinnamon stick**
10 cloves
6 allspice berries
1 small wineglass brandy

Put the wine into an enamel or stainless steel saucepan with the ginger, cinnamon, cloves and allspice berries. Set it on a low heat and let it get really warm, but don't let it boil. Let it infuse over the heat for 10 minutes. Put the brandy into the bottom of a large jug and strain in the wine. Serve the punch straight away in thick, half-pint glasses.

Preparation: 20 minutes

BEER

Dusk sends the pickers home to camp,
But the country works while London sleeps.
Within the oast the sulphurous furnace roars;
Men shovel coal, and clang the doors,
And in an inner room play cards and dice
Beneath a smoking lamp.

(V. Sackville-West)

THE SKILL of the barley grower and the maltster, the hop-stringer and the hop-drier, and the brewer who puts all the ingredients together, combine to produce the barrels of foaming, tawny beer that finally roll out of the breweries and into the cellars of the local public house.

Malting barley, with its high starch content, is grown mainly in the east and south of England and in parts of Scotland. It is sown in winter or spring and harvested in July and August. From the farm, the threshed barley grains are taken to the maltings where they are soaked until they begin to germinate and then toasted in big, steamy kilns smelling of breakfast cereal. Each brewer requires a different type of malt for his own special brew of beer. Some want it dark, for a rich, malty flavour, but others prefer the toasting to be only a light one.

If it were not for the hops, then there would have been no beer. We would all still have been drinking ale, which was originally a brew made only from malt and yeast. Hops give beer its bitter flavour and preserve it in the barrel. In the hop gardens in Kent, Sussex, Hampshire, Hereford and Worcester, the tiny hop shoots, looking like small red asparagus tips, begin to appear in March and, as they are a climbing plant, they have to be strung, like runner beans. The new method of stringing is to hook the strings over the top wire from the ground, using a long bamboo pole with a hook on the end, but in parts of Kent you can still find stilt-walking hop-stringers. The foot platforms on the stilts are ten feet high and to get on them the stilt walker has to lean them up against one of the hop poles and climb up a ladder. Then he works along the wire sideways, tying each string in two half hitches; on a good day, with no wind, he can tie five hundred strings in three quarters of an hour. 'It is an enjoyable job,' we were told by one who had been doing it for thirty years, 'because you are nearer the sun.'

Three weeks in September are devoted to hop picking. Until about twenty-five years ago, this was all done by hand and in order to get the crop in on time, the whole village would turn out into the fields. In Kent and Sussex their numbers were swelled by people from the

BEER

The malt store at the top of a nineteenth-century tower brewery

The warmth and friendliness of a country pub

BEER

This is a very simple recipe for mulled ale. We have tried it in smaller quantities and it is best with a rather sweet sherry and dark mild ale.

JUMP UPON BETTY
Grate a nutmeg into a jug, to which put one bottle of sherry. Boil a quart of ale and pour into it. Be careful not to break the head of the ale in boiling.
(From the Receipt Book of Susannah Stacey, recorded in Marcus Woodward's *The Mistress of Stanton's Farm*)

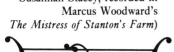

East End of London who came down for a working holiday. They would all sit along the rows of hops on upturned baskets and boxes and when the long hop bines were cut down they would strip off all the bright green flowers by hand and put them into bushel baskets. When the baskets were full the pickers would shout for the tally man who inspected the work to see that no leaves or twigs were mixed in with the hops. If he was satisfied, he would make a mark on the picker's tally stick and empty the basket into a large bin. From the bin the hops were put into small sacks called pokes, which were loaded onto a cart and taken up to the oast house.

Today, the first two steps in the picking process are the same. The bottom of the hop string is cut with a hook, and the top is cut with a pole-pulling knife. The bines are pulled down and then the machine does all the rest. It strips the flowers from the bines, blows out all the leaves and twigs and finally sends the sulphury-smelling, papery flowers bouncing up a conveyor and down a chute into the pokes, which are made of nylon now instead of hessian but are still the same size.

Before we moved to our present house, we used to caretake an oast house in return for being able to keep our cars in it, but we always had to vacate it at the end of August when it was made ready for drying. The three men responsible for drying the hops live in the oast for the duration of the picking, so they make up beds in one of the small rooms, check the cooker, make sure there is a supply of coal for the small fire and clean the dart board. They supply their own food, but the farmer gives them a box of new, red Worcester apples and a barrel of beer.

The hops are loaded into the oast through a window in the upper storey and are tipped into one of the three round kilns that open off the long wooden room. When we looked out of the kitchen window and saw black smoke coming from the pointed kilns we knew drying had begun. The smoke comes from the brimstone that is lit at the same time as the diesel burners to kill off any insects and to keep the hops a bright green. The burners rumble away for about eight hours and then the kiln door is opened. There is a heavy, damp, warm smell and the round room contains nothing but the papery, soft, green hops. The skilled hop-man can tell just by rubbing them between his fingers whether or not they are dry enough and if they are, the burners are switched off and the hops swept out with a traditional birch broom onto the floor of the upper storey which becomes the cooling floor. In about four or five hours, when they are quite cold, the hops are swept across the smooth, wooden floor and pressed hard into a tall, narrow sack called a pocket which is eventually dropped down onto the floor below. The men use a long broom, which consists of a large, twiggy birch branch and a wood-framed shovel with a hessian carrying surface called a scuppet (because it scoops it). In an old oast, with a wooden floor and the autumn sun streaming in through the windows and lighting up the clouds of pale green dust, the scene is absolutely timeless.

The two oldest varieties of hops have the delightful names of Fuggles and Goldings. Many brewers still ask for these specifically, although the newer ones, such as Challenger and Target, may eventually take over since you need less of them to have the same bittering effect. The brewing process has changed very little since it was first evolved and some of the terms and the names of the equipment, like wort, liquor, mash, sparge, and underback, are the same in breweries today as they were in country cottages at the turn of the century.

Until tea became cheap and could be bought at the village shop, beer was the everyday drink for all the family and it was the housewife who usually took charge of the regular brewing. The children had the small beer, made by using the malt for a second time, the adults had one of a moderate strength and, for special occasions, such as Christmas or the harvest supper, the brew was made strong and rich. In 1881 a law was passed stating that no one could brew beer at home over an original gravity of 1016 without a licence. Most beers today average around 1035–40, so this was very weak indeed, and the law gradually caused the decline of home brewing. The men turned to the local public house for their refreshment and the women turned to tea. In country districts, however, beer was still brewed, and it is doubtful whether it was always as weak as the law required. My grandfather certainly used to make his own strong brew, and he used to station my father and my aunt one at either end of the street in case the revenue man or a policeman walked past and smelled it. What they would have done had one of them appeared I don't know, but it is hard to imagine the whole brew being poured quickly down the drain!

In 1963, the licensing laws were finally relaxed and, almost overnight, home brewing became a popular pastime. But brewing does not take place on as large a scale as it once did in country homes and most people prefer to make only one or two gallons at a time. The beer kits available have made the process a very easy one, although the enthusiast can still buy the basic ingredients and make up his own

---

This is a Scottish dish, often eaten at harvest time:

MEAL-AND-ALE
2 quarts (2·28 l) ale
8 oz (225 g) oatmeal
6 oz (175 g) treacle
whisky to taste

Fill a large earthenware bowl with ale, and add the treacle, slightly warmed. Stir in the oatmeal until the mixture is smooth. Pour as much whisky in it as desired. The dish is prepared in the morning to be served up at the end of the harvest feast. A ring is always put inside **and the one who gets it will be the first to be married.**

(Whitbread's *Receipts and Relishes*)

Oh, I have been to Ludlow Fair
And left my necktie God knows
*   where,*
And carried half-way home, or
*   near,*
Pints and quarts of Ludlow
*   beer:*
Then the world seemed none so
*   bad*
And I myself a sterling lad;
And down in lovely muck I've
*   lain,*
Happy till I woke again.

(A. E. Housman)

Hop gardens at picking time

recipe. You can also alter the flavour and strength of the kit beers by adding extra hops or malt extract or using malt grains in place of the extract. We once made a superb cherry ale by boiling up two pounds of crushed morello cherries with the hops in a barley wine kit and then following the basic kit instructions. We put it into screw-topped quart bottles with a teaspoon of brown sugar in each one and then left it until Christmas Day. It was a deep, reddy brown and very strong, with a rich, cherry flavour. The recipe we give for cock ale sounds awful, but it is quite delicious, very smooth and rich, and does not taste at all of chicken.

Much has been written about brewery beer in recent years and there have been many arguments about real beer and keg. The true countryman's drink has always been the unfiltered, cask-conditioned beer and for its preservation and present revival we have to thank the Campaign for Real Ale. One of the prettiest breweries in the country is Ridleys at Hartford End in Essex. It is called the 'Brewery in the Fields' as it is surrounded by fields of wheat and grazing cattle. The

155

Filling wooden casks with beer

wooden building is a typical nineteenth-century tower brewery and the process starts at the top and works down.

In the beamed roof is the malt store where the sacks are piled high on rough wooden floors and below this is the mill where it is ground. At a quarter to six in the morning on the next floor down, the ground malt is mixed in the mash tun with boiling water and left to steep for two hours. Mashing is the key operation and the more malt that is used, the stronger the beer will be. The water, which has now become the wort, is drained away and the steamy malt, smelling of grapenuts, is sparged with streams of water, filtering down and frothing into the underback on the floor below. From the underback the wort is pumped into a copper where it is boiled up with the hops, the final strength of flavour depending on the length of time for which it is boiled. Then it is filtered and put into large, wooden fermenting vessels, the yeast is added and a thick, living, working crust develops on the top. The brewery still uses wooden casks and these are filled on the ground floor and stacked up on the cobbles outside to be taken away to the brewery's pubs, which are all in the Essex area.

You can still find village pubs that, despite the efforts of some breweries to dress them up in plastic and chrome, have survived almost untouched since the last century. They have wooden counters with black handpumps, wooden furniture, dark beams and cream walls. The public bar has brown lino and the saloon a red carpet, and any horse brasses or similar decorations are the genuine article. Here, people meet at the end of a long day's work to unwind amongst friendly faces, and you will always find someone to listen to your latest successes or give a sympathetic ear to your troubles. In the public bar you can hear tales of sporting dogs and ferrets and learn the way the harvest goes. It is the headquarters of the local football team who arrive after Saturday's game, either jubilant or downtrodden, and talking of the unfair 'ref' or the amazing penalty that won the match. The saloon bar, on weekday nights, is quiet and comfortable, but at weekends come the visitors, who share for a few hours this part of village life.

Recipes for Beer

Beery potatoes

A strong light ale gives these potatoes a good, hearty flavour. They are best with beef casseroles and with cheese dishes.

1½ lbs (675 g) medium-sized old potatoes
1½ oz (40 g) butter
½ pint (275 ml) strong light ale
1 tablespoon (15 ml) chopped chives
12 chopped sage leaves
pinch sea salt
freshly ground black pepper

Peel the potatoes and slice them into ¼-inch (6-mm) thick rounds. Put them into a saucepan with half the butter, the herbs, beer and seasonings. Set them, tightly covered, on a moderate heat for 20 minutes, stirring them around occasionally to prevent them from sticking.

By the end of the cooking time all the beer should be absorbed and the potatoes just tender. Lower the heat down to the lowest point. Mash the potatoes, with the pan still on the stove, working in the rest of the butter as you do so and turning off the heat if they begin to stick. Serve them hot.

Preparation: 20 minutes
Cooking: 20 minutes

Herrings soused in beer

This is an excellent way of using up old beer. Serve the herrings with a salad as a main course for four people, or by itself as a first course for eight.

4 medium-sized herrings
½ teaspoon (2·5 ml) black peppercorns
½ teaspoon (2·5 ml) allspice berries
½ teaspoon (2·5 ml) coarse sea salt
1 medium onion
½ pint (255 ml) stale beer
8 cocktail sticks

Heat the oven to Reg 3/350°F/180°C. Fillet the herrings. Crush the spices and salt together with a small pestle and mortar. Quarter and thinly slice the onion and put half into the bottom of a fairly deep ovenproof dish, such as a soufflé dish. Sprinkle the herrings with the crushed spices and put a small amount of onion on the tail end of each one. Roll up the fillets, tail first, and secure them with cocktail sticks. Pack them in the dish in a single layer and pour in the beer. Cover the herrings with foil and bake them for 30 minutes. Take them out of the oven and let them cool completely, still covered. Chill them for 24 hours.

Preparation: 30 minutes
Cooking: 30 minutes
Chilling: 24 hours

Steak marinated in beer

If you only have steak as the occasional treat, then make the most of it. You find so many French recipes for steak – Bordelaise and au poivre – that it's good to give it a robust, English, country flavour. It will be none the less appetising for it either!

1½ lbs (675 g) rump steak cut into 4 serving pieces
½ pint (275 ml) strong, draught bitter
2 large onions, coarsely chopped
1 tablespoon (15 ml) chopped thyme
1 tablespoon (15 ml) chopped parsley
1 tablespoon (15 ml) chopped marjoram
2 chopped sage leaves
8 oz (225 g) mushrooms
1 oz (25 g) butter

Mix the beer in a bowl with the herbs and onions. Put in the pieces of steak and leave them for at least three hours at room temperature, turning them several times. Quarter the mushrooms. Lift the steak out of the marinade and then take out the onions, using a perforated spoon. Heat the butter in a frying-pan on a high heat. Put in the pieces of steak and brown them well on both sides. Continue cooking them, lowering the heat if necessary, until they are done to your liking. Remove them and keep them warm. With the pan on a moderate heat, mix in the onions and cook them, stirring them about, for 1 minute. Put in the mushrooms and cook them for 1 minute more. Pour in the marinade and bring it to the boil. Turn down the heat and let it simmer for 2 minutes. Pour the onions, mushrooms and marinade over the steak.

Marinade: 3 hours
Preparation and cooking: 40 minutes

Spiced brisket in mild ale

Ask a friendly publican to fill up a jar with dark mild ale so you can make this recipe of gently spiced, tender and very flavoursome brisket. As it takes rather a long time to cook, drink the rest of the mild while the meat is in the oven!

1 piece lean, rolled brisket, weighing about $2\frac{1}{4}$ lbs (1 kg)
6 cloves
6 black peppercorns
6 allspice berries
pinch sea salt
1 small onion, cut in half but not peeled
1 bayleaf
$\frac{1}{2}$ pint (275 ml) dark mild ale

Heat the oven to Reg 3/325°F/ 160°C. Crush the spices and salt together and rub them into the surface of the beef. Put the meat into a casserole with the onion and bayleaf. Pour the mild over the top. Set the casserole on top of the stove and bring the mild to the boil. Cover the casserole and put it into the oven for 2 hours. Then take out the beef and keep it warm. Strain the juices into a saucepan and let them simmer gently while you carve the beef and arrange it on a serving dish. Pour the juices over the top.

Preparation: 15 minutes
Cooking: 2 hours

Topside simmered with roots in beer

This is one of the best beef dishes you will ever make. All the flavours blend together to make a robust, winter meal. Serve a bright, fresh vegetable with it, such as spring greens, Brussel tops, curly kale or green cabbage. As for potatoes – bake them in their jackets.

1 piece topside of beef weighing $2-2\frac{1}{2}$ lb (1 kg)
8 oz (225 g) swede
8 oz (225 g) parsnips
1 large carrot
1 large onion
1 clove garlic, finely chopped
1 oz (25 g) beef dripping
$\frac{1}{2}$ pint (275 ml) bitter beer
2 bayleaves

2 tablespoons (30 ml) chopped parsley
1 tablespoon (15 ml) Worcester sauce
1 tablespoon (15 ml) grated horseradish

Dice all the vegetables. Melt the dripping in a flameproof casserole on a high heat. Put in the beef and brown it all over. Remove it and lower the heat. Stir in the vegetables and garlic. Cover them and let them sweat for 7 minutes. Pour in the beer and bring it to the boil. Replace the meat, tuck in the bayleaves, cover and simmer on top of the stove for 1 hour 15 minutes. Remove the beef and stir the parsley, Worcester sauce and horseradish into the vegetables. Let the vegetables simmer, uncovered, while you carve the beef. Arrange the beef on a serving dish and pour the vegetables over the top.

Preparation: 35 minutes
Cooking: 1 hour 30 minutes

Beef and carrots in beer jelly

This is a good way of dealing with braising steak or topside if the weather is warm and you don't fancy a hot stew. It is very attractive and makes a superb dish for a dinner party.

$1\frac{1}{2}-2$ lbs (675–900 g) good quality braising steak or topside
12 oz (350 g) new carrots
6 allspice berries
8 black peppercorns
1 onion, peeled and stuck with 5 cloves
$\frac{1}{2}$ pint (275 ml) bitter beer
bouquet garni
1 bayleaf
1 clove garlic, crushed with a pinch sea salt
2 teaspoons (10 ml) powdered gelatine

Heat the oven to Reg 3/325°F/ 170°C. Have the beef cut into slices about $\frac{1}{4}$ inch (6 mm) thick. Scrub and thinly slice the carrots. Crush the allspice berries and peppercorns together. Put the beef into a fairly wide-based casserole and scatter in the spices. Cover the beef with the carrots and put the onion somewhere in the middle. Pour in the beer, tuck in the bouquet garni and bayleaf and make sure the garlic is evenly distributed in the liquid. Cover the casserole and put it into the oven for 2 hours.

Discard the bouquet garni and bayleaf. Lift out the beef and arrange it on a flat serving plate. Cover it with the carrots. Skim the juices in the casserole. Soak the gelatine in 3 tablespoons (45 ml) of the juices. Stir it back into the casserole with the rest. Set the casserole on a low heat and stir until the gelatine dissolves. Let the jelly cool and spoon half of it over the beef and carrots. Put the beef into the fridge for the jelly to set. Spoon the rest of the jelly over the beef and return it to the fridge to set completely. Bring the beef back to room temperature for 30 minutes before serving.

Preparation: 40 minutes
Cooking: 2 hours
Chilling: 1 hour

Chicken in beer

Long, slow cooking in beer makes a chicken soft and tender and gives it and the vegetables a rich, warming flavour. The colours of the casserole are rich autumn reds and browns.

1 roasting chicken weighing 3 lb (1·4 kg)
4 oz (125 g) lean bacon
1 large onion
4 oz (125 g) carrots
1 small white turnip
1 large parsnip

2 sticks celery
½ oz (15 g) butter
½ pint (275 ml) bitter beer
1 large bouquet garni

Heat the oven to Reg 4/350°F/ 180°C. Joint the chicken and finely dice the bacon and vegetables. Melt the butter in a large, flameproof casserole on a moderate heat. Put in the bacon, brown it and set it aside. Put in the chicken pieces, skin side down first, and brown them on both sides. Remove them and put them with the bacon. Lower the heat and mix in the vegetables. Stir them around, uncovered, until they are just beginning to brown. Pour in the beer and bring it to the boil. Replace the chicken and the bacon and tuck in the bouquet garni. Cover the casserole and put it into the oven for 1 hour 30 minutes.

Preparation: 30 minutes
Cooking: 1 hour 30 minutes

Chicken, ale and parsley pie

Chicken and bacon always make light and savoury pies. This one will feed up to six people.

rough puff pastry made with
    8 oz (225 g) wholemeal flour
1 roasting chicken weighing
    3½ lb (1·575 kg)
8 oz (225 g) collar bacon, in
    one piece
8 oz (225 g) carrots
½ oz (15 g) butter or 2
    tablespoons (30 ml)
    rendered chicken fat
1 large onion, thinly sliced
½ pint (275 ml) bitter beer
4 tablespoons (60 ml)
    chopped parsley
¼ nutmeg, grated
beaten egg for glaze

Heat the oven to Reg 7/425°F/ 210°C. Make the pastry and chill it. Joint the chicken. Bone the joints and cut the meat into 1½-inch (4-cm) pieces, removing any tough skin. Cut the bacon into ½-inch (1·5-cm) dice. Put them into a small saucepan and cover with water. Set it on a low heat, bring it to the boil and simmer for 2 minutes. Drain the bacon, refresh it with cold water and drain it again. Thinly slice the carrots. Melt the butter or heat the fat in a large frying-pan on a high heat. Put in the chicken, in two batches, and brown it, moving it around all the time. Remove it and lower the heat. Stir in the carrots and onion, cover them and let them sweat for 10 minutes. Pour in the beer and bring it to the boil. Add the chicken, bacon and parsley and grate in the nutmeg. Transfer everything to a large pie dish and put a pie funnel in the centre. Cover the pie with the pastry. Decorate the top with trimmings and brush it with beaten egg. Bake the pie for 45 minutes and serve it hot.

Preparation: 1 hour
Cooking: 45 minutes

The wassail bowl

Next crown the bowl full
With gentle lamb's wool
Add sugar nutmeg and ginger
With store of ale too
And thus ye must do
To make the Wassail a
swinger.

The wassail bowl is dark and rich and cheering and best drunk really hot. The crab-apples don't actually float on the top but they melt into the beer, giving it flavour and body. It is excellent as a warmer on bonfire night, but at Christmas, when there might not be any crab-apples left, use small, cored, cooking apples.

12 crab-apples
2 tablespoons (30 ml)
    Barbados sugar
4 pints (2·5 l) brown ale
¼ pint (275 ml) cream sherry
½ oz (15 g) root ginger,
    broken
½ nutmeg, grated
½ teaspoon (2·5 ml) ground
    cinnamon

Put the crab-apples into an ovenproof dish with the sugar, and bake them in a moderate oven for 20 minutes. Heat up the rest of the ingredients in a large saucepan but do not allow to boil. Pour the wassail into a large punch bowl and add the apples.

Preparation: 40 minutes

Homemade beer

This makes a golden bitter-type beer. Adding the sugar to the bottles makes sure it is nice and lively and also makes it a little stronger.

1 gallon (4·6 l) water
1 oz (25 g) hops
1 teaspoon (5 ml) dried
    brewer's yeast
12 oz (350 g) demerara sugar
    plus 8 teaspoons (40 ml)
    for the bottles
8 oz (225 g) golden syrup
8 oz (225 g) malt extract

Put the water into a large pan with the hops, sugar and syrup. Bring them to the boil and keep them on a rolling boil for 20 minutes. Strain the liquid into a large container and stir in the malt. When the liquid is lukewarm, stir in the yeast. Leave the brew in a warm place until it has stopped working, skimming off some of the yeasty crust if it looks like bubbling over the top. Strain and bottle it after eight days and put 1 teaspoon of sugar into each bottle. Leave the beer for three weeks and make sure all the sediment has settled to the bottom before opening.

Nettle beer

Instead of hops, boil up 2 lbs (900 g) young nettle leaves with the water, sugar and syrup. This makes a lighter flavoured beer and was a country practice for many years, even after the introduction of hops.

Cock ale

Putting ground-up chicken bones soaked in wine into the brew makes it really strong and thick. A friend of ours also tried it with a piece of veal and finished up with something that you had to drink in wineglasses!

Soak the crushed wing tips, bones, neck and parson's nose of a cooked chicken in $\frac{1}{2}$ pint white wine (apple is best) for 12 hours. Strain the liquid off and add it to the homemade beer after you have put in the yeast. Tie the chicken mush in a muslin bag and leave it dangling in the beer container until the beer has finished fermenting.

N.B. Don't use a chicken that has been cooked with a strong flavoured stuffing such as sage and onion.

CIDER

Then fill up the jug boys, and let it go round,
Of drinks not the equal in England is found,
So pass round the jug, boys,
and pull at it free,
There's nothing like cider,
rough cider, for me!
(Traditional)

ALTHOUGH CIDER is today only associated with the West Country and perhaps Herefordshire, it was, until the beginning of this century, the everyday drink of the farm workers and other country people in all the apple-growing and adjacent counties of England. It was then the duty of every farmer to provide some kind of liquid refreshment for his workers, especially at times like harvest and haymaking when work was hardest and throats were dry. Making cider with any available apples enabled him to send all his malting barley to market and therefore saved him a good deal of money. The cider-making process was also simpler than brewing beer and was only carried out once a year.

Cider was in the pottery jug on the table when a man came home from work; it was in the stone jar that lay in the cool shade of a hawthorn hedge at harvest time; it was heated and mixed with herbs to drive away colds and was drunk as a cure for rheumatism; it was watered down as a drink for the children, and tough meat was marinated in it. A barrel of cider was tapped for the harvest supper and at Christmas it was mulled with spices and poured into the wassail bowl. Cider was a universal liquid and although very few academics have written about it or poets waxed lyrical over it, it is often referred to in rhymes, ballads and wassailing songs. In the cider counties at Christmas, New Year or Twelfth Night, the apple orchards were wassailed to bring good luck to the next year's crop; and drinking cider or eating specially made caraway cakes soaked in cider became a ritual in other good luck ceremonies such as that of wassailing the wheat fields in Gloucestershire.

After the first world war, when life in the countryside was becoming more mechanised, many of the farmers stopped making their own cider. It was usually left to one person in the district to take all the apples and press them for everyone else. By the 1930s, when the custom of the boss providing the drink was dying out, less and less cider was made in this way and many of the presses were stopped forever. But there were still cider orchards and often a surplus of eating and cooking apples, so in the principal apple counties (Cornwall, Devon,

Sweet cyder is a great thing,
A great thing to me,
Spinning down to Weymouth town
By Ridgway thirstily,
And maid and mistress summoning
Who tend the hostelry:
O cyder is a great thing,
A great thing to me,!
(Thomas Hardy, 'Great Things')

CIDER

Somerset, Dorset, Gloucestershire, Herefordshire, Norfolk, Kent and Sussex) some farmers carried on and apple pressing still takes place on their farms today. Some simply brew a few barrels a year and keep them in the barn purely for family, friends and workers. Others sell their cider to local customers and perhaps to one or two pubs in the vicinity. There is nothing better than going into a pub in some out-of-the-way country village and finding unexpectedly a barrel of 'the real thing' put up behind the bar.

Some small producers have expanded over the years and become like the smaller, independent brewers. None of their character has been lost and, to a large extent, the traditional pressing and fermenting methods are still used. They sell cider in gallon and half-gallon jars and five-gallon barrels to pubs and off-licences in their own and neighbouring counties, and if you are local, you can call in and buy direct. Some farm producers have become even larger concerns, selling over a wider area. There are also the firms who were set up specifically to make cider such as Bulmers of Hereford who are the largest and probably the oldest, and Merrydown in Sussex who have only been in production since 1939. The National Association of Cidermakers have twenty members on their list who produce cider commercially and these include the larger farms, but the number of smaller producers has never been counted.

For many years, large orchards of apples were grown specifically for cider making and these were supplemented with cooking and eating apples. The old cider apples have delightful names, each with different qualities. The best ciders were said to be those made from one variety of apple only, although, as a certain J. Philips of Hereford wrote in a long piece about cider making in 1790, 'There are those that a compounded Fluid drain from different mixtures.... Woodcock, Pippin, Moyle, Rough Eliot, Sweat Pearmain, the blended streams (each mutually correcting each) create a pleasurable medley.'

The terms used to describe the cider apples and the flavours they produce – sweet, bittersweet, sharp and bittersharp – have been the same for centuries and are still used by the big cider makers. Sweet ciders were once made with Woodbine, Sweet Coppin and Sweet Alford; bittersweet, which have a low acid and high tannin content, with Eggleston Styre, Knotted Kernel, Royal Wilding, Silver Cup and, more recently, Dabinett, Yarlington Mill and Tremlett's Bitter. Sharp ciders with a high acid and low tannin content were made from Cap of Liberty (like many, of French origin), Old Foxwhelp, Dymock Red and Frederick. (This last was also said to be the best for apple jelly.) Kingston Blacks made a bittersharp cider, high in both tannin and acid. Other varieties included Dog's Nose, Ruby Streak, Redstreak, 'the Moyle of sweetest honey'd taste', and Ratheripes ('rathe' meaning 'early'). Nowadays, although a small acreage of cider apples is grown, much of our cider is made from a mixture of cooking and eating apples which are the windfalls or small, misshapen rejects from the packhouses. The combination of sweet and sharp works admirably.

We don't know the source of this recipe but it was recorded in an extraordinary book about cider by E. Birkett in 1952 called *The Golden Wine of Old Britain*. It looks as though the 'old fowl' was eaten instead of being left to disappear into the liquid.

To make use of an old fowl:

Braise with raisins, cloves and spice, then steep for ten to fourteen days in nine gallons of strong Cyder. Take out and drain then braise again. The liquor is strained and bottled, and left for several months in order to mature, when this, having absorbed much of the fowl's goodness, is a great fortifying drink.

FOOD FROM THE COUNTRY

When being harvested, apples for cider do not have to be carefully picked by hand. They can be shaken down from the trees, as a little bruising does no harm. At one time the trees were beaten with stout sticks or shaken manually, the apples fell on the ground and were picked up by hand. Now they are mostly picked up mechanically and in orchards where the trees are widely spaced the apples fall into a catching frame which is attached to a mechanical shaker. Once picked, the apples should be stored for a while so they can mellow in the soft, autumn sun. When they were hand-shaken they were simply piled in heaps in the orchard. This can still be the case in small cider farms, but in the factories they are stored in enormous concrete silos. This mellowing process is essential as the sugar content (which will eventually turn to alcohol) increases, and the apples become softer so more juice can be extracted. It used to be November before the apples were ready, and the traditional day to begin pressing was the first of the month. Pressing now lasts from September until Christmas and sometimes right round to March if the harvest has been a good one and a lot of apples have been kept in cold store.

The basic cider-making process has not changed, whether on a small or a large scale. The apples are pressed and the juice fermented. The really old cider presses took the form of a round stone trough. In the centre was a post, attached to which was a stone wheel. When the apples were tipped into the trough, the wheel was rotated by an old and patient horse. The juice was collected underneath and put into barrels. Perhaps the oldest example of this type of press, the trough made from one enormous piece of granite, belongs to Symonds' Cider and English Wine Co. of Stoke Lacey in Herefordshire. The stone presses were used for many years, even after the first specially constructed cider mill came into operation in the seventeenth century. This consisted of a wooden cylinder that was rotated by hand to pulp the apples. The pulp was then placed between layers of straw in a screw press. This pulping and pressing method has hardly changed at all since then.

The cider farm at Stoke Lacey uses just such a system. They start very early on the coldest mornings of the year. Apparently the colder the day the better the pressing and it can be so cold that the juice freezes in the press. Literally tons of mellowed bitter-sweet cider apples are bounced up a conveyor to a pulper in which they are jumbled and mashed. From there they go to a hopper, and from the hopper they splosh out onto a wicker mat covered with a thick hessian, nylon or mohair cloth. The cloth is folded over and another mat and cloth are put on ready for the next batch. These layers are eventually put into an electric press and reduced to one third their original thickness in half an hour. Even before it is put into the press, the juice flows out continually, and it is syphoned off through a pipe to a tank and thence to wooden vats. The dry pulp left between the mats is called apple cheese. It was once the custom to run water through it and press it again to make a slightly sharp, non-alcoholic and refreshing drink. It

*There was an old man
And he had an old cow,
And how to keep her, he didn't
    know how;
So he built a barn
To keep that cow warm
And a little more cyder will do
    us no harm!*

(Traditional)

Some suggestions for serving from *The Golden Wine of Old Britain*, which was written at a time when specific cider apple varieties were used.

With trout: White Norman. *With lamb and dill sauce:* Eggleston Styre or Royal Wilding. *With game and goose:* Kingston Black. *With cheese and savouries:* Old Foxwhelp

'... the three English cheeses – in order of merit – a rich, buttery well-seasoned (not under 12 months) Lancashire, or Cheshire or Cheddar, each ad lib, of course; a red-skinned onion, a few leaves of well-grown spinach, and a glass or two of Cyder.'

CIDER

(**above**) *Bitter-sweet cider apples*

(**left**) *Apple pulp in the press – the first stage*

Freshly-pressed apples flow into the tank before being siphoned out into the vats

The juices begin to flow

was given to the children and was very useful as a cooking liquid. Now the cheese is mostly used for animal feed.

A good cider, it was once said, relies only on the apples and their correct weathering and pressing. The simplest way of making cider was, and still is, to leave the juice in wooden barrels with the bung open until it had fermented naturally and then stop them up and leave them for six months. You then have a refreshing, fairly dry drink, which is just slightly lively but not altogether sparkling. This is the true rough cider. This natural fermenting method is still used on many of the smaller farms to make a dry cider; those who prefer it stronger and sweeter add sugar or raisins. Kentish vintage cider is made with plenty of sugar and left to mature for three years so it is rich and strong and tawny-gold, and it should only be drunk in wineglasses – although at the farm it is drunk by the half-pint. To control the flavour and the strength of a cider that is sold on a large scale, all the different barrels are mixed together before bottling or putting into smaller barrels, and the whole batch, if necessary, is sweetened together. The larger cider makers prefer not to rely on the natural yeasts for fermentation, but destroy these first and add their own. This ensures that their product is always the same.

Any cider that didn't come up to standard in the old days was

'improved' by some means or other and who knows what goes on with the privately produced barrels today! In Devon, spices, treacle or fresh beef were once added, in Cornwall a quart of sheep's blood, in Kent black cherries, and in Herefordshire gingerbread, milk, a few quarts of wheat, eggs or blackberries. Raisins are still used instead of sugar, and at one time these were soaked first in brandy. To sweeten new cider, burning brimstone was put into the barrel (these were the days in which sugar was scarce), but unfortunately it also left behind an unpleasant taste of sulphurous acid. When you drink any kind of farm cider, you glow from the inside out and it can give you an immense sense of well-being. It can also live up to its Somerset name of Tanglefoot!

Dry cider and vintage cider are invaluable in the country kitchen, both in their own right and also as substitutes for dry white wine or sherry. If you are unable to track down any made on a farm, then there are some very good still, dry, commercially made ciders, and there are several kinds of strong vintage to be had in third-pint bottles. Cider is renowned for its ability to break down meat, which was demonstrated when the piece of beef put in to 'improve' it was found to have completely disappeared in a few months. Any tough cut of pork, beef or even lamb, or any game that you suspect might be rather elderly, can be tenderised by placing it in a marinade of dry cider. Expensive cuts, too, will have their flavour and texture much improved. Use the marinade for braising the tougher meats or for making a sauce for roasts and grills. Even if you haven't marinated the meat, cider is a very effective braising or pot-roasting liquid for meats. Use it also in sauté dishes, and half and half with stock for making gravy for roast meat. Vegetables can be braised in the oven in cider or simmered in it, with a knob of butter, on top of the stove. Oily

This sounds rather like our apple mead (page 127). It was, by all accounts, very useful in the kitchen.

A Rich and Pleasant Wine
Take new cider from the press, mix it with as much honey as will support an egg, boil gently fifteen minutes but not in an iron, brass or copper pot. Skim it well; when cool, let it be tunned, but don't quite fill. In March following, bottle it, and it will be fit to drink in six weeks; but it will be less sweet if kept longer in the cask. You will have a rich and strong wine, and it will keep well. This will serve for any culinary purposes which milk, or sweet wine, is directed for.

Honey is a fine ingredient to assist and render palatable, new crabbed austere cider.

(Domestic Cookery, 1814)

Bill Symonds with his old horse-driven granite cider press, not now in use, but exhibited at agricultural shows

fish – mackerel and herrings – are superb cooked in cider. Bake them in cider either whole or filleted, or use the cider as a marinade before grilling them.

Fruit for tarts or mousses can be cooked in cider instead of water; and cider can also be used for the syrup for a fruit compote or fresh fruit salad. If you are serving dried fruit, soak it for 12 hours first in cider and eat it without cooking. Dry cider can also be effectively used as the liquid in bread or scones and it can be mixed into cakes. Vintage cider is superb in fruit cakes or in any cake where sherry or Madeira is called for. When making a syllabub, beat vintage cider into whipped cream instead of brandy. You can also use it to make a sweet butter to go with plain cakes or steamed puddings.

Recipes for Cider

Cider-braised pigeons

Root vegetables and cider give pigeons a homely country flavour and the long braising makes them deliciously moist and tender.

4 pigeons
4 large sage leaves
1 medium onion
1 medium carrot
1 stick celery and a few
   leaves
1 small piece swede
1 small white turnip
1 oz (25 g) pork dripping
1 pint (575 ml) dry cider
1 bouquet garni
3 tablespoons (45 ml)
   chopped parsley

Heat the oven to Reg 4/350°F/ 180°C. Truss the pigeons and put a sage leaf into each one. Roughly chop the vegetables. Melt the dripping in a large, flameproof casserole on a high heat. Put in the pigeons and brown them well. Remove them and lower the heat. Mix in the vegetables, cover them and let them sweat for 7 minutes. Set the pigeons on top and pour in the cider. Bring it to the boil and tuck in the bouquet garni. Cover the casserole and put it into the oven for 2 hours. Lift out the pigeons and keep them warm. Strain the juices in the casserole, pressing down hard on the vegetables. Reheat the juices if necessary. Put the pigeons into a warm serving dish, pour the juices over the top and use the chopped parsley as decoration.

Preparation: 25 minutes
Cooking: 2 hours

Leg of venison marinated in cider

Leg of venison becomes extremely tender after a long while in a cider marinade. This is a homely country stew, rich, delicious and warming.

1½ lbs (675 g) leg of venison
MARINADE:
½ pint (275 ml) dry cider
¼ nutmeg, grated
4 chopped sage leaves
1 small onion, thinly sliced
sea salt and freshly ground
   black pepper
COOKING:
up to ¼ pint (150 ml) dry cider
   or stock
1 oz (25 g) butter
1 medium onion, thinly
   sliced
8 oz (225 g) carrots, thinly
   sliced
4 chopped sage leaves
¼ nutmeg, grated
sea salt and freshly ground
   black pepper

Cut the venison into slices ½ inch (1·5 cm) thick. Mix the ingredients for the marinade together. Put the venison into the marinade, cover it and leave it in a cool place for 48 hours.

Heat the oven to Reg 4/350°F/ 180°C . Lift the venison out of the marinade and dry it with kitchen paper. Strain the marinade and make it up to ½ pint (275 ml) with extra cider or with stock. Melt the butter in a large, flameproof casserole on a high heat. Put in as many pieces of venison as will fit in one layer and brown them on both sides. Remove them and brown the rest in the same way.

Take these out too, lower the heat and put in the onion and carrots. Cook them until the onion begins to soften. Pour in the marinade and bring it to the boil. Add the sage, nutmeg, salt and pepper and replace the venison. Cover the casserole and put it into the oven for 1 hour 30 minutes.

Preparation (1): 15 minutes
Marinade: 48 hours
Preparation (2): 20 minutes
Cooking: 1 hour 30 minutes

Vintage pork and button onions

The sweet vintage cider used in this recipe cooks to a lovely dark brown glaze.

1½–2 lbs (675–900 g) lean pork
   (either spare rib chops or
   lean end of the belly)
20 button onions
1 oz (25 g) pork dripping
7 fl oz (200 ml) vintage cider
6 chopped sage leaves

Cut the pork into ¾-inch (2-cm) dice and peel the onions. Melt the dripping in a large, heavy frying-pan or sauté pan, put in the pork pieces and brown them. Remove them and set them aside. Lower the heat, put in the onions and cook them until they are just beginning to brown. Raise the heat again, pour in the cider and bring it to the boil. Replace the pork and add the sage. Cover the pan and set it on a very low heat for 20 minutes.

Preparation: 25 minutes
Cooking: 20 minutes

Pork, liver and cider loaf

This mixture makes a very light textured loaf with a rich flavour. Serve it with the cider sauce which makes a good, sharp contrast. Serve them both hot.

1 lb (450 g) streaky pork rashers
8 oz (225 g) pig's liver
2 oz (50 g) bacon pieces
2 oz (50 g) wholemeal breadcrumbs
4 tablespoons (60 ml) dry cider
½ oz (15 g) pork dripping
1 medium onion, finely chopped
12 chopped sage leaves
10 black peppercorns, coarsely crushed
large pinch sea salt

Heat the oven to Reg 4/350°F/ 180°C. Put the pork, liver and bacon through the fine blade of a mincer. Soak the bread-crumbs in the cider. Melt the dripping in a frying-pan on a low heat. Mix in the onion and cook it until it is soft. Mix it into the pork with the soaked crumbs, sage, peppercorns and salt. Pile the mixture into a 2-lb (900-g) loaf tin and smooth the top. Bake the loaf, uncovered, for 2 hours. Serve it hot, cut into slices, with cider sauce.

Preparation: 30 minutes
Cooking: 2 hours

Cider sauce

This smooth, glossy sauce has an underlying sharpness which goes superbly with the pork loaf and with plainly cooked pork. Use it instead of gravy for roasts, make it into a sauce for chops, or even pour it over sausages.

1 oz (25 g) pork dripping
1 small onion, finely chopped
1 small carrot, finely chopped
1 stick celery, finely chopped
1 tablespoon (15 ml) wholemeal flour
¾ pint (450 ml) dry cider
1 bouquet of sage

Melt the dripping in a saucepan on a low heat. Stir in the onion, carrot and celery and cook them until they are just beginning to brown. Stir in the flour and brown it. Stir in the cider and bring it to the boil. Add the sage, cover and simmer for 45 minutes. Strain the sauce, return it to the saucepan and simmer for 2 minutes more.

Preparation: 15 minutes
Cooking: 47 minutes

Leeks braised with mustard and cider

Cider, leeks and mustard are the perfect combination to serve with pork.

1½ lbs (675 g) good fat leeks, about 1½ inches (4 cm) in diameter
1 oz (25 g) butter
2 teaspoons (10 ml) mustard powder
¼ pint (150 ml) dry cider
2 tablespoons (30 ml) chopped parsley

Heat the oven to Reg 4/350°F/ 180°C. Cut the leeks into short lengths so they are as wide as they are long. Wash them well. Heat the butter in a flameproof casserole on a low heat. Stir in the mustard and keep stirring until it thickens. Mix in the leeks. Pour in the cider and bring it to the boil. Mix in the parsley. Cover the casserole and put it into the oven for 45 minutes.

Preparation: 20 minutes
Cooking: 45 minutes

Apple and cider syllabub

Use a strong, fairly sweet, vintage cider for this light textured syllabub.

2 large Bramley apples
6 cloves
½ pint (275 ml) double cream
2 fl oz (120 ml) vintage cider
2 oz (50 g) stoned dates
2 oz (50 g) sultanas

Heat the oven to Reg 5/375°F/ 190°C. Core the apples and stick the cloves into the holes. Put them onto a heatproof dish and bake them for 30 minutes. Skin them and rub the pulp through a sieve. Mix it with the cream and beat them together using an electric mixer on a slow speed. After about 2 minutes, add the cider. Keep beating until the mixture is light and thick. Finely chop the dates and sultanas and mix them into the syllabub. Pile the syllabub into a serving dish and put it into a cool place for 2 hours before serving to let some of the fruits' sweetness seep into the mixture.

Cooking: 30 minutes
Preparation: 30 minutes
Chilling: 2 hours

Old English cider cake

This recipe for cider cake has been claimed by both Oxfordshire and Herefordshire, but as it is so simple we suspect that it has been made in many other counties besides. Nutmeg and cider are the only flavourings used but the combination is extremely effective, giving the cake an unusual, spicy flavour. Wholemeal flour and Barbados sugar improve its moist, light texture considerably. Serve it plain, cut into slices, or thickly spread with vintage cider butter. It keeps very well wrapped in foil or in an airtight tin.

8 oz (225 g) butter
8 oz (225 g) Barbados sugar
4 eggs, beaten
1 lb (450 g) wholemeal flour
2 teaspoons (10 ml) bicarbonate of soda
1 nutmeg, grated
½ pint (275 ml) dry cider
butter for greasing

Heat the oven to Reg 4/350°F/180°C. Cream the butter and beat in the sugar until the mixture is light and fluffy. Add the eggs, a little at a time. Beat in half the flour, mixed with the bicarbonate of soda. Thoroughly mix in the cider and then fold in the remaining flour. Put the mixture into a buttered tin, 8 inches by 11 inches (20 cm by 28 cm) and 2 inches (5 cm) high. Smooth the top. Bake the cake for 45 minutes and turn it onto a wire rack to cool.

Preparation: 30 minutes
Cooking: 45 minutes

Vintage cider butter

This is a variation on brandy and rum butters. Serve it spooned over the Christmas pudding or over mince pies. At other times of the year it can top plainer puddings or be spread on plain cakes like the one above.

8 oz (225 g) unsalted butter
3 tablespoons (45 ml) clear honey
3 tablespoons (45 ml) vintage cider

Beat the butter to a fluffy cream. Beat in the honey, 1 tablespoon (15 ml) at a time, and then the vintage cider, 1 teaspoon (5 ml) at a time. Pile the butter into an earthenware bowl and chill it lightly before serving.

Preparation: 30 minutes

Gooseberry and elderflower mousse

Sweet, strong cider and elderflowers add sweetness and flavour to a light gooseberry mousse. Ordinary sweet cider can be used if vintage is unobtainable.

1¼ lbs (600 g) green gooseberries
6 tablespoons (90 ml) vintage cider
3 sprigs elderflowers
MOUSSE:
½ oz (15 g) gelatine
4 tablespoons (60 ml) vintage cider
2 oz (50 g) honey
1 egg, separated
¼ pint (150 ml) double cream
FOR DECORATION:
green glacé cherries and angelica

Put the gooseberries into a saucepan with the cider and elderflowers. Set them, covered, on a low heat and cook them until they are soft and can be beaten to a purée (about 15 minutes). Rub them through a sieve. Put them back into the rinsed-out pan with the honey. Set the pan on a low heat and let the honey melt into the gooseberries. Meanwhile, dissolve the gelatine in the 4 tablespoons (60 ml) cider. Stir it into the gooseberries and honey and keep stirring until it has melted. Take the pan from the heat and beat in the egg yolk. Return it to the heat and stir until the mixture thickens but does not boil. Leave it to cool.

Lightly whip the double cream and whip the egg white until it is stiff. Fold first the cream and then the white into the gooseberries. Pour the mousse into a lightly greased mould and leave it in the bottom of the fridge or in a cool place to set.

It looks very pretty turned out and decorated with the cherries and angelica.

Preparation and cooking: 40 minutes
Cooling and setting: 2 hours

Apple and ginger upside down cake

This is a good sticky ginger cake. Serve it for tea, or as a dessert with yoghurt or whipped cream.

3 oz (75 g) butter
2 oz (50 g) honey
1 egg, beaten
1 teaspoon (5 ml) ground ginger
1 teaspoon (5 ml) ground cinnamon
6 oz (175 g) 81% or 85% wheatmeal self-raising flour
4 oz (125 g) black treacle or molasses
2 tablespoons (30 ml) vintage cider
1 large cooking apple
4 pieces preserved stem ginger
butter for greasing a 7-inch (18-cm) cake tin

Heat the oven to Reg 3/325°F/170°C. Cream the butter in a bowl and beat in the honey. Gradually beat in the egg. Mix the spices with the flour and beat these in, a little at a time. Add the treacle or molasses and then the cider. Peel, quarter, core and slice the apple, and slice the ginger into thin pieces. Arrange half the sliced apple and ginger in the base of the prepared tin, leaving a few gaps between. Put in half the cake mixture and arrange the rest of the apple and ginger on top. Add the remaining cake mixture and smooth the top. Bake the cake for 1 hour 30 minutes and turn it out carefully onto a wire rack to cool.

Preparation: 30 minutes
Cooking: 1 hour 30 minutes

Mulled cider

Mulled cider is ideal for winter parties, when guests have travelled a long way in the cold.

3 pints (1·725 l) dry cider
2 large oranges
20 cloves
6 tablespoons (120 ml) honey
1 piece cinnamon stick
   about 6 inches (15 cm)
   long, broken
$\frac{1}{4}$ pint (150 ml) brandy

Stick the cloves into the oranges and cut the oranges into thick slices. Put the cider into a large saucepan with the oranges, honey and cinnamon stick. Set it on a gentle heat and bring it slowly to simmer-

ing point. Keep the cider at this temperature for 10 minutes to bring out the flavour of the spices, but don't let it boil. Warm the brandy gently in a small frying-pan. Set it alight and while it is still flaming, pour it into the cider. Ladle it out into sturdy mugs as soon as the flames have died.

Preparation: 30 minutes

Cider wassail

This is a really traditional wassail bowl of cider. It might not be suitable for the summer months, but after a cold night's carol singing round the village at Christmas, it is the most cheering of cups.

4 large Bramley apples
16 cloves
3 pints (1·725 ml) dry cider
1 pint (575 ml) vintage cider
2 eggs, beaten

Core the apples and stick four cloves into each one where the core has been removed. Bake the apples in a hot oven for 30 minutes so they are fluffy and burst their skins. Rub the pulp through a sieve. Put it into a saucepan, flameproof casserole or preserving pan and stir in both types of cider. Heat it on a moderate heat until the cider is just below boiling point. Put the eggs into a medium-sized bowl and half-fill another bowl with cider mixture. Quickly pour the cider from the one into the eggs in the other and keep pouring backwards and forwards 'from a great height' so you eventually get a mixture that is light and frothy. Pour the froth into the rest of the cider and heat the mixture through again, without boiling.

Preparation: 20 minutes
Cooking of the apples: 30 minutes

ABOUT THE PHOTOGRAPHS

All the photographs in this book were taken on a $2\frac{1}{4}$-inch square single lens reflex camera (Hasselblad). This format was chosen because on the one hand it is big enough to give good quality reproduction and on the other hand the equipment is small enough to lug over hills and through mud without getting a hernia.

I always carry two camera bodies, a standard lens (80 mm), a telephoto (150 mm), a wide-angle (50 mm) and a super wide (38 mm). With exposure meter, various filters, etc, it all weighs about 22 lbs, which feels more like 2 tons at the end of the day! For interior photographs on location, I carry a bag of flash units and, of course, a tripod. This, I find, is the minimum of equipment needed to give sufficient control to the photographer, especially when it comes to the relationship between foreground and background. Unfortunately, not many work places are all that photogenic and you cannot normally choose where to stand, so the lenses have to work for you. I have heard a lot of rubbish talked about how you can do everything on one lens but this only applies when you have complete control over the subject matter involved. This is certainly not the case with cows, pigs or a working dairy.

I always use Kodak film because I'm used to it and I can get hold of it quickly. Ektachrome transparency materials were used throughout. Some of the colour transparencies have been reproduced in black and white in the book. I used colour materials balanced for daylight, to achieve natural looking colours from electronic flash and daylight. I usually allow extra exposure for any tungsten lights to appear as a warm glow. Neon lights are a photographer's nightmare and reproduce erratically!

A very wide variety of types of work was involved in doing this book, from controlled studio shots where everything can be adjusted at will to landscapes with animals where, as soon as you get out of the car, having seen the perfect set-up with sheep or whatever in exactly the right place, the blighters get up and run into the next field behind a hedge! The best technique for this kind of work is to have the camera all ready beside you in the car, shutter speed and aperture set for quick action. At other times, landscapes can involve sitting still waiting patiently for a cloud to move away or for it to stop deluging with rain.

Perhaps at this point I ought to mention equipment, bags and clothing. The best kind of bag is the soft canvas type with pockets you can get to from the top. The hard metal cases are great for storing equipment, but to carry any distance over rough terrain, they are murder. As to clothing, you can't beat an oiled cotton jacket with huge pockets, the type worn for shooting. In fact, mine serves both purposes beautifully. For the feet, what would anyone do without wellies? I even wear mine in the darkroom.

Talking about darkrooms, all the transparencies were processed by me in my own hand-tank set-up, partly because I don't trust anybody else, but mainly because I like to see the results as soon as possible.

It is said that photography – like other arts – is ninety-nine per cent perspiration and one per cent inspiration. Well, after a couple of years of enjoyable, if sometimes exasperating, work, the table was groaning under a huge pile of transparencies out of which the seventy-odd that appear in this book were selected. I hope you get as much enjoyment out of looking at them as I did from taking them.

MICK DUFF

ACKNOWLEDGEMENTS

We have been greatly helped by the following people and would like to extend our grateful thanks to them all.

First, a special thanks to Eric Humphrey of the British Farm Produce Council for pointing us in all the right directions and for always being on the other end of the phone when he was needed.

These people have given us information covering a range of subjects:

John Acock, Acock and Freeman Ltd, Four Ayes Farm, Bicknor, Kent

Jane Anderson of the Meat Promotion Executive

The Apple and Pear Development Council

Mr Atkinson of T. D. Ridley and Sons (Brewers) Ltd, Hartford End, Essex

Jean Bailey of the *Amateur Winemaker*

Richard and Joyce Barnes, Biddenden Vineyards, Kent

Ken and Audrey Beevor, Hazel Street Beefarm, Stockbury, Kent

Philip Butcher, Assistant Director General of the National Union of Farmers

Rachel and Curly Carley, Home Farm, Sandway, Kent

Richard 'Butch' Chantler, Wye, Kent

Gay Christopherson, Swanton Mill, Mersham, Ashford, Kent

Laurie Coates

Mr and Mrs Robert Crockford, The Brookside, Windermere

John Davis and Mr and Mrs David Stapleton, Pinneys Smokehouses Ltd, Brydekirk

Mike Davidson, Ivy House Farm, Grafty Green, Kent

Mr Dennet, Preston Bakery, Kent (since retired)

Members of Doddington and Shorne Shoots, Kent

Raymond Duveen and Bob Morley of the English Farmhouse Cheese Information Service

The Eggs Authority

The Free Range Egg Association

The Game Conservancy

Mr and Mrs Gould, Gould Farm, East Pennard, Shepton Mallet, Somerset

James Graham, Secretary of the Cereals Commission, NFU

Mid and Ted Grimshaw, Lenham Heath, Kent

John Harrison, Manor Farm, Rainham, Kent

Derek, Jane and Lyn Haslup, Shepherds Farm, Lenham Heath, Kent

Carl Hayes

Madge and Den Hill, Aylesbury, Bucks

Alcwyn James, Llwyncelyn Farm, Llandeilo, Dyfed

Bill Jordan, W. Jordan and Son Ltd, Holme Mills, Biggleswade, Beds

Joe Lewis, Southernden Farm, Headcorn, Kent

Dennis Longley, QDP, Egerton, Kent

Michael and Marie Luck, Frogshole Farm, Benenden, Kent

The fishing ghillie at the Maesllwych Arms Hotel, Glasbury-on-Wye

Jack Milstead, Sunnyside Farm, Nettlestead, Kent

Colin Morris, Harrietsham, Kent

Vic Morris

The National Game Dealers Association

Mr and Mrs John Notman, Tubslake Farm, Hawkhurst, Kent

Peter Oughton

Mr and Mrs John Pattinson and Clive Pattinson, Calthwaite Hall, Calthwaite, Penrith, Cumbria

John Pearson

Ann Petch and Carol Bigg of 'The Whole Hog', Easthele Farm, King's Nympton, Devon

Martin Pitt, Levetts Farm, Clench Common, Marlborough, Wilts

Quality Milk Producers Ltd

John Roach, Horticultural Division, NFU

Michael and Deidre Rust, Court Lodge Farm, Hastingleigh, Kent

David and Avril Salisbury, London End Farm, Keysoe, Beds

Fred Scott, West Moor Farm, Rainham, Kent

Mr and Mrs Neil Smith, 'The Red Lion', Charing Heath, Kent

The Stilton Cheesemakers Association

Mr P. Stockdale, Websters Dairy Ltd, Saxelby, Leicestershire

Peter J. Tait, NFU of Scotland

Wendy Taylor, Secretary, The Royal Smithfield Club

Ruth Thompson, Oak Cottage Herb Farm, Nesscliff, Shropshire

John Thorley, Secretary, The National Sheep Society, Purple Heather Farm, Cholesbury, Tring, Herts

Stanley Thorp and Philip Thorp of Crump Way Ltd, Somerset

Nick Wainford of the British Bacon Bureau

Jack Ward of the Merrydown Wine Company Ltd and the English Vineyards Association

John and Sue Webb, Charing Heath, Kent

Wolfgang of Miller Howe, Windermere

SOURCES

The publisher and authors are grateful to all those owners of copyright works which have been quoted in the text.

INTRODUCTION John Milton, 'L'Allegro'; Kathleen Thomas, *Purse Barley*   **PORK, HAM AND BACON** Ben Jonson, *Bartholomew Fair*; Marcus Woodward, *The Mistress of Stanton's Farm*; George Ewart Evans, *Ask the Fellows who Cut the Hay*; R. E. Davies, *Pigs and Bacon Curing*   **BEEF AND VEAL** Alison Uttley, *Recipes from an old Farmhouse*; 'The Twelve Oxen' (traditional); Helen Edden, *County Recipes of Old England*   **LAMB AND MUTTON** Thomas Love Peacock, 'War Song of Dinas Vawr'; Thomas Farrall; Mrs Loudon, *The Lady's Country Companion*; Whitbread's *Receipts and Relishes*; 'The Derby Ram' (traditional)   **POULTRY** John Clare, 'The Shepherd's Calendar' (April); Florence Irwin, *The Cookin' Woman*; Hannah Glasse, *The Art of Cookery Made Plain and Easy*; William Allingham, 'Four Ducks on a Pond'   **GAME** Major Hugh Pollard, *The Sportsman's Cookery Book*; Rebecca Price, *The Compleat Cook*   **FISH** James Hogg, 'A Boy's Song'; Isaak Walton, *The Compleat Angler*; Major Hugh Pollard, *The Sportsman's Cookery Book*; May Byron, *Pot Luck*   **EGGS** A. Hawkshawe, 'The Clucking Hen'; W. M. W. Fowler, *Countryman's Cooking*; Marcus Woodward, *The Mistress of Stanton's Farm*   **DAIRY PRODUCTS** Robert Louis Stevenson, 'The Cow'; Richard Dehan, *Maids in a Market Garden*; Dorothy Hartley, *Here's England*; Alison Uttley, *Recipes from an old Farmhouse*   **VEGETABLES** John Clare, 'The Shepherd's Calendar' (July); Hannah Glasse, *The Art of Cookery Made Plain and Easy*; Florence Irwin, *The Cookin' Woman*; Alison Uttley, *Recipes from an old Farmhouse*   **FRUITS AND NUTS** John Keats 'Ode to Autumn'; Mrs C. W. Earle, *Pot Pourri from a Surrey Garden*; Humphrey Phelps, *Just across the Fields*; Rebecca Price, *The Compleat Cook*; Richard Church, *The Little Kingdom*   **HERBS AND FLOWERS** William Shakespeare, *The Winter's Tale*: Mrs C. F. Leyel, *Herbal Delights*; Elvira, *Kentish Yesterdays*   **HONEY** W. B. Yeats, 'The Lake Isle of Innisfree'; John Clare, 'The Shepherd's Calendar' (May); Florence White, *Good Things in England*; André Launay, *The Merrydown Book of Country Wines*   **CEREALS** Lucy Diamond, 'A Rhyme of Harvest'; Thirza Wakely, 'Spring Work at the Farm'; Mrs Loudon, *The Lady's Country Companion*; Elvira, *Kentish Yesterdays*; K. Fisher, 'Story of the Corn'   **WINE** (Oscar Wilde, *De Profundis*); *Cook and Housewife's Manual, 1829;* Flora Thompson, *Lark Rise to Candleford*   **BEER** V. Sackville-West, 'The Land'; Marcus Woodward, *The Mistress of Stanton's Farm*; Whitbread's *Receipts and Relishes*; A. E. Housman, 'A Shropshire Lad'   **CIDER** Thomas Hardy, 'Great Things'; E. Birkett, *The Golden Wine of Old Britain*; Nathaniel Howard, 1804; *Domestic Cookery, 1814.*

INDEX

INDEX

FOOD FROM THE COUNTRY

INDEX

181